HEATH
ALGEBRA 2
AN INTEGRATED APPROACH
LARSON, KANOLD, STIFF

EXTRA PRACTICE
COPYMASTERS

David C. Falvo

McDougal Littell

Evanston, Illinois • Boston • Dallas

In 1–6, use the graph to determine which inequality symbol, $<$ or $>$, should be placed between the two real numbers.

1. -3 ☐ 5

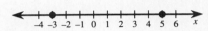

2. -8 ☐ -11

3. $\frac{7}{2}$ ☐ $\frac{3}{4}$

4. $-\frac{8}{3}$ ☐ $-\frac{7}{5}$

5. $\sqrt{2}$ ☐ $\sqrt{3}$

6. -2.5 ☐ -4.2

In 7–12, plot the real numbers on the real number line.

7. 0 and 4

8. -3 and 1

9. -5 and -9

10. $\frac{10}{3}$ and $\frac{17}{4}$

11. $-\frac{25}{2}$ and $-\frac{14}{5}$

12. $-\sqrt{2}$ and $-\frac{2}{5}$

In 13–21, state the property that is illustrated.

13. $(3 + 5) + 5 = 3 + (5 + 5)$

14. $9 + (-9) = 0$

15. $(-3)(7) = (7)(-3)$

16. $6 + 11 = 11 + 6$

17. $6 \cdot \frac{1}{6} = 1$

18. $9(5 + 7) = 9 \cdot 5 + 9 \cdot 7$

19. $-5 + 0 = -5$

20. $4(1) = 4$

21. $(4 \cdot 3) \cdot 5 = 4 \cdot (3 \cdot 5)$

22. Find the sum of 4 and 6.

23. Find the sum of -2 and 9.

24. Find the difference of -2 and 5.

25. Find the difference of 7 and -3.

26. Find the product of 5 and 4.

27. Find the product of -9 and 8.

28. Find the quotient of 21 and 7.

29. Find the quotient of 12 and -2.

30. *Wedding Cake* A wedding cake has five tiers. The bottom two tiers are each 5 inches high and the top three tiers are each 4 inches high. How tall is the cake?

31. *Eating Pizza* Eight friends buy 4 pizzas. Each pizza is cut into 6 pieces. Each person eats the same number of pieces. How many pieces does each person eat?

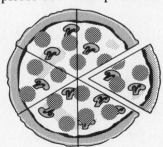

In 1–6, evaluate the expression.

1. $2x - 3$ when $x = 0$

2. $4 - 7x$ when $x = -2$

3. $y(2 + y)$ when $y = -5$

4. $3t - 0.5(t + 1)$ when $t = 3$

5. $(25a - 3) \div 8$ when $a = 3$

6. $2n \div (1 - n)$ when $n = 5$

In 7–15, write the expression using exponents.

7. $2 \cdot 2 \cdot 2$

8. $5 \cdot 5 \cdot 5 \cdot 5 \cdot 5 \cdot 5$

9. $3x \cdot 3x$

10. $(-9)(-9)(-9)(-9)$

11. $a \cdot a \cdot a \cdot a \cdot a$

12. $(-x)(-x)(-x)$

13. $(2y \cdot 2y \cdot 2y) + 7$

14. $(4b \cdot 4b) + (2a \cdot 2a)$

15. $(x \cdot x \cdot x)(y \cdot y)$

Geometry   **In 16 and 17, find an expression for the area of the figure.**

16.

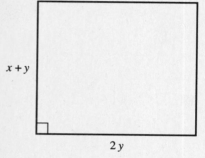

$x + y$

$2y$

17.

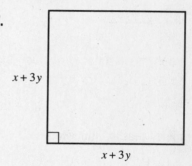

$x + 3y$

$x + 3y$

18. Evaluate the expression obtained in Exercise 16 when $x = 2$ and $y = 3$.

19. Evaluate the expression obtained in Exercise 17 when $x = 5$ and $y = 2$.

In 20–28, use order of operations to evaluate the expression.

20. $3 - 2 \cdot 5$

21. $11 + 8 \div 2$

22. $4 \cdot 3 + 6 \cdot 5$

23. $3 \cdot (2 + 1) - 4$

24. $14 \div (7 - 5) + 1$

25. $-1 + (3 + 2)^2$

26. $(5 - 2)^3 - 3 \cdot 4$

27. $(4 + 3)(-1 + 5)^2$

28. $(-8 + 6) \div (3 - 1)^2$

Weekly Earnings   **In 29 and 30, use the following information.**

For 1980 through 1990, the average weekly earnings (in dollars) for workers in the United States can be modeled by

$E = 14.5t + 270,$

where $t = 0$ represents 1980.

29. Approximate the average weekly earnings in 1980.

30. Approximate the average weekly earnings in 1990.

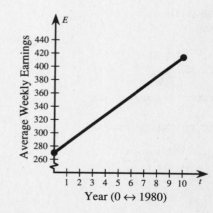

In 1–6, solve the linear equation by adding (or subtracting) the same number to both sides.

1. $x + 3 = 0$

2. $x - 7 = 2$

3. $5 + x = 4$

4. $-18 + x = 6$

5. $5 = x + 2$

6. $-3 = x - 11$

In 7–12, solve the linear equation by multiplying (or dividing) both sides by the same number.

7. $6x = 24$

8. $5x = -15$

9. $\frac{1}{3}x = 6$

10. $-\frac{4}{3}x = 8$

11. $3 = -9x$

12. $4 = 12x$

In 13–24, solve the linear equation.

13. $2x + 3 = 7$

14. $5x - 2 = 13$

15. $6 - x = 4$

16. $x + 4 = 2x + 9$

17. $3x - 1 = x + 4$

18. $4 + 5x = x - 8$

19. $-(x + 1) = 2(3x - 1)$

20. $3(x - 2) = 5(4 + x)$

21. $2(7 - x) = 6(1 + 2x)$

22. $-4(3 - x) + 6 = 2(x - 3)$

23. $2(x + 1) = 4 - 3(2x + 1)$

24. $3(1 - x) - (3 + x) = 8$

25. *Geometry* The perimeter of the figure shown below is 35 feet. Find its dimensions.

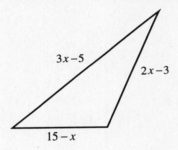

26. *Geometry* The perimeter of the figure shown below is 38 feet. Find its dimensions.

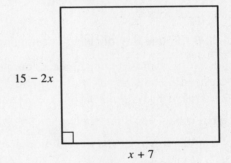

27. *Weekly Pay* You have a job that pays $5.60 an hour. You get $8.40 an hour for overtime (anything over 40 hours). Use the verbal model below to determine how many hours you need to work to earn $287.

| Hourly wage | · | 40 hours | + | Overtime wage | · | Overtime hours | = | Total pay |

28. *Plumbing Bill* The bill from your plumber was $134. The cost for labor was $32 per hour. The cost for materials was $46. Use the verbal model below to determine how many hours the plumber worked.

Cost for labor   Cost for materials

| Total bill | = | Hourly fee | · | Number of hours | + | Materials cost |

Party Supplies In 1–4, use the following information.

You have $120 to purchase soda pop for a party. Each case of 24 cans costs $7.50. Assuming there is no sales tax, how many cases can you purchase? Use the following verbal model.

Total cost	=	Price per case	·	Number of cases

1. Assign labels to each part of the verbal model.

2. Use the labels to translate the verbal model into an algebraic equation.

3. Solve the equation.

4. Answer the question.

Vacation Trip In 5–8, use the following information.

On a trip to the Grand Canyon, you drove 168 miles in $3\frac{1}{2}$ hours. What was your average speed? Use the following verbal model.

Distance traveled	=	Rate of travel	·	Time traveled

5. Assign labels to each part of the verbal model.

6. Use the labels to translate the verbal model into an algebraic equation.

7. Solve the equation.

8. Answer the question.

New Carpeting In 9–13, use the following information.

You just added a family room to your home. You have budgeted $450 for carpeting. If you need 30 square yards of carpeting, how much can you spend per square yard?

9. Create a verbal model for this problem.

10. Assign labels to each part of the verbal model.

11. Use the labels to translate the verbal model into an algebraic equation.

12. Solve the equation.

13. Answer the question.

Sharing the Driving In 14–18, use the following information.

You and a friend share the driving on a 300-mile trip. Your friend drives for three hours at an average speed of 52 miles per hour. How fast must you drive for the remainder of the trip if you want to reach your hotel in three more hours?

14. Create a verbal model for this problem.

15. Assign labels to each part of the verbal model.

16. Use the labels to translate the verbal model into an algebraic equation.

17. Solve the equation.

18. Answer the question.

In 1–6, solve for the indicated variable.

1. *Distance*

   Solve for t: $d = rt$

2. *Simple interest*

   Solve for r: $I = Prt$

3. *Height of an equilateral triangle*

   Solve for s: $h = \dfrac{\sqrt{3}s}{2}$

4. *Volume of a right circular cone*

   Solve for h: $V = \dfrac{\pi r^2 h}{3}$

5. *Area of a trapezoid*

   Solve for b_1: $A = \dfrac{h}{2}(b_1 + b_2)$

6. *Lateral surface area of a frustrum of a right circular cone*

   Solve for R: $S = \pi s(R + r)$

Geometry **In 7 and 8, solve the formula for the indicated variable.**

7. *Volume of a swimming pool*

   Solve for h: $V = \pi r^2 h$

8. *Surface area of a kite*

   Solve for w: $S = \frac{1}{2}(wh_1 + wh_2)$

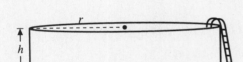

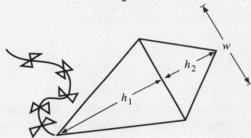

9. Use the formula obtained in Exercise 7 to calculate the depth of the swimming pool if $r = 10$ feet and $V = 1413.72$ cubic feet.

10. Use the formula obtained in Exercise 8 to calculate the width of the kite if $h_1 = 16$ inches, $h_2 = 28$ inches, and $S = 506$ square inches.

Hot Air Balloons **In 11–13, use the following information.**

In 1794, the French Army sent soldiers up in hot air balloons to observe enemy troop movements. One such balloon, the L'Entrepenant, had a volume of $\frac{256\pi}{3}$ cubic meters.

11. Solve the formula for the volume of a sphere for r^3. Then use this new formula to calculate the radius of the L'Entrepenant balloon.

    $V = \frac{4}{3}\pi r^3$

12. What was the diameter of the L'Entrepenant balloon?

13. Use the formula for the surface area of a sphere to approximate the surface area of the L'Entrepenant balloon.

    $S = 4\pi r^2$

Name _____

In 1–6, match the inequality with its graph.

1. $x \leq 0$

2. $-2 < x < 3$

3. $x < -2$ or $x > 3$

4. $x > -2$

5. $x < 3$

6. $x \geq 0$

a.
```
←———┼——┼——┼——┼——┼——┼——⊕——┼——→ x
   -3 -2 -1  0  1  2  3  4
```

b.
```
←———┼——⊕——┼——┼——┼——┼——⊕——┼——→ x
   -3 -2 -1  0  1  2  3  4
```

c.
```
←———┼——⊕——┼——┼——┼——┼——⊕——┼——→ x
   -3 -2 -1  0  1  2  3  4
```

d.
```
←———┼——┼——┼——●——┼——┼——┼——┼——→ x
   -3 -2 -1  0  1  2  3  4
```

e.
```
←———┼——┼——┼——●——┼——┼——┼——┼——→ x
   -3 -2 -1  0  1  2  3  4
```

f.
```
←———┼——┼——⊕——┼——┼——┼——┼——┼——→ x
   -3 -2 -1  0  1  2  3  4
```

In 7–12, solve the inequality using one transformation.

7. $x + 3 < 1$

8. $x - 5 \geq 2$

9. $4 \leq 7 + x$

10. $2x > 6$

11. $\frac{1}{2}x \leq 5$

12. $3x > -9$

In 13–18, solve the inequality using two transformations.

13. $2x - 1 > -5$

14. $3x + 2 < 8$

15. $5x - 8 \geq -3$

16. $\frac{1}{2}x + 4 \leq 7$

17. $\frac{2}{3}x - 5 > 1$

18. $6 + 3x \leq 5$

In 19–24, solve the inequality using two transformations. Remember to reverse the inequality when you multiply or divide by a negative number.

19. $3 - x < 2$

20. $-x + 5 \geq 6$

21. $4 - 2x \leq 0$

22. $-3x + 5 > -1$

23. $7 - 9x < 12$

24. $-5x + 1 \geq 1$

In 25–33, solve the inequality and sketch its graph.

25. $3x - 1 \leq 2x + 2$

26. $4 - 2x > x + 1$

27. $5x - 7 \leq 7x - 6$

28. $5 \leq \frac{1}{2}x - 1 \leq 8$

29. $-2 < 2x - 5 < 3$

30. $-4 < 2 - x < 6$

31. $x - 4 \leq 2$ or $x + 4 \geq 12$

32. $x - 1 < -3$ or $2x + 1 > 3$

33. $1 - 2x \leq -3$ or $3 - x \geq 5$

34. *Bird Eggs*   The largest egg laid by any bird is that of the ostrich. An ostrich egg can reach 8 inches in length. The smallest egg is that of the vervain hummingbird. Its eggs are approximately 0.4 inches in length. Write an inequality that represents the various lengths of bird eggs. Then graph the inequality.

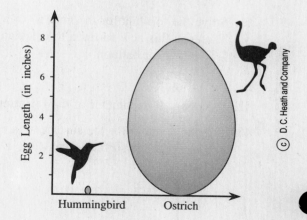

In 1–6, transform the absolute value equation into two linear equations.

1. $|x + 2| = 7$

2. $|2x - 1| = 5$

3. $|5x + 11| = 6$

4. $\left|\frac{1}{2}t - 3\right| = 1$

5. $|5 - t| = 3$

6. $|1 - 4t| = 9$

In 7–12, solve the absolute value equation. Begin by transforming the absolute value equation into two linear equations.

7. $|x + 3| = 5$

8. $|3x - 2| = 8$

9. $|2x + 6| = 14$

10. $\left|\frac{1}{2}t - 4\right| = 1$

11. $|11 - 3t| = 2$

12. $|7t + 3| = 4$

In 13–18, transform the absolute value inequality into a compound inequality.

13. $|x + 7| < 3$

14. $|2x - 4| \le 10$

15. $|5 - 3x| < 7$

16. $|x - 4| > 5$

17. $|5x + 1| \ge 4$

18. $|2 - x| > 9$

In 19–24, solve the absolute value inequality. Begin by transforming the absolute value inequality into a compound inequality.

19. $|x - 5| < 1$

20. $|3x + 2| \le 7$

21. $|4 - x| < 5$

22. $|x + 8| \ge 3$

23. $|2x - 1| > 5$

24. $|11 - 3x| > 4$

25. *Touring a Ship* The diagram below shows the water line of a large ship. From the diagram, we see that the ship extends 27 feet above the water and 27 feet below the water. Suppose you toured the entire ship. Write an absolute value inequality that represents all the distances you could have been from the water line.

26. *Water Temperature* Most fish can adjust to a change in the water temperature of up to $15°F$ if the change is not sudden. Suppose a lake trout is living comfortably in water that is $58°F$. Write an absolute value inequality that represents the range of temperatures at which the lake trout can survive.

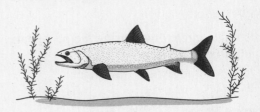

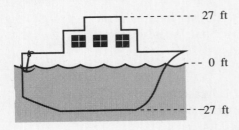

27 ft

0 ft

–27 ft

27. *Hours of Daylight* According to the *Old Farmer's Almanac*, the hours of daylight in Fairbanks, Alaska, range from approximately $3\frac{1}{2}$ hours in mid-December to approximately 21 hours in mid-June. Write an absolute value inequality that represents the hours of daylight in Fairbanks.

1. **Home Runs** A baseball coach recorded the number of home runs per game for each game in the regular season. The coach then constructed a line plot for the data, as shown at the right. Suppose you attended one of the eighteen games. Is it most likely that the team hit 0, 1, 2, or 3 home runs during that game?

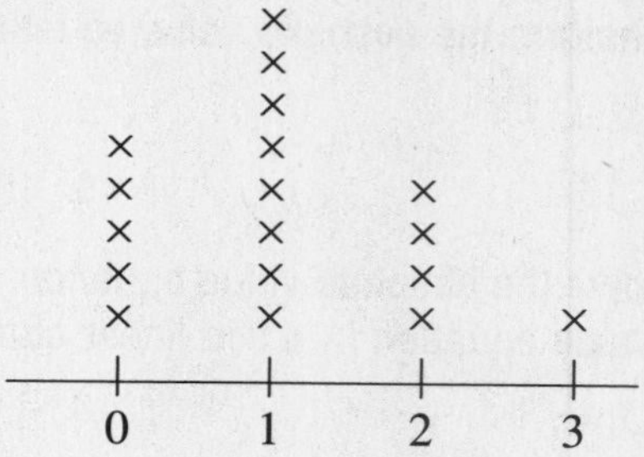

```
              x
              x
              x
      x       x
      x       x       x
      x       x       x
      x       x       x
      x       x       x       x
    --+-------+-------+-------+--
      0       1       2       3
```

2. **Birdwatching** Each weekend for three months a group of birdwatchers went to a different location to view the red-bellied woodpecker in its natural environment. On each occasion they recorded the number of red-bellied woodpeckers they saw. The results are shown in the table at the right. Construct a frequency distribution and a line plot for this data.

June	6	4	8	8	
July	5	6	3	7	
August	3	5	5	3	5

Phobias In 3–5, use the following information.

According to the *Unofficial U.S. Census* by Tom Heymann, the things shown below at the right elicit fear in the greatest number of Americans.

3. Construct a bar graph that represents the number of people who fear each of the six scary things.

4. Calculate each category's percent of the total number of people.

5. Construct a circle graph using the percentages that you found in Exercise 4.

Scary thing	Number afraid
Snakes	100,983,000
Public speaking	64,038,000
High places	46,797,000
Mice	39,408,000
Flying in an airplane	39,400,000
Spiders and insects	27,093,000
	317,719,000

6. **Gasoline Prices** In 1988, the average price of regular unleaded gasoline in Delaware was 58.6 cents per gallon. In 1989, the average price per gallon rose to 67.1 cents, and in 1990, the average price was 74.4 cents per gallon. Some 4800 miles away in Hawaii, the average price of regular unleaded gasoline was 84.6 cents per gallon in 1988, 83.4 cents per gallon in 1989, and 90.3 cents per gallon in 1990. Construct a double bar graph that shows the price per gallon of regular unleaded gasoline for Delaware and Hawaii for the years 1988–1990.

Name _____

In 1–3, identify the coordinates of each point. State which quadrant each point lies in.

1.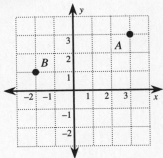

2.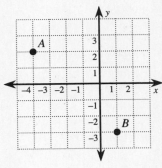

3.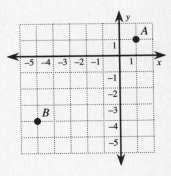

In 4–11, plot the point in a coordinate plane.

4. $(2, 5)$

5. $(-1, 3)$

6. $(4, -2)$

7. $(-3, 0)$

8. $(-4, -1)$

9. $(0, 6)$

10. $(\frac{1}{2}, 3)$

11. $(-2.5, -4)$

In 12 and 13, complete the table of values for the given equation.

12. $y = 2x + 3$

x	−2	−1	0	1	2
y					

13. $y = -\frac{1}{2}x + 4$

x	−2	−1	0	1	2
y					

In 14–19, construct a table of values and sketch the graph of the equation.

14. $y = 5x + 1$

15. $y = 3x - 7$

16. $y = -2x$

17. $y = -x + 2$

18. $y = \frac{1}{2}x + 3$

19. $y = -3x - 5$

In 20–25, sketch both lines on the same coordinate plane. Then find the point at which the two lines intersect.

20. $x = 3, \quad y = 3$

21. $x = -5, \quad y = 2$

22. $x = 1, \quad y = -3$

23. $y = 0, \quad x = 6$

24. $y = -1, \quad x = -4$

25. $y = 5, \quad x = 0$

26. *Hooded Warbler*   The breeding range of the hooded warbler is shown in the diagram at the right. Each unit on the coordinate plane that is superimposed over the map represents approximately 100 miles. Write equations for the vertical and horizontal sides of the rectangle that enclose the breeding range.

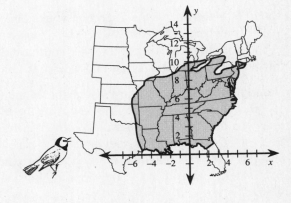

In 1–3, estimate the slope of the line if it exists.

1.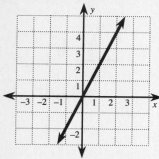

2.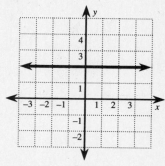

3.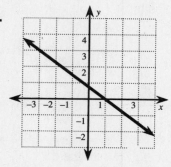

In 4–9, find the slope of the line containing the given points.

4. (2, 3), (5, 9)

5. (1, 4), (3, −2)

6. (−2, 7), (−3, −1)

7. (5, −1), (−7, 5)

8. (−11, 0), (4, −5)

9. (3, 4), (0, 0)

In 10–13, find the slope of each line and determine which line is steeper.

10. Line 1 contains (−2, 1) and (3, 6).
Line 2 contains (4, 5) and (2, −3).

11. Line 1 contains (3, −1) and (5, −5).
Line 2 contains (−2, −2) and (1, −11).

12. Line 1 contains (0, 3) and (−2, 4).
Line 2 contains (−8, 6) and (4, −6).

13. Line 1 contains (10, 2) and (−5, −3).
Line 2 contains (4, −1) and (12, 0).

In 14–22, determine whether the line containing the given points is horizontal, vertical, rises to the right, or falls to the right.

14. (4, −2), (3, −3)

15. (9, −2), (−3, −2)

16. (−3, 5), (5, 3)

17. (7, 5), (7, −8)

18. (10, 5), (4, 15)

19. (0, 4), (−3, 4)

20. (−9, −11), (−5, 5)

21. (−1, 6), (−1, 7)

22. (7, 0), (1, 12)

23. *Parallel Lines* If two nonvertical lines are parallel, what do we know about their slopes?

24. *Perpendicular Lines* If two nonvertical lines are perpendicular, what do we know about their slopes?

25. *Picking Strawberries* One afternoon your family goes out to pick strawberries for jam. At 1:00 P.M., you have picked 3 quarts. You finish picking at 3:00 P.M. and have 28 quarts of strawberries. At what average rate was your family picking?

26. *Washington Monument* The Washington Monument is 555 feet tall. The figure at the right shows that the monument is composed of a 500-foot pillar topped by a 55-foot pyramid. The base of the pillar is 55 feet wide. The base of the pyramid is 34 feet wide. Use this information to approximate the slope of the sides of the pillar and the slope of the sides of the pyramid.

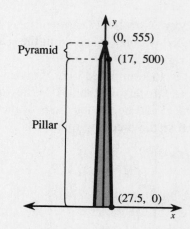

In 1–6, find the *x*-intercept of the line by letting *y* = 0 and solving for *x*.

1. $x - 3y = 4$ **2.** $2x + 5y = -8$ **3.** $-6x + y = 3$

4. $7x - 8y = 12$ **5.** $-3x + 9y = 18$ **6.** $4x - 5y = 1$

In 7–12, find the *y*-intercept of the line by letting *x* = 0 and solving for *y*.

7. $3x + 2y = 6$ **8.** $x - 5y = 7$ **9.** $4x + y = -1$

10. $-9x + 8y = -2$ **11.** $14x - 6y = 9$ **12.** $-2x + 7y = 21$

In 13–18, find the *x*-intercept and *y*-intercept of the line. Then use the intercepts to sketch the line.

13. $2x - y = 4$ **14.** $-3x + 4y = 12$ **15.** $5x + 2y = -8$

16. $x + 6y = 3$ **17.** $7x - 2y = -6$ **18.** $-4x + 8y = 20$

In 19–24, write the equation in slope-intercept form by solving the equation for *y*.

19. $-7x + y = -1$ **20.** $4x + 2y = 3$ **21.** $-3x + 5y = 15$

22. $-6x + 9y = 18$ **23.** $2x - y = 2$ **24.** $8x - 2y = 6$

In 25–30, identify the slope and *y*-intercept of the line and then use them to sketch the line.

25. $y = 3x - 1$ **26.** $y = -x + 6$ **27.** $y = \frac{2}{3}x + 2$

28. $y = -\frac{1}{4}x + 3$ **29.** $y = \frac{5}{3}x - 4$ **30.** $y = -\frac{7}{2}x - 3$

31. *Saving Change*   Each time you get dimes or quarters for change, you throw them into a jar. You are hoping to save $50. Write a model that shows the different numbers of dimes and quarters that you could accumulate to reach your goal.

32. *Commission Sales*   A salesperson receives a 3% commission on furniture sold at a sale price and a 4% commission on furniture sold at the regular price. The salesperson wants to earn a $250 commission. Write a model that shows the different amounts of sale-priced and regular-priced furniture that can be sold to reach this goal.

Teeter-Totter   In 33–35, use the following information.

The center post on a teeter-totter is 2 feet high. When one side rests on the ground, each end of the teeter-totter is 7 feet from the center post (see figure).

33. Find the slope of the teeter-totter as it is shown in the figure.

34. Find the *y*-intercept of the line that follows the path of the teeter-totter.

35. Use the slope and *y*-intercept found above to write an equation of the line that follows the path of the tetter-totter. Use the form $y = mx + b$.

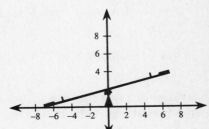

© D.C. Heath and Company

In 1–6, write an equation of the line that has the given slope and y-intercept.

1. $m = 1$, y-intercept: -3 **2.** $m = -5$, y-intercept: 2 **3.** $m = -\frac{1}{2}$, y-intercept: -4

4. $m = \frac{4}{3}$, y-intercept: 6 **5.** $m = 8$, y-intercept: 0 **6.** $m = 0$, y-intercept: 5

In 7–12, write an equation of the line that has the given slope and passes through the given point.

7. $(2, 1)$, $m = -2$ **8.** $(-4, 3)$, $m = 5$ **9.** $(7, -5)$, $m = 1$

10. $(-1, -10)$, $m = 3$ **11.** $\left(\frac{1}{2}, 4\right)$, $m = -8$ **12.** $\left(\frac{2}{3}, 0\right)$, $m = -4$

In 13–15, write an equation of the line shown in the figure.

13.
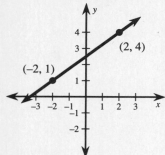

14.
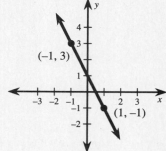

15.
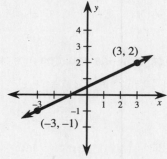

In 16–21, the variables x and y vary directly. Use the model y = kx to find k and write an equation that relates the variables.

16. When $x = 2$, $y = 6$.   **17.** When $x = -1$, $y = 5$.   **18.** When $x = 4$, $y = -10$.

19. When $x = 1$, $y = 0.25$.   **20.** When $x = -8$, $y = 2$.   **21.** When $x = 0.3$, $y = 0.9$.

Measuring Speed In 22 and 23, use the following information.

The speed of an automobile in miles per hour varies directly with its speed in kilometers per hour. A speed of 64 miles per hour is equivalent to a speed of 103 kilometers per hour.

22. Write a linear model that relates your speed in miles per hour to your speed in kilometers per hour.

23. You are driving through Canada and see the speed limit sign shown at the right. You are traveling 55 miles per hour. Are you speeding?

Chicken Consumption In 24 and 25, use the following information.

For 1983 through 1989, the per capita consumption of chicken in the U.S. increased at a rate that was approximately linear. In 1983, the per capita consumption was 36.9 pounds, and in 1989, it was 47 pounds.

24. Write a linear model for the per capita consumption of chicken in the U.S. Let $t = 3$ represent 1983.

25. What would you expect the per capita consumption of chicken to be in 1995?

MAXIMUM
80
km/h

In 1–4, determine whether the ordered pairs are solutions of the inequality.

1. $2x - 3y \leq 2$; $(0, -1)$, $(3, 2)$

2. $x + 2y > 4$; $(2, 1)$, $(-3, 6)$

3. $5x + y \geq -3$; $(-3, 6)$, $(2, -5)$

4. $3x - 10y < -8$; $(6, 3)$, $(-4, -2)$

In 5–12, write an equation that corresponds to the given inequality.

5. $x > -3$

6. $y \leq 7$

7. $y \geq -2x$

8. $\frac{1}{2}x < 5$

9. $2x + y \geq 5$

10. $6x + 2y < 1$

11. $3x - 4y > -8$

12. $-5x - 3y \leq 3$

In 13–20, write an equation that corresponds to the given inequality. Then sketch the graph of the inequality.

13. $x \geq 1$

14. $x < -\frac{1}{2}$

15. $2x > 6$

16. $-3x \geq 15$

17. $y < 4$

18. $y \geq -5$

19. $\frac{1}{3}y \geq -2$

20. $-y > -7$

In 21–28, write an equation in slope-intercept form that corresponds to the given inequality. Then sketch the graph of the inequality.

21. $y < 2x - 1$

22. $y \geq \frac{1}{2}x + 5$

23. $4x + y \leq -2$

24. $x + 2y > 4$

25. $-5x + 5y > 1$

26. $3x - y \leq 7$

27. $2x - 4y > 8$

28. $6x - 3y \geq -1$

Defrosting Meat In 29–31, use the following information.

According to the *Joy of Cooking* cookbook, you should always defrost meat in the original wrappings on a refrigerator shelf. You should allow 5 hours for each pound, less for thinner cuts. Using inequality notation we have $t \leq 5p$, where t is the time in hours and p is the number of pounds of meat being defrosted.

29. Sketch the graph of the inequality. Use t on the vertical axis and p on the horizontal axis.

30. What are the coordinates of a $2\frac{1}{2}$-pound roast that has been defrosting for 12 hours?

31. Is it possible that the roast in Exercise 30 is completely defrosted? Explain your answer.

Fund Raiser In 32–35, use the following information.

An environmentalist group is planning a fund raiser. The group wants to purchase caps and T-shirts with their logo on them and sell them at a profit. They can buy caps for $3 each and T-shirts for $5 each. They have $800 to spend.

32. Write an inequality that represents the number of caps, x, and T-shirts, y, that the group can buy.

33. Sketch the graph of the inequality.

34. Suppose the group purchased 50 caps and 150 T-shirts. What point on the coordinate plane represents this purchase?

35. Is the point in Exercise 34 a solution of the inequality?

In 1–6, find the vertex of the graph. Begin by setting the expression inside the absolute value symbols equal to zero.

1. $y = 2|x| - 3$

2. $y = |x - 1| + 2$

3. $y = |2x + 3| - 5$

4. $y = \frac{1}{2}|3 - x| + 4$

5. $y = |\frac{1}{2}x + 3| - 6$

6. $y = 5|4 - 2x| + 1$

In 7–10, complete the table.

7. $y = 2|x| + 5$

x	−3	−2	−1	0	1	2	3
y							

8. $y = |x + 1| - 3$

x	−7	−5	−3	−1	1	3	5
y							

9. $y = |2x - 1| - 2$

x	−5	−3	−1	$\frac{1}{2}$	2	4	6
y							

10. $y = -2|3x + 1| + 4$

x	−5	−3	−1	$-\frac{1}{3}$	1	3	5
y							

In 11–16, determine whether the graph opens up or down.

11. $y = -3|x|$

12. $y = 3|x + 1|$

13. $y = |2x + 1| - 10$

14. $y = 4|x - 1| + 3$

15. $y = -2|3x + 1| + 7$

16. $y = |3 - 2x| + 1$

In 17–28, sketch the graph of the equation.

17. $y = |x| - 4$

18. $y = |x - 4|$

19. $y = |x + 2| - 3$

20. $y = |2x + 1| + 3$

21. $y = 2|x - 3|$

22. $y = -|x + 5|$

23. $y = |4 - x| + 5$

24. $y = 3|1 - 3x| + 2$

25. $y = -2|x + 7| - 4$

26. $y = |\frac{1}{2}x| - 2$

27. $y = |\frac{2}{3}x + 2| + 1$

28. $y = \frac{1}{2}|x - 1| + 2$

A-Frame Home In 29 and 30, use the following information.

The roof line of an A-frame home follows the path given by $y = -\frac{11}{6}|x| + 22$. Each unit on the coordinate plane represents one foot.

29. Find the vertex of the graph.

30. What does the y-value of the vertex tell us about the home?

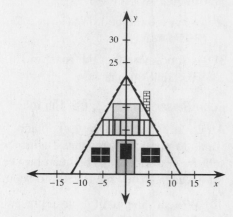

Fine Dining In 31–33, use the following information.

An exclusive restaurant is open from 3:00 P.M. to 10:00 P.M. Each evening, the number of people served, s, increases steadily and then decreases according to the model

$$s = -30|t - 6.5| + 105$$

where $t = 0$ corresponds to 12:00 noon.

31. Sketch the graph of this model.

32. Find the vertex of the graph.

33. Explain what each coordinate of the vertex represents.

In 1–3, construct a scatter plot for the given data. Then state whether *x* and *y* have a positive correlation, a negative correlation, or no correlation.

1.

x	−3	−2.5	−2	−1.75	−1.5	−1	−0.5	0	0.5	0.75	1	1.5
y	0.25	0.5	1	1.5	1.25	2	2.5	2.5	3	3.25	3.5	3.75

2.

x	0	0.5	1	1.25	1.5	2	2.5	3	3.25	3.5	4	4.25
y	2.75	3	2.5	2	1.75	1	1.25	1.5	2.5	3	3.25	3

3.

x	−2	−1	−0.5	0	0.25	1	1.5	2.5	2.75	3.5	4	4.5
y	1	1.25	0.5	0	−1	−1.25	−2	−2.25	−2	−3	−3.25	−3.5

In 4–6, write an equation of the line that best fits the scatter plot.

4.

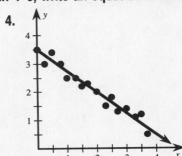

5.

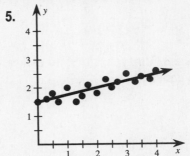

6.

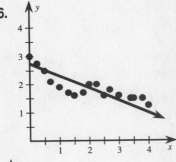

7. *100-Meter Freestyle* The winning times for the men's 100-meter freestyle in the Olympic Games for 1948–1988 are shown in the scatter plot at the right. Approximate the best-fitting line for this data.

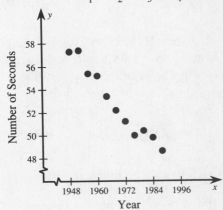

Broccoli Consumption In 8–10, use the following.

The data table shows the per capita consumption of broccoli, *b* (in pounds), for the years 1980 through 1989.

Year, *t*	1980	1981	1982	1983	1984
Pounds, *b*	1.6	1.8	2.2	2.3	2.7

Year, *t*	1985	1986	1987	1988	1989
Pounds, *b*	2.9	3.5	3.6	4.2	4.5

8. Construct a scatter plot for the data. Let *t* = 0 represent 1980.

9. Approximate the best-fitting line for the data.

10. If this pattern were to continue, what would the per capita consumption of broccoli be in 1995?

In 1–3, state whether the linear system has one solution, many solutions, or no solution.

1. $\begin{cases} 2x - 8y = -16 \\ -x + 4y = -8 \end{cases}$

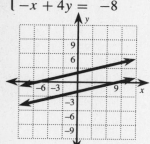

2. $\begin{cases} x + 3y = 1 \\ 3x - y = 13 \end{cases}$

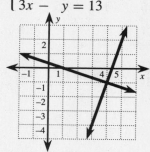

3. $\begin{cases} 5x + 2y = -4 \\ -10x - 4y = 8 \end{cases}$

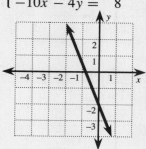

In 4–6, decide whether the ordered pair is a solution of the linear system.

4. $(1, 5)$

$\begin{cases} 3x - y = -2 \\ -4x + 2y = 5 \end{cases}$

5. $(-2, 3)$

$\begin{cases} 3x + 5y = 9 \\ -2x + 3y = 13 \end{cases}$

6. $(-3, -4)$

$\begin{cases} 4x - 7y = 16 \\ -6x + y = 14 \end{cases}$

In 7–12, sketch the graph of the linear system. Use your graph to estimate the solution. Check your solution in each equation.

7. $\begin{cases} x + 2y = 3 \\ -7x + 3y = -21 \end{cases}$

8. $\begin{cases} 2x - 3y = 2 \\ -5x + 2y = -16 \end{cases}$

9. $\begin{cases} 3x - y = -8 \\ -2x + 5y = 1 \end{cases}$

10. $\begin{cases} 3x + 5y = -19 \\ 5x - 2y = 20 \end{cases}$

11. $\begin{cases} 4x - 3y = -14 \\ -2x + 5y = 14 \end{cases}$

12. $\begin{cases} x - 7y = -28 \\ 9x + 2y = 8 \end{cases}$

13. **Amusement Park** A group of 42 people go to an amusement park. The admission fee for adults is $16. The admission fee for children is $12. The group spent $568 to get into the park. How many adults and how many children were in the group?

Break-Even Analysis In 14–17, use the following information.

You purchase a skateboard shop for $110,000. You estimate that monthly costs will be $3800. The monthly revenue is expected to be $5600.

14. Let R represent the revenue you bring in during the first t months. Write a model for R.

15. Let C represent your costs, including the purchase price, during the first t months. Write a model for C.

16. Sketch the graphs of the revenue and costs equations on the same coordinate plane.

17. How many months will it take you to break even?

Name _____

In 1–6, use substitution to solve the system.

1. $\begin{cases} 2x - 5y = 9 \\ \quad y = 3x - 7 \end{cases}$

2. $\begin{cases} -3x + 4y = 1 \\ \quad x = 2y + 1 \end{cases}$

3. $\begin{cases} 6x + 2y = 11 \\ \quad y = -4x + 6 \end{cases}$

4. $\begin{cases} x - 2y = -1 \\ 5x - 7y = 4 \end{cases}$

5. $\begin{cases} 4x + 3y = 3 \\ 2x + y = -3 \end{cases}$

6. $\begin{cases} 10x - 16y = 17 \\ \quad x + y = 3 \end{cases}$

In 7–12, use a linear combination to solve the system.

7. $\begin{cases} 5x + y = 6 \\ -5x + 3y = -22 \end{cases}$

8. $\begin{cases} 2x - 3y = 4 \\ 8x + 3y = 1 \end{cases}$

9. $\begin{cases} 4x + y = -5 \\ 4x + 3y = 9 \end{cases}$

10. $\begin{cases} 2x - 7y = -10 \\ 3x + 2y = 10 \end{cases}$

11. $\begin{cases} 3x - 4y = 12 \\ 6x + 2y = -11 \end{cases}$

12. $\begin{cases} 5x - 2y = -15 \\ 7x + 5y = 18 \end{cases}$

In 13–18, use any convenient method to solve the system.

13. $\begin{cases} 4x + 7y = -10 \\ 3x - 7y = -4 \end{cases}$

14. $\begin{cases} -2x + 3y = 8 \\ \quad x - 5y = -4 \end{cases}$

15. $\begin{cases} 6x + y = 0 \\ 15x + 2y = 9 \end{cases}$

16. $\begin{cases} 6x - 3y = 1 \\ 4x - 2y = 7 \end{cases}$

17. $\begin{cases} 3x - 8y = 1 \\ 6x + 2y = 11 \end{cases}$

18. $\begin{cases} 4x - 16y = 4 \\ -3x + 12y = -3 \end{cases}$

19. ***Albums and Cassettes*** For 1980 through 1990, the manufacturers' shipments of long-playing albums, A (in millions), and audio cassettes, C (in millions), can be modeled by the equations

$A = -31.8t + 322$ **Album shipments**

$C = \quad 42.8t + 110$ **Cassette shipments**

where $t = 0$ represents 1980. In what year did the number of cassettes being shipped surpass the number of albums being shipped?

20. ***Treasure Map*** You are given the treasure map shown at the right and the riddle below.

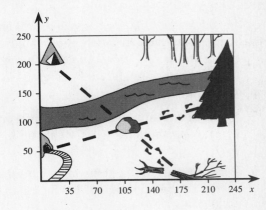

> *A young man traveled from the mighty pine,*
>   *down along the river to the old coal mine.*
> *An old man traveled from the broken tree,*
>   *up across the river to the great tepee.*
> *A treasure can be found where the two paths cross,*
>   *under a big stone covered with moss.*

The young man's path is given by

$-4x + 11y = 550$.

The old man's path is given by

$13x + 11y = 2420$.

Find the coordinates of the point where the treasure can be found.

1. **Vacation Trip** You and a friend share the driving on a 280-mile trip. Your average speed is 58 miles per hour. Your friend's average speed is 53 miles per hour. You drive one hour longer than your friend. How many hours did each of you drive? Use the following verbal model.

| Verbal Model | | Your speed | · | Your time | + | Friend's speed | · | Friend's time | = | 280 miles |

| | Your time | = | Friend's time | + | 1 hour |

Decorating a Gym In 2–5, use the following information.

You are in charge of decorating for the spring dance. You purchase 10 bags of balloons and 6 rolls of crêpe paper for $20.10. You soon realize that this is not enough to decorate the entire gym. On your second trip to the store, you spend $12.80 on 4 bags of balloons and 8 rolls of crêpe paper. What was the price for each item? Assume the sales tax is included in the price.

2. Write a verbal model for this problem.

3. Assign labels to the verbal model.

4. Use the labels to write a linear system that represents the problem.

5. Solve the system and answer the question.

6. **Golf Bags** A sporting goods store receives a shipment of 124 golf bags. The shipment includes two types of bags, full-size and collapsible. The full-size bags cost $38.50 each. The collapsible bags cost $22.50 each. The bill for the shipment is $3430. How many of each type of golf bag are in the shipment?

Milk Consumption In 7–9, use the following information.

The table at the right shows the per capita consumption of whole and lowfat milk for the years 1980 and 1990. Over the ten-year period, the consumption of whole milk decreased at a rate that was approximately linear. During that same time, the consumption of lowfat milk increased at a rate that was approximately linear.

Per Capita Milk Consumption

	1980	1990
Whole milk	17 gal	10.5 gal
Lowfat milk	9.2 gal	15.2 gal

7. Write an equation in slope-intercept form that represents the per capita consumption, W, of whole milk. Let $t = 0$ represent 1980.

8. Write an equation in slope-intercept form that represents the per capita consumption, L, of lowfat milk. Let $t = 0$ represent 1980.

9. Estimate the year that the consumption of lowfat milk surpassed the consumption of whole milk.

Name _____

In 1–3, match the system of inequalities with its graph.

1. $\begin{cases} y \le x \\ y \ge -2 \\ x \le 3 \end{cases}$

2. $\begin{cases} y \ge x \\ y \ge -2 \\ x \le 3 \end{cases}$

3. $\begin{cases} y \le x \\ y \le -2 \\ x \le 3 \end{cases}$

a.

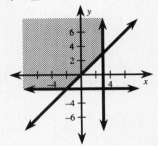

b.

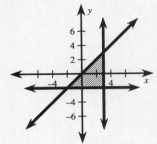

c.

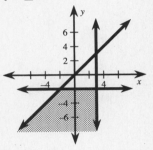

In 4–11, sketch the graph of the system of linear inequalities.

4. $\begin{cases} x > -2 \\ y \le 4 \end{cases}$

5. $\begin{cases} y < 2 \\ y > -3 \end{cases}$

6. $\begin{cases} x \ge 0 \\ x < 5 \end{cases}$

7. $\begin{cases} y \le 2x \\ x < 3 \end{cases}$

8. $\begin{cases} y \le 5 \\ x > -3 \\ y \le 2x - 2 \end{cases}$

9. $\begin{cases} x \ge -3 \\ x \le 4 \\ y < x + 5 \end{cases}$

10. $\begin{cases} y > \frac{1}{2}x - 4 \\ y \le -x + 3 \\ y \le 2x \end{cases}$

11. $\begin{cases} x + y < 1 \\ 2x - y < 4 \\ x \ge -2 \end{cases}$

In 12–14, sketch the graph of the system of linear inequalities. Label each vertex.

12. $\begin{cases} y \ge 3x - 4 \\ y \le -\frac{1}{2}x + 3 \\ x > -2 \end{cases}$

13. $\begin{cases} 2x + y < 3 \\ x - y > -6 \\ y \ge 0 \end{cases}$

14. $\begin{cases} x + 2y \le 10 \\ 2x + y \le 8 \\ 2x - 5y < 20 \end{cases}$

15. **Field Trip** Your class has rented busses for a field trip. Each bus seats 44 passengers. The rental company's policy states that you must have at least 3 adult chaperones on each bus. Let x represent the number of students on each bus. Let y represent the number of adult chaperones on each bus. Write a system of linear inequalities that shows the various numbers of students and chaperones that could be on each bus. (Each bus may or may not be full.)

16. **Iceberg** The diagram at the right shows the cross section of an iceberg. Write a system of inequalities that represents the portion of the iceberg that extends above the water.

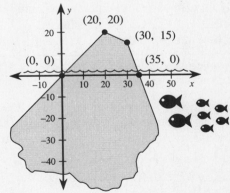

In 1–3, you are given the graph of the constraint inequalities. Find the minimum and maximum values of the objective quantity.

1. $C = x - y$

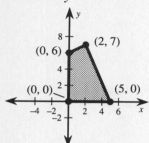

2. $C = x + 2y$

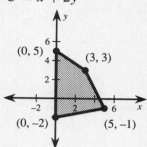

3. $C = -2x + y$

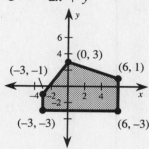

In 4–9, sketch the graph of the constraint inequalities. Label the vertices. Then find the minimum and maximum values of the objective quantity.

4. Objective quantity:
$$C = 3x - y$$
Constraints:
$$\begin{cases} x \geq 0 \\ y \geq 0 \\ 2x + y \leq 6 \end{cases}$$

5. Objective quantity:
$$C = 2x + 4y$$
Constraints:
$$\begin{cases} x \leq 3 \\ x + y \geq 3 \\ 2x - 3y \geq -9 \end{cases}$$

6. Objective quantity:
$$C = x + 5y$$
Constraints:
$$\begin{cases} 3x + 2y \leq 8 \\ 2x - y \geq -4 \\ x - 4y \leq -2 \end{cases}$$

7. Objective quantity:
$$C = 4x - 3y$$
Constraints:
$$\begin{cases} x \geq 0 \\ x \leq 5 \\ y \geq 0 \\ 2x - 5y \geq -15 \end{cases}$$

8. Objective quantity:
$$C = 2x + 3y$$
Constraints:
$$\begin{cases} x \geq 0 \\ y \geq 1 \\ 4x + y \geq 6 \\ x + 2y \geq 5 \end{cases}$$

9. Objective quantity:
$$C = 5x + 2y$$
Constraints:
$$\begin{cases} x \leq 4 \\ 2x + y \geq 3 \\ x - 3y \leq -2 \\ -x + 2y \leq 6 \end{cases}$$

Candy Factory In 10–13, use the following information.

Your candy factory is making chocolate-covered peanuts and chocolate-covered pretzels. For each case of peanuts, you make $40 profit. For each case of pretzels, you make $55 profit. The table below shows the number of machine hours and man hours needed to produce one case of each type of candy. It also shows the maximum number of hours available.

Production hours	Peanuts	Pretzels	Maximum hours
Machine hours	2	6	150
Man hours	5	4	155

10. Write an equation that represents the profit (the objective quantity).

11. Write a system of inequalities that represents the constraints of this problem.

12. Sketch the graph of the constraints found in Exercise 11 and label the vertices.

13. How many cases of each product should you make to maximize profits?

In 1–3, solve the system of linear equations.

1. $\begin{cases} x - 2y + 3z = -4 \\ y - z = 3 \\ z = -1 \end{cases}$

2. $\begin{cases} x + 3y = 1 \\ y + 2z = 5 \\ z = 3 \end{cases}$

3. $\begin{cases} x + 5y - 7z = 6 \\ y - 3z = 7 \\ z = -4 \end{cases}$

In 4–7, perform the indicated row operation.

4. Interchange Equation 1 and 2.

$\begin{cases} 2y + 4z = 6 & \textbf{Equation 1} \\ x - 3y + z = -1 & \textbf{Equation 2} \\ 3y + 5z = 7 & \textbf{Equation 3} \end{cases}$

5. Multiply Equation 2 by $\frac{1}{2}$.

$\begin{cases} x - 3y + z = -1 & \textbf{Equation 1} \\ 2y + 4z = 6 & \textbf{Equation 2} \\ 3y + 5z = 7 & \textbf{Equation 3} \end{cases}$

6. Add -3 times Equation 2 to Equation 3.

$\begin{cases} x - 3y + z = -1 & \textbf{Equation 1} \\ y + 2z = 3 & \textbf{Equation 2} \\ 3y + 5z = 7 & \textbf{Equation 3} \end{cases}$

7. Multiply Equation 3 by -1.

$\begin{cases} x - 3y + z = -1 & \textbf{Equation 1} \\ y + 2z = 3 & \textbf{Equation 2} \\ -z = -2 & \textbf{Equation 3} \end{cases}$

In 8–10, write the system of linear equations in triangular form.

8. $\begin{cases} x - 3y + 2z = 15 \\ y - 5z = 4 \\ 2y - 7z = -1 \end{cases}$

9. $\begin{cases} x + 2y - z = 4 \\ -x + y + 4z = 5 \\ 2y - z = 0 \end{cases}$

10. $\begin{cases} x + y + z = 8 \\ 3x + 4y + z = 19 \\ 2x - 2y + 8z = 28 \end{cases}$

In 11–16, solve the system of linear equations.

11. $\begin{cases} x - y + 2z = 4 \\ x - 3z = 1 \\ 2y - z = -15 \end{cases}$

12. $\begin{cases} x + y - z = 6 \\ 2y - 3z = 4 \\ -y + 2z = -1 \end{cases}$

13. $\begin{cases} x + 2y - z = 3 \\ x - 3y + z = -1 \\ -x + y - 3z = 5 \end{cases}$

14. $\begin{cases} x - 2y - z = 3 \\ x + y + 2z = 9 \\ 2x + 3y + z = 0 \end{cases}$

15. $\begin{cases} 2x + 3y + 2z = 1 \\ x + 4y - z = 7 \\ 3x + y + 3z = -2 \end{cases}$

16. $\begin{cases} x - 2y + 3z = -7 \\ 4x + 5y + z = 4 \\ -x + y - 2z = 5 \end{cases}$

17. **Pet Store Supplies** A pet store receives a shipment of pet foods at the beginning of each month. Over a three-month period, the store received 1770 pounds of dog food, 1165 pounds of cat food, and 365 pounds of bird seed. Use the information in the table to find the number of pounds of pet food in each of the three shipments.

	1st Shipment	2nd Shipment	3rd Shipment
Dog food	60%	50%	50%
Cat food	25%	35%	45%
Bird seed	15%	15%	5%

In 1–4, determine the order of the matrix.

1. $\begin{bmatrix} 3 & 5 & -7 \\ 1 & 2 & 9 \\ -2 & 6 & 1 \\ 4 & -3 & 5 \end{bmatrix}$ 2. $\begin{bmatrix} 4 & 9 \\ -5 & 1 \\ 2 & -6 \end{bmatrix}$ 3. $\begin{bmatrix} 4 \\ 3 \end{bmatrix}$ 4. $\begin{bmatrix} 1 & 4 & 5 & -2 \\ -6 & 2 & 0 & 3 \\ 3 & 8 & -1 & 4 \end{bmatrix}$

In 5–8, perform the indicated operation. Remember, to add or subtract matrices, you add or subtract corresponding entries.

5. $\begin{bmatrix} 1 & 3 \\ -2 & 5 \\ 2 & 4 \end{bmatrix} + \begin{bmatrix} 4 & 9 \\ 7 & 1 \\ -2 & 6 \end{bmatrix}$ 6. $\begin{bmatrix} 1 & 3 \\ 2 & 4 \end{bmatrix} - \begin{bmatrix} -5 & 2 \\ 7 & 1 \end{bmatrix}$

7. $\begin{bmatrix} 4 & 3 & -2 \\ 1 & 5 & 4 \\ 2 & 7 & 6 \end{bmatrix} - \begin{bmatrix} 1 & 2 & 5 \\ 4 & -1 & 3 \\ 6 & 7 & 9 \end{bmatrix}$ 8. $[6 \quad -2 \quad 1 \quad 8] + [7 \quad 5 \quad -3 \quad 2]$

In 9–12, multiply the matrix by the indicated scalar. Remember, to multiply a matrix by a scalar, you multiply each entry in the matrix by the scalar.

9. $3\begin{bmatrix} 1 & 4 \\ -3 & 2 \end{bmatrix}$ 10. $-2\begin{bmatrix} -\frac{1}{2} & 0 & 2 \\ 3 & 4 & -1 \\ -2 & \frac{3}{2} & 5 \end{bmatrix}$ 11. $10\begin{bmatrix} 0.2 \\ 1.3 \\ 0.5 \end{bmatrix}$ 12. $-5\begin{bmatrix} 1 & 4 & -2 & 3 \\ 0 & -5 & 1 & 4 \end{bmatrix}$

In 13–16, simplify the expression.

13. $\left(\begin{bmatrix} 1 & 2 \\ 0 & -1 \end{bmatrix} - \begin{bmatrix} -3 & -4 \\ 2 & 5 \end{bmatrix}\right) + \begin{bmatrix} 2 & 5 \\ 3 & 9 \end{bmatrix}$ 14. $\begin{bmatrix} 1 & 3 \\ 2 & 0 \\ 5 & 6 \end{bmatrix} - \left(\begin{bmatrix} 9 & 2 \\ 4 & -1 \\ -3 & 1 \end{bmatrix} + \begin{bmatrix} -7 & 3 \\ 0 & 1 \\ 5 & 3 \end{bmatrix}\right)$

15. $2\left(\begin{bmatrix} 3 & 2 & 5 \\ -1 & 6 & -2 \end{bmatrix} + \begin{bmatrix} 1 & 3 & -4 \\ 6 & 4 & 2 \end{bmatrix}\right)$ 16. $-3\begin{bmatrix} 1 & 4 \\ -2 & 6 \end{bmatrix} - \left(\begin{bmatrix} 0 & 3 \\ 2 & 6 \end{bmatrix} + \begin{bmatrix} -3 & 2 \\ 5 & -1 \end{bmatrix}\right)$

Health Club Membership In 17 and 18, use the following information.

A health club offers three different membership plans. With Plan A, you can use all club facilities: the pool, fitness center, and racket club. With Plan B, you can use the pool and fitness center. With Plan C, you can only use the racket club facilities. The matrices below show the annual cost for a Single and a Family membership for the years 1990–1992.

1990

	Single	Family
Plan A	336	624
Plan B	228	528
Plan C	216	384

1991

	Single	Family
Plan A	384	720
Plan B	312	576
Plan C	240	432

1992

	Single	Family
Plan A	420	792
Plan B	360	672
Plan C	288	528

17. You purchased a Single Plan A membership in 1990, a Family Plan B in 1991, and a Family Plan A in 1992. How much did you spend for your membership over the three years?

18. You purchased a Family Plan C membership in 1990, and upgraded to the next highest plan each year. How much did you spend for your membership over the three years?

Name _____

In 1–4, state the order of each matrix and determine whether the product AB is defined. If it is, state the order of AB.

1. $A = \begin{bmatrix} 1 & -2 \\ 3 & 4 \\ 4 & 1 \end{bmatrix}$ $B = \begin{bmatrix} 4 & 9 & -3 \end{bmatrix}$

2. $A = \begin{bmatrix} 1 & 4 & -2 \\ 3 & -1 & 0 \end{bmatrix}$ $B = \begin{bmatrix} 3 & 1 & -2 \\ 5 & 2 & 4 \\ -3 & -6 & 7 \end{bmatrix}$

3. $A = \begin{bmatrix} 5 \\ -2 \\ 3 \\ 1 \end{bmatrix}$ $B = \begin{bmatrix} 1 & 7 \end{bmatrix}$

4. $A = \begin{bmatrix} 2 & 4 \\ 3 & 2 \\ -1 & 6 \\ 0 & -3 \end{bmatrix}$ $B = \begin{bmatrix} 1 & 7 & 3 & -4 \\ 6 & -2 & 6 & 1 \\ 5 & 4 & 8 & 0 \end{bmatrix}$

In 5 and 6, complete the multiplication to find the product.

5. $\begin{bmatrix} 3 & 1 \\ 4 & -2 \end{bmatrix}\begin{bmatrix} 2 & 1 & 0 \\ 3 & -2 & 4 \end{bmatrix} = \begin{bmatrix} (3)(2)+(1)(3) & (3)(1)+(1)(-2) & (3)(0)+(1)(4) \\ \boxed{} & \boxed{} & \boxed{} \end{bmatrix}$

6. $\begin{bmatrix} 1 \\ -2 \\ 3 \end{bmatrix}\begin{bmatrix} -4 & 6 \end{bmatrix} = \begin{bmatrix} 1(-4) & 1(6) \\ \boxed{} & \boxed{} \\ \boxed{} & \boxed{} \end{bmatrix}$

In 7–12, find the product.

7. $\begin{bmatrix} 1 & -2 \\ 6 & 4 \end{bmatrix}\begin{bmatrix} 3 & 1 \\ 5 & 2 \end{bmatrix}$

8. $\begin{bmatrix} 2 & 0 & 1 \\ -3 & 1 & 2 \\ 0 & 0 & 4 \end{bmatrix}\begin{bmatrix} -2 & -1 & 2 \\ 1 & 0 & 3 \\ 0 & -4 & 1 \end{bmatrix}$

9. $\begin{bmatrix} -1 & 3 \\ 2 & 2 \end{bmatrix}\begin{bmatrix} 1 & 3 & 4 \\ -2 & 0 & 5 \end{bmatrix}$

10. $\begin{bmatrix} -3 & 4 & 1 & 2 \end{bmatrix}\begin{bmatrix} 1 \\ 2 \\ -5 \\ 3 \end{bmatrix}$

11. $\begin{bmatrix} 1 & -2 \\ 3 & 0 \\ 2 & 4 \end{bmatrix}\begin{bmatrix} 2 & -1 & 4 & 2 \\ 1 & 0 & 5 & -3 \end{bmatrix}$

12. $\begin{bmatrix} 4 & -1 \\ 0 & 2 \\ 3 & 1 \\ 6 & -2 \end{bmatrix}\begin{bmatrix} 3 \\ 2 \end{bmatrix}$

In 13–16, simplify the expression.

13. $4\begin{bmatrix} \frac{1}{2} & -1 \\ -\frac{3}{4} & \frac{3}{2} \end{bmatrix}\begin{bmatrix} -3 & -5 \\ 4 & 2 \end{bmatrix}$

14. $\begin{bmatrix} 1 & 3 \\ -2 & 0 \end{bmatrix}\begin{bmatrix} 5 & 2 \\ 1 & -1 \end{bmatrix} + \begin{bmatrix} 1 & 3 \\ -2 & 0 \end{bmatrix}\begin{bmatrix} -3 & 5 \\ 2 & -2 \end{bmatrix}$

15. $\begin{bmatrix} 2 & -4 & 0 \\ 0 & 3 & 6 \\ -1 & 5 & 1 \end{bmatrix}\left(\begin{bmatrix} 1 & 2 \\ -3 & 0 \\ 5 & 1 \end{bmatrix} + \begin{bmatrix} 3 & -1 \\ 0 & 2 \\ 4 & 5 \end{bmatrix} \right)$

16. $\left(\begin{bmatrix} 3 \\ -1 \\ 0 \end{bmatrix} + \begin{bmatrix} 2 \\ 5 \\ 1 \end{bmatrix} \right)\begin{bmatrix} 4 & 4 \end{bmatrix}$

17. Senior Play The senior class play was performed on three different evenings. The attendance for each evening is shown in the table at the right. Adult tickets sold for $3.50. Student tickets sold for $2.50. Use matrix multiplication to determine how much money was taken in each night.

	Adults	Students
Opening night	420	300
Second night	400	450
Final night	510	475

In 1–4, evaluate the determinant of the 2 × 2 matrix.

1. $\begin{bmatrix} 6 & 2 \\ -1 & 3 \end{bmatrix}$
2. $\begin{bmatrix} -1 & 5 \\ 3 & 4 \end{bmatrix}$
3. $\begin{bmatrix} -4 & 6 \\ -2 & 3 \end{bmatrix}$
4. $\begin{bmatrix} 0 & -1 \\ 7 & 8 \end{bmatrix}$

In 5–7, evaluate the determinant of the 3 × 3 matrix. **Expand by minors** along the indicated row or column.

5. Expand along Row 1.

$\begin{bmatrix} 1 & 0 & 1 \\ 5 & 9 & 2 \\ 7 & -3 & 6 \end{bmatrix}$

6. Expand along Column 2.

$\begin{bmatrix} 3 & -1 & 2 \\ 2 & 1 & 0 \\ 5 & 0 & 4 \end{bmatrix}$

7. Expand along Row 2.

$\begin{bmatrix} 3 & 5 & -2 \\ 2 & 1 & 1 \\ 5 & -3 & 4 \end{bmatrix}$

In 8–10, evaluate the determinant of the 3 × 3 matrix. **Use the expansion by minors method.**

8. $\begin{bmatrix} 1 & -2 & 5 \\ 4 & 5 & -1 \\ 3 & 1 & 0 \end{bmatrix}$
9. $\begin{bmatrix} 1 & 4 & 3 \\ 0 & 2 & 5 \\ 2 & -1 & 4 \end{bmatrix}$
10. $\begin{bmatrix} 1 & 0 & 1 \\ -2 & 5 & -2 \\ 3 & 6 & 3 \end{bmatrix}$

In 11–13, evaluate the determinant of the 3 × 3 matrix. **Use the diagonals method.**

11. $\begin{bmatrix} 4 & 3 & -1 \\ -2 & 1 & 0 \\ 5 & 6 & -3 \end{bmatrix}$
12. $\begin{bmatrix} 1 & 2 & 3 \\ 4 & 5 & 1 \\ 6 & 4 & 2 \end{bmatrix}$
13. $\begin{bmatrix} -1 & 2 & 0 \\ 5 & 1 & 6 \\ 0 & 3 & -5 \end{bmatrix}$

In 14–16, use a determinant to find the area of the triangle.

14.

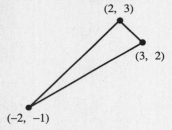

(2, 3)
(3, 2)
(−2, −1)

15.

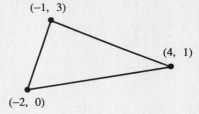

(−1, 3)
(4, 1)
(−2, 0)

16.

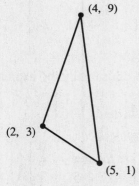

(4, 9)
(2, 3)
(5, 1)

17. *New Hampshire* The figure at the right shows a map of the state of New Hampshire. Use the triangle superimposed over the map to approximate the area of the state. Each unit on the map represents one mile. Compare your answer to the actual area of the state.

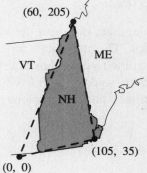

(60, 205)
ME
VT
NH
(105, 35)
(0, 0)

In 1–5, decide whether the matrices are inverses of each other.

1. $\begin{bmatrix} 5 & -3 \\ 3 & -2 \end{bmatrix}$, $\begin{bmatrix} 2 & -3 \\ 3 & -5 \end{bmatrix}$

2. $\begin{bmatrix} 2 & 1 \\ -1 & 1 \end{bmatrix}$, $\begin{bmatrix} 1 & -1 \\ 1 & 2 \end{bmatrix}$

3. $\begin{bmatrix} 4 & 1 \\ 7 & 2 \end{bmatrix}$, $\begin{bmatrix} 2 & -1 \\ -7 & 4 \end{bmatrix}$

4. $\begin{bmatrix} 1 & 4 & -2 \\ 3 & 0 & 5 \\ 3 & 1 & 4 \end{bmatrix}$, $\begin{bmatrix} -5 & -18 & 20 \\ 3 & 10 & -11 \\ 3 & 11 & -12 \end{bmatrix}$

5. $\begin{bmatrix} 1 & 0 & 2 \\ 0 & 3 & 6 \\ -2 & 4 & 8 \end{bmatrix}$, $\begin{bmatrix} 0 & 3 & -2 \\ -1 & 1 & -2 \\ 2 & -3 & 4 \end{bmatrix}$

In 6–9, find the inverse of the 2 × 2 matrix.

6. $\begin{bmatrix} 4 & 5 \\ 7 & 9 \end{bmatrix}$

7. $\begin{bmatrix} 3 & -4 \\ 2 & -3 \end{bmatrix}$

8. $\begin{bmatrix} 1 & 0 \\ 0 & 2 \end{bmatrix}$

9. $\begin{bmatrix} -6 & 3 \\ 5 & -3 \end{bmatrix}$

In 10–13, find A^{-1} and use it to solve the matrix equation.

10. $\underbrace{\begin{bmatrix} 1 & 2 \\ 2 & 3 \end{bmatrix}}_{A} X = \underbrace{\begin{bmatrix} 4 & -1 \\ 5 & 2 \end{bmatrix}}_{B}$

11. $\underbrace{\begin{bmatrix} 5 & -4 \\ -11 & 9 \end{bmatrix}}_{A} X = \underbrace{\begin{bmatrix} -1 & 0 \\ 3 & 2 \end{bmatrix}}_{B}$

12. $\underbrace{\begin{bmatrix} 6 & 7 \\ 5 & 6 \end{bmatrix}}_{A} X = \underbrace{\begin{bmatrix} 1 & 0 & -2 \\ 3 & 1 & 4 \end{bmatrix}}_{B}$

13. $\underbrace{\begin{bmatrix} 3 & -4 \\ 4 & -6 \end{bmatrix}}_{A} X = \underbrace{\begin{bmatrix} 1 & -3 & 4 \\ -2 & 0 & 6 \end{bmatrix}}_{B}$

Encoding Messages **In 14–16, use the following information.**

The message, MEET ME AT SUNSET, is to be encoded using the matrix

$A = \begin{bmatrix} 5 & -3 \\ 2 & -1 \end{bmatrix}$.

14. Convert the message into 1 × 2 uncoded row matrices.

15. Multiply each of the uncoded row matrices found in Exercise 14 by A to obtain the coded row matrices.

16. Write the message in code.

Decoding Messages **In 17–20, use the following information.**

You are the detective in a "Who Done It?" mystery. A crime has been committed and you have narrowed the suspects down to the six characters shown at the right. Use the inverse of

$A = \begin{bmatrix} 2 & 3 \\ 1 & 2 \end{bmatrix}$

to decode each clue. Then use the clues to determine which character committed the crime.

Miss L. Toe   Mrs. Ippi   Miss Behave

Mr. Meister   Mr. Ed   Mr. Crumpet

17. 38 67 9 18 38 57 43 72 40 60 2 3 27 41 28 42

18. 46 73 10 15 51 79 20 39 38 57 26 45 21 41 43 67 38 57

19. 46 73 10 15 17 26 38 57 39 66 35 56 8 16 11 21 36 54

20. "Who done it?"

Name _____

In 1–6, write the linear system as a matrix equation.

1. $\begin{cases} x - y = 3 \\ -2x + y = 4 \end{cases}$

2. $\begin{cases} 3x - y = -1 \\ 4x + y = 15 \end{cases}$

3. $\begin{cases} 6x - 3y = 39 \\ 5x + 9y = -25 \end{cases}$

4. $\begin{cases} x - y + z = -2 \\ 2x \quad + 3z = 4 \\ 3y - z = 7 \end{cases}$

5. $\begin{cases} 3x + y - 2z = 1 \\ x - 2y + z = 12 \\ x + 4y \quad = -18 \end{cases}$

6. $\begin{cases} 5x - 3y + z = 6 \\ 2x + 2y + 3z = -1 \\ x - 5y - 4z = 9 \end{cases}$

In 7–9, write the linear system as a matrix equation. Then use the inverse of the coefficient matrix to solve the system.

7. $\begin{cases} x + y = 2 \\ 2x + y = -1 \end{cases}$

8. $\begin{cases} 3x - 2y = 8 \\ 4x - 3y = 10 \end{cases}$

9. $\begin{cases} 5x - 2y = -9 \\ -7x + 3y = 14 \end{cases}$

In 10–12, write the linear system as a matrix equation. Then use the inverse of the coefficient matrix to solve the system. In each case, the inverse has been provided.

10. $\begin{cases} 2x + y - z = 3 \\ 3x \quad + z = -5 \\ 5x + 2y - 2z = 5 \end{cases}$

$A^{-1} = \begin{bmatrix} -2 & 0 & 1 \\ 11 & 1 & -5 \\ 6 & 1 & -3 \end{bmatrix}$

11. $\begin{cases} x + y - z = 2 \\ 9x + 6y - 7z = 24 \\ -6x - 4y + 5z = -15 \end{cases}$

$A^{-1} = \begin{bmatrix} -2 & 1 & 1 \\ 3 & 1 & 2 \\ 0 & 2 & 3 \end{bmatrix}$

12. $\begin{cases} x + y - 2z = -9 \\ 2x + y + z = 0 \\ -x - 2y + 6z = 21 \end{cases}$

$A^{-1} = \begin{bmatrix} 8 & -2 & 3 \\ -13 & 4 & -5 \\ -3 & 1 & -1 \end{bmatrix}$

Stock Investment In 13–16, use the following information.

You have $10,000 to invest in three types of stock. The expected annual returns for the three stocks are shown in the table below. You want the combined investment in Stock X and Stock Y to be three times the amount invested in Stock Z. You are hoping to obtain an average return of 8.5%.

Stock	Expected return
Stock X	6%
Stock Y	8%
Stock Z	12%

13. Write a linear system that represents the given information.

14. Write the system as a matrix equation.

15. Use an inverse matrix and a graphing calculator to solve the system.

16. How much should you invest in each type of stock?

In 1–3, write the augmented matrix for the linear system.

1. $\begin{cases} 2x + y - z = 4 \\ 3x + 2y + z = 6 \\ -x + y + 3z = -1 \end{cases}$

2. $\begin{cases} x - 2y + 3z = 10 \\ x \quad\quad - z = 2 \\ x + 3y - 4z = -9 \end{cases}$

3. $\begin{cases} 3x - 2y - 7z = 3 \\ 3y - z = -6 \\ x - 2y - 5z = -15 \end{cases}$

In 4–6, write the linear system that is represented by the augmented matrix.

4. $\begin{bmatrix} 1 & -1 & 4 & \vdots & 3 \\ 0 & 1 & 4 & \vdots & 5 \\ 0 & 0 & 1 & \vdots & -2 \end{bmatrix}$

5. $\begin{bmatrix} 2 & -3 & 0 & \vdots & 11 \\ 0 & 1 & 4 & \vdots & -1 \\ 0 & 0 & 1 & \vdots & 6 \end{bmatrix}$

6. $\begin{bmatrix} 1 & -2 & 7 & \vdots & -21 \\ 0 & 3 & 0 & \vdots & 15 \\ 0 & 0 & 1 & \vdots & -4 \end{bmatrix}$

In 7–12, write the augmented matrix for the linear system. Use elementary row operations to write the system in triangular form. Then use substitution to solve for each variable.

7. $\begin{cases} x + 2y - z = 12 \\ x + 3y - z = -6 \\ 2y + z = 5 \end{cases}$

8. $\begin{cases} 2x - 3y - 5z = 1 \\ x - 2y = 12 \\ -4x + 6y + 7z = -23 \end{cases}$

9. $\begin{cases} x - y + z = -8 \\ 2x + 3y - 3z = 4 \\ x + 2y + 7z = 13 \end{cases}$

10. $\begin{cases} 3x + 2y - 4z = 0 \\ x - y + 2z = 10 \\ 2x - 3y + 5z = 14 \end{cases}$

11. $\begin{cases} x \quad\quad - 2z = 7 \\ x + 3y + 4z = -5 \\ 5x - y + 3z = 9 \end{cases}$

12. $\begin{cases} 5x + 2y + 3z = 20 \\ 2x - 3y + 4z = -2 \\ x - 2y + 3z = 16 \end{cases}$

Nursery Shipment **In 13–15, use the following information.**

A nursery receives a shipment of 246 trees. The shipment includes pine trees, fruit trees, and maple trees. There are twice as many pine trees as there are fruit trees. The maple trees make up half of the shipment.

13. Write a system of equations that represents the information given above. Let x, y, and z represent the number of pine trees, fruit trees, and maple trees, respectively.

14. Write the augmented matrix for the linear system in Exercise 13.

15. Use the augmented matrix in Exercise 14 to solve the system.

16. ***Pewter Alloys*** Pewter is an alloy that consists mainly of tin. It also contains small amounts of antimony and copper. Three pewter alloys contain the percents of tin, antimony, and copper shown in the matrix at the right. You have 1296 pounds of tin, 69 pounds of antimony, and 35 pounds of copper. How much of each alloy can you make?

Percents by Weight

	Alloy X	Alloy Y	Alloy Z
Tin	0.90	0.94	0.92
Antimony	0.08	0.03	0.06
Copper	0.02	0.03	0.02

In 1–6, find the determinant of the coefficient matrix.

1. $\begin{cases} 4x - 5y = -13 \\ -3x + 4y = 10 \end{cases}$

2. $\begin{cases} 3x + 7y = 4 \\ x + 3y = 0 \end{cases}$

3. $\begin{cases} 2x - y = 16 \\ 6x + 2y = 78 \end{cases}$

4. $\begin{cases} x + y - z = 2 \\ x - 2y + z = 8 \\ -y + z = 3 \end{cases}$

5. $\begin{cases} x + 2y = 7 \\ -3x + 5y + z = 11 \\ 5x - 2y - z = 0 \end{cases}$

6. $\begin{cases} 2x + y - 3z = -4 \\ x + 2y + z = 2 \\ x + 3y + 4z = 10 \end{cases}$

In 7–12, use Cramer's rule to solve the linear system. (Hint: Use the determinants calculated in Exercises 1–6.)

7. $\begin{cases} 4x - 5y = -13 \\ -3x + 4y = 10 \end{cases}$

8. $\begin{cases} 3x + 7y = 4 \\ x + 3y = 0 \end{cases}$

9. $\begin{cases} 2x - y = 16 \\ 6x + 2y = 78 \end{cases}$

10. $\begin{cases} x + y - z = 2 \\ x - 2y + z = 8 \\ -y + z = 3 \end{cases}$

11. $\begin{cases} x + 2y = 7 \\ -3x + 5y + z = 11 \\ 5x - 2y - z = 0 \end{cases}$

12. $\begin{cases} 2x + y - 3z = -4 \\ x + 2y + z = 2 \\ x + 3y + 4z = 10 \end{cases}$

13. **Children's Literature** A. A. Milne (1882–1956), an English author, became famous for his children's stories and poems. One of Milne's most famous works, *Winnie-the-Pooh,* is based on his son Christopher Robin, and the young boy's stuffed animals. Two years after the first book was published, the Pooh stories continued in the book *The House at Pooh Corner.* Solve the linear system given below to find the year that each of these great books were published. (Use Cramer's rule.)

$$\begin{cases} x - y = -2 \\ \frac{1}{6}x - \frac{1}{8}y = 80 \end{cases}$$

Registered Voters In 14–17, use the following information.

In 1988, there were 6.047 million people registered to vote in Florida. Of these, x million were registered democrats, y million were registered republicans, and z million were registered as independent. The value of x is 0.908 million more than the value of y. The value of y is 1.935 million more than z.

14. Write an equation using the variables x, y, and z, that represents the total number of registered voters.

15. Write an equation that relates the number of registered democrats, x, to the number of registered republicans, y.

16. Write an equation that relates the number of registered republicans, y, to the number of people registered as independent, z.

17. Show how Cramer's rule can be used to find the values of x, y, and z.

In 1–12, write the equation in the form $x^2 = d$. Then solve for x.

1. $2x^2 = 2$

2. $-4x^2 = -36$

3. $\frac{1}{2}x^2 = 32$

4. $x^2 - 3 = 1$

5. $x^2 + 2 = 7$

6. $16 - x^2 = -9$

7. $3x^2 - 1 = 5$

8. $\frac{1}{3}x^2 + 5 = 32$

9. $\frac{2}{3}x^2 - 8 = 16$

10. $2x^2 - 11 = x^2 + 5$

11. $x^2 + 1 = 3x^2 - 13$

12. $2(x^2 + 4) = 10$

Geometry In 13 and 14, use the Pythagorean Theorem to find x. Round your answer to two decimal places.

13.

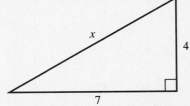

14.

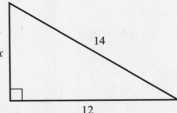

Falling Object In 15–17, find the time it takes an object to hit the ground when it is dropped from a height of s feet. Use the falling-object model $h = -16t^2 + s$.

15. $s = 80$

16. $s = 160$

17. $s = 320$

18. Compare your answers in Exercises 15–17. Does an object that is dropped from $2s$ feet take twice as long to reach the ground as an object that is dropped from s feet? Explain your answer.

19. **Cost of a New Car** From 1970 to 1990, the average cost of a new car, C (in dollars), can be approximated by the model $C = 30.5t^2 + 4192$ where t is the year, with $t = 0$ corresponding to 1970. During which year was the average cost of a new car $12,000?

Short Cut In 20–22, use the following information.

Suppose your house is on a large corner lot. The children in the neighborhood cut across your lawn, as shown in the figure at the right. The distance across the lawn is 35 feet.

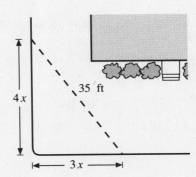

20. Use the Pythagorean Theorem to find x.

21. Find the distance the children would have to travel if they did not cut across your lawn.

22. How many feet do the children save by taking the "short cut?"

In 1–6, write the quadratic equation in standard form, identify the leading coefficient, and determine whether the graph opens up or down.

1. $y = 2x^2 + x - 1$

2. $y = 3 - x - x^2$

3. $y = 4 + 3x - 5x^2$

4. $y = -2x + 1 + x^2$

5. $y = 4 - 3x^2$

6. $y = x + 9x^2$

In 7–12, find the vertex and the axis of symmetry of the parabola.

7. $y = x^2 + 2x - 1$

8. $y = 2x^2 - 8x + 3$

9. $y = -x^2 - 6x + 8$

10. $y = x^2 - x + 4$

11. $y = -x^2 + 4$

12. $y = 2x^2 + 4x$

In 13–16, complete the table of values.

13. $y = x^2 - 2x + 1$

x	−2	−1	0	1	2	3	4
y							

14. $y = -2x^2 + 8x - 3$

x	−1	0	1	2	3	4	5
y							

15. $y = x^2 + 4$

x	−3	−2	−1	0	1	2	3
y							

16. $y = x^2 - 6x$

x	0	1	2	3	4	5	6
y							

In 17–25, sketch the graph of the parabola. Label the vertex.

17. $y = x^2$

18. $y = x^2 + 1$

19. $y = -x^2 + 2$

20. $y = x^2 - 2x$

21. $y = 2x^2 - 12x$

22. $y = -x^2 + 8x + 2$

23. $y = x^2 + 14x - 9$

24. $y = -2x^2 - 4x + 7$

25. $y = 3x^2 + 3x - 1$

26. *Area of a Building Lot*   You want to purchase the property shown in the map at the right. Each tick mark on the coordinate system represents 50 feet. Use the map to approximate the area of the lot.

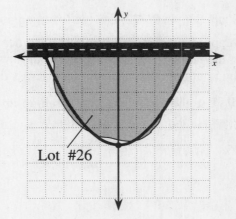

Lot #26

Minimum Cost **In 27–29, use the following information.**

A manufacturer of lighting fixtures has daily production costs modeled by

$$y = 0.25x^2 - 10x + 800$$

where y is the total cost in dollars and x is the number of fixtures produced.

27. Sketch the graph of the model. Label the vertex.

28. What is the minimum daily production cost, y?

29. How many fixtures should be produced each day to yield a minimum cost?

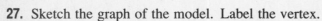

© D. C. Heath and Company

In 1–6, write the perfect-square trinomial as the square of a binomial.

1. $x^2 + 2x + 1$ **2.** $x^2 - 4x + 4$ **3.** $x^2 - 16x + 64$

4. $x^2 + 3x + \frac{9}{4}$ **5.** $x^2 - \frac{1}{2}x + \frac{1}{16}$ **6.** $x^2 + 5x + \frac{25}{4}$

In 7–12, determine what must be added to each expression so that it becomes a perfect-square trinomial.

7. $x^2 + 6x + \boxed{?}$ **8.** $x^2 - 14x + \boxed{?}$ **9.** $x^2 + 8x + \boxed{?}$

10. $x^2 - x + \boxed{?}$ **11.** $x^2 - 22x + \boxed{?}$ **12.** $x^2 + 7x + \boxed{?}$

In 13–18, write the equation in the form $x^2 + bx = -c$. Then solve the equation by completing the square.

13. $x^2 - 2x - 2 = 0$ **14.** $x^2 + 4x - 1 = 0$ **15.** $x^2 - 6x + 2 = 0$

16. $x^2 + 12x + 3 = 0$ **17.** $x^2 + x - 2 = 0$ **18.** $x^2 - x - 1 = 0$

In 19–24, write the equation in the form $ax^2 + bx = -c$. Then divide each term by a and solve the equation by completing the square.

19. $2x^2 - 2x - 4 = 0$ **20.** $3x^2 + 9x - 12 = 0$ **21.** $2x^2 - 4x - 10 = 0$

22. $-5x^2 + 10x + 20 = 0$ **23.** $4x^2 - 4x - 2 = 0$ **24.** $3x^2 - 12x + 1 = 0$

Geometry In 25 and 26, find the dimensions of the figure. Round your answer to three decimal places.

25. Rectangle area = 178 square feet

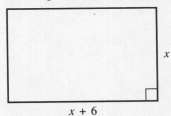

26. Triangle area = 23 square centimeters

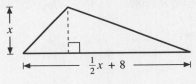

No Passing Zone In 27–30, use the following information.

A "No Passing Zone" sign has the shape of an isosceles triangle. The width of the sign is 7 inches greater than its height. The top and bottom edges of the sign are 44 inches.

27. Use the Pythagorean Theorem to write an equation that relates x, $2x + 7$, and 44.

28. Solve the equation in Exercise 27 by completing the square. (Hint: Use decimal representations and a calculator to simplify your work.)

29. What is the height of the sign?

30. What is the width of the sign?

Name _____

In 1–6, write the equation in standard form. Identify *a*, *b*, and *c*.

1. $2x^2 - 5 = x$　　　**2.** $x^2 = 5x - 6$　　　**3.** $3x = 7 - 3x^2$

4. $3x^2 + 5 = x^2 - 4x$　　　**5.** $2 - x = 8x - x^2$　　　**6.** $-5x^2 + 2 = x^2 - 1$

In 7–12, find the discriminant, $b^2 - 4ac$, of the quadratic equation.

7. $x^2 - x + 3 = 0$　　　**8.** $-x^2 + 2x - 1 = 0$　　　**9.** $3x^2 + x - 2 = 0$

10. $4x^2 - 12x + 9 = 0$　　　**11.** $5x^2 - 2x + 4 = 0$　　　**12.** $-2x^2 + 3x + 5 = 0$

In 13–18, find the discriminant and use it to determine the number of real solutions of the equation.

13. $x^2 - 2x - 3 = 0$　　　**14.** $x^2 + 5x + 2 = 0$　　　**15.** $-x^2 + 3x - 5 = 0$

16. $-4x^2 + 20x - 25 = 0$　　　**17.** $3x^2 - 2x + 1 = 0$　　　**18.** $2x^2 - x + 4 = 0$

In 19–24, use the quadratic formula to solve the equation.

19. $x^2 - x - 1 = 0$　　　**20.** $-2x^2 + 3x + 2 = 0$　　　**21.** $2x^2 + x - 4 = 0$

22. $4x^2 - 9x + 2 = 0$　　　**23.** $10x^2 + 2x - 5 = 0$　　　**24.** $-8x^2 + 7x + 2 = 0$

In 25–30, write the equation in standard form. Then use the quadratic formula to solve the equation.

25. $3x^2 - 4x = 2x^2 + 2$　　　**26.** $x^2 - 5 = 2x - 1$　　　**27.** $4 - 2x^2 = x - 3$

28. $x^2 - 3x + 2 = 4x^2 - 3$　　　**29.** $9x - x^2 = x^2 + 4x - 1$　　　**30.** $6x^2 + 5 = 2x^2 - 3x + 7$

Geometry In 31 and 32, use the quadratic formula to find the dimensions of the figure. Round your answer to three decimal places.

31. Rectangle area = 24.5 square inches

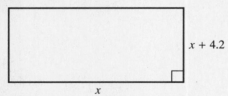

$x + 4.2$

x

32. Parallelogram area = 63.9 square centimeters

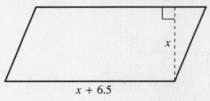

x

$x + 6.5$

Throwing an Object on the Moon In 33–35, use the following information.

An astronaut standing on the surface of the moon throws a rock into the air with an initial velocity of 27 feet per second. The astronaut's hand is 6 feet above the surface of the moon. The height of the rock is given by $h = -2.7t^2 + 27t + 6$.

33. How many seconds is the rock in the air?

34. Suppose the astronaut had been standing on the earth's surface. Write a vertical motion model for the height of the rock after it is thrown.

35. Use the model in Exercise 34 to determine how many seconds the rock remains in the air when thrown from the earth's surface.

In 1–8, write the number using the imaginary unit *i*.

1. $\sqrt{-16}$ 2. $\sqrt{-36}$ 3. $\sqrt{-121}$ 4. $-\sqrt{-64}$

5. $\sqrt{-6}$ 6. $\sqrt{-7}$ 7. $\sqrt{-11}$ 8. $-\sqrt{-15}$

In 9–16, use the fact that $i^2 = -1$ to simplify the expression.

9. $3i^2$ 10. $(3i)^2$ 11. $-5i^2$ 12. $(-5i)^2$

13. $\left(\sqrt{-4}\right)^2$ 14. $\left(\sqrt{-49}\right)^2$ 15. $\left(\sqrt{-13}\right)^2$ 16. $\left(\sqrt{-11}\right)^2$

In 17–22, solve the equation. Use the imaginary unit *i* to write your solutions.

17. $x^2 = -16$ 18. $x^2 = -81$ 19. $x^2 + 144 = 0$

20. $x^2 + 5 = 4$ 21. $-2x^2 + 3 = 11$ 22. $x^2 - 7 = 4x^2 + 5$

In 23–28, add (or subtract) the complex numbers.

23. $(5 + 3i) + (2 + 4i)$ 24. $(3 - 2i) + (1 + i)$ 25. $(7 + 2i) - (3 + 3i)$

26. $(5 + i) - (3 - 8i)$ 27. $i + (11 - 5i)$ 28. $i - (6 + i) + (4 - 2i)$

In 29–34, use the Distributive Property to multiply the complex numbers.

29. $i(4 + i)$ 30. $3i(-1 + 2i)$ 31. $-4i(3 - 7i)$

32. $(1 + 3i)(1 - i)$ 33. $(5 - i)(1 - 2i)$ 34. $(2 + 3i)(3 + 4i)$

In 35–37, identify the complex numbers in the complex plane.

35. 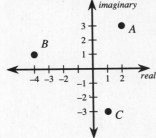   36. 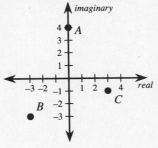   37.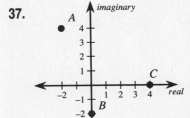

38. **What's for Lunch?** Plot the complex numbers in the complex plane provided at the right. Some points are plotted twice (i.e., $A = M$, $B = T$, and $G = K$). Connect the points in alphabetical order. Determine what's for lunch.

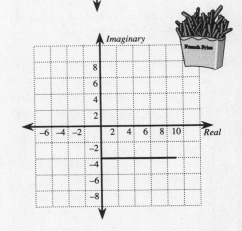

$A = -3i$	$F = -1 - 7i$	$K = -2 - 4i$	$P = 1$
$B = 9 - 3i$	$G = -2 - 4i$	$L = -4i$	$Q = 8$
$C = 9 - 4i$	$H = -6$	$M = -3i$	$R = 10 - 2i$
$D = 11 - 4i$	$I = -2 + 8i$	$N = -1 - 3i$	$S = 10 - 3i$
$E = 10 - 7i$	$J = 4 + 8i$	$O = -1 - 2i$	$T = 9 - 3i$

Name _____

In 1–6, decide whether the complex number is a solution of the equation.

1. $x^2 - 2x + 2 = 0, \ 1 - i$ **2.** $x^2 - 4x - 5 = 0, \ 2 + i$

3. $x^2 - 6x + 10 = 0, \ 3 + i$ **4.** $x^2 - 2x + 17 = 0, \ 1 - 4i$

5. $x^2 - 4x - 13 = 0, \ 2 - 3i$ **6.** $x^2 - 6x + 13 = 0, \ 3 + 2i$

In 7–15, use the quadratic formula to solve the equation. Use the imaginary unit *i* to write your solutions.

7. $x^2 - 2x + 2 = 0$ **8.** $x^2 - 12x + 37 = 0$ **9.** $x^2 + 8x + 17 = 0$

10. $-x^2 + 2x - 10 = 0$ **11.** $4x^2 - 4x + 5 = 0$ **12.** $9x^2 - 36x + 37 = 0$

13. $9x^2 - 24x + 17 = 0$ **14.** $3x^2 + 5 = x^2 + 2x$ **15.** $x^2 - 2x = 5x - 13$

In 16–21, find all real solutions of the equation. Round your answers to two decimal places.

16. $x^2 + 5x - 7 = 0$ **17.** $x^2 - 5x - 3 = 0$ **18.** $-x^2 + 2x + 4 = 0$

19. $5x^2 - 9x - 11 = 0$ **20.** $0.5x^2 + 1.2x - 2.5 = 0$ **21.** $3.45x^2 - 0.24x - 7.31 = 0$

22. *Fencing Your Garden* It takes 80 feet of fencing to enclose your garden. According to your calculations, you will need 350 square feet to plant everything you want. Is your garden big enough? Explain your answer.

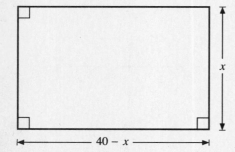

23. *New Carpeting* You have new carpeting installed in a rectangular room. You are charged for 20 square yards of carpeting and 48 feet (16 yards) of tack strip. Do you think these figures are correct? Explain your answer.

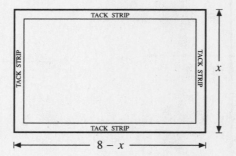

24. *Charitable Contributions* According to a survey conducted in 1990 by *Independent Sector*, the percent of their incomes that Americans give to charities is related to their household incomes. For families with annual incomes between \$5000 and \$100,000, the percent is modeled by

$$P = 0.0014x^2 - 0.1529x + 5.855$$

where P is the percentage of annual income given and x is the annual income in thousands of dollars. At what annual income do Americans give 1%, $P = 1$, of that income to charity? Explain your answer.

In 1–4, determine whether the ordered pair is a solution of the inequality.

1. $y < x^2 - 2x + 4$, $(1, 2)$

2. $y > 2x^2 + x - 5$, $(-2, 1)$

3. $y \leq -2x^2 + 5x + 6$, $(4, -4)$

4. $y \geq -3x^2 - 4x + 1$, $(-3, -6)$

In 5–7, match the inequality with its graph.

5. $y \geq -x^2 + 4x - 3$

a.

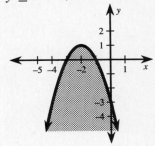

6. $y \leq -x^2 - 4x - 3$

b.

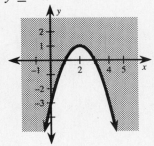

7. $y \leq x^2 + 2x - 3$

c.

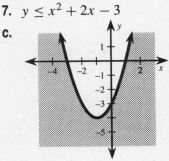

In 8–16, sketch the graph of the inequality.

8. $y \leq 2x^2 + 1$

9. $y \geq x^2 + 2x$

10. $y > 3x^2 - 6x$

11. $y < x^2 - 2x + 1$

12. $y \leq -x^2 + 6x - 7$

13. $y \geq 3x^2 + 6x + 2$

14. $y > -x^2 - 6x - 9$

15. $y \geq 2x^2 + 4x - 2$

16. $y < -2x^2 - 8x - 5$

In 17–22, sketch the intersection of the graphs of the inequalities.

17. $y \geq x^2$

   $y \leq -x^2 + 3$

18. $y \geq 2x^2 - 4$

   $y \leq -x^2 - 1$

19. $y \leq -x^2 + 4$

   $y \geq x^2 - 2x + 1$

20. $y \leq -x^2 + 4$

   $y \geq x^2 + 2x + 1$

21. $y > x^2 + 4x + 1$

   $y \leq -x^2 - 2x + 1$

22. $y \geq 2x^2 - 12x + 16$

   $y < -x^2 + 2x + 3$

Gift Shop Logo In 23–26, use the following information.

You are using a computer to create a logo for a gift shop called *On the Wings of a Dove*. The logo you have designed is shown at the right.

23. Sketch the intersections of the graphs of the inequalities.

   a. $y \geq 0.33x^2 - 2x + 4$

   $y \leq -0.09x^2 + 1.3x$

   b. $y \geq 0.33x^2 + 2x + 4$

   $y \leq -0.09x^2 - 1.3x$

24. Which region in Exercise 23 represents the dove's left wing?

25. Which region in Exercise 23 represents the dove's right wing?

26. Which two inequalities (when intersected) make up the dove's tail?

Name _____

In 1 and 2, identify the domain and range of the relation.

1. {(1, −4), (2, −3), (3, −2), (4, −1), (5, 0)}   **2.** {(0, 2), (1, −3), (2, −1), (3, 2), (4, 1)}

In 3–5, use a set of ordered pairs to describe the relation.

3.
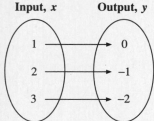

4.
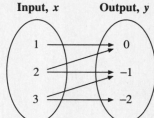

5.
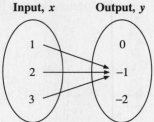

In 6 and 7, sketch a graph of the relation.

6.

Input, x	0	1	2	3	4	5
Output, y	−2	4	−1	−2	3	2

7.

Input, x	3	3	7	5	1	5
Output, y	2	4	6	8	10	12

In 8–10, use a mapping diagram to describe the relation.

8.
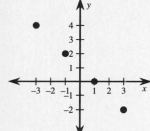

9.
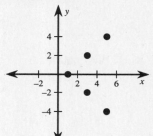

10.
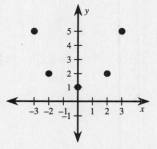

11. Which of the relations in Exercises 6 and 7 is a function?

12. Which of the relations in Exercises 8–10 are functions?

In 13 and 14, determine whether the relation is a function.

13. {(1, −1), (2, −1), (3, −1), (4, −1)}

14. {(2, 3), (2, 4), (2, 5), (2, 6), (2, 7)}

In 15–20, find the indicated value of f(x).

15. $f(x) = x + 2$, $f(-1)$

16. $f(x) = 2x - 1$, $f(2)$

17. $f(x) = x^2 - 3$, $f(3)$

18. $f(x) = x^2 + 2x$, $f(-2)$

19. $f(x) = 2x^2 - x + 1$, $f(0)$

20. $f(x) = -3x^2 + x - 2$, $f(4)$

21. *Movie Theaters*   For 1984 through 1989, the number of movie theaters, M (in thousands), in the United States is shown in the table. Was the number of movie theaters a function of the year?

Year	1984	1985	1986	1987	1988	1989
Movie Theaters, M	20	21	22	24	23	23

In 1–6, find the set of all *x*-values that make sense in the function.

1. $f(x) = 3x + 2$

2. $f(x) = x^2 - 2x + 1$

3. $f(x) = \dfrac{3}{x}$

4. $f(x) = \sqrt{2x}$

5. $f(x) = \dfrac{x}{x - 1}$

6. $f(x) = \sqrt{x + 2}$

In 7–10, find *f*(*x*) + *g*(*x*). Simplify your answer.

7. $f(x) = 4x$, $g(x) = 1 - x$

8. $f(x) = 2x + 3$, $g(x) = x^2 - 1$

9. $f(x) = x^2 + 3$, $g(x) = x^2 - 2x - 1$

10. $f(x) = x^2 - 2x + 3$, $g(x) = x^2 + x - 4$

In 11–14, find *f*(*x*) – *g*(*x*). Simplify your answer.

11. $f(x) = 2x$, $g(x) = x + 3$

12. $f(x) = x^2 - x$, $g(x) = x^2 - 2$

13. $f(x) = x + 1$, $g(x) = -x^2 + 2x + 3$

14. $f(x) = 2x^2 - 3x + 4$, $g(x) = x^2 + x$

In 15–18, find *f*(*x*) · *g*(*x*). Simplify your answer.

15. $f(x) = 2x - 1$, $g(x) = 3$

16. $f(x) = x + 1$, $g(x) = 3x - 2$

17. $f(x) = x^2 + x - 1$, $g(x) = 2x$

18. $f(x) = -x^2 + 2x + 2$, $g(x) = x + 1$

In 19–22, find *f*(*x*) ÷ *g*(*x*).

19. $f(x) = 3x$, $g(x) = x + 2$

20. $f(x) = x^2 + 1$, $g(x) = x - 2$

21. $f(x) = x - 2$, $g(x) = x^2 + x - 4$

22. $f(x) = 3x^2 - x + 1$, $g(x) = x + 3$

In 23–26, use the three-step process described in the text to find *f*(*g*(*x*))
and *g*(*f*(*x*)).

23. $f(x) = 3x$, $g(x) = 2x + 1$

24. $f(x) = x + 1$, $g(x) = 3x - 2$

25. $f(x) = x^2 + 1$, $g(x) = x - 2$

26. $f(x) = x^2 + x - 3$, $g(x) = x + 1$

Furniture Sale   In 27–31, use the following information.

You have a coupon for $100 off the price of a sofa. When you arrive at
the store, you find that the sofas are on sale for 25% off.

27. Let *x* represent the original price of the sofa. Use
function notation to describe your cost, $f(x)$, using
only the coupon.

28. Let *x* represent the original price of the sofa. Use
function notation to describe your cost, $g(x)$, with only
the 25% discount.

29. Form the composition of the functions *f* and *g* that
represents your cost if you use the coupon first, then
take the 25% discount.

30. Form the composition of the functions *f* and *g* that
represents your cost if you use the discount first, then
use the coupon.

31. Would you pay less for the sofa if you used the coupon
first or took the 25% discount first?

In 1–4, find the inverse of the relation.

1. $\{(1, 3), (4, -2), (-1, 0), (2, 1), (-3, -4)\}$ **2.** $\{(0, 1), (1, -2), (2, 4), (3, -1), (4, 0)\}$

3. $\{(-3, 5), (-5, 4), (2, 7), (-1, -2), (4, 1)\}$ **4.** $\{(\frac{1}{2}, 6), (0, 4), (-\frac{2}{3}, 2), (-1, 1), (3, 0)\}$

In 5–10, find an equation for the inverse of the relation.

5. $y = 2x$ **6.** $y = -x + 5$ **7.** $y = 3x + 1$

8. $y = 4x - 9$ **9.** $y = \frac{1}{2}x + 6$ **10.** $y = x^2 + 3$

In 11–13, find the inverse of the function. Then sketch the inverse on the given coordinate system. Is the inverse a function of x?

11. $f(x) = 4x + 3$ **12.** $f(x) = \frac{1}{2}x - 1$ **13.** $f(x) = x^2 + 2$

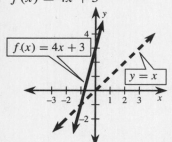 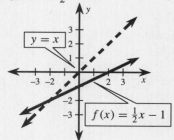 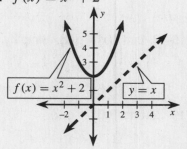

In 14–19, use the horizontal line test to determine whether the inverse of f is a function of x.

14. $f(x) = -3x + 5$ **15.** $f(x) = 2x^2 - 3$ **16.** $f(x) = 1 - x^2$

17. $f(x) = |x|$ **18.** $f(x) = 3 - 2x$ **19.** $f(x) = \frac{1}{2}x + 4$

In 20–25, verify that f and g are inverses of each other by showing that $f(g(x)) = g(f(x))$.

20. $f(x) = 2x$, $g(x) = \dfrac{x}{2}$ **21.** $f(x) = 1 - x$, $g(x) = 1 - x$

22. $f(x) = x - 2$, $g(x) = x + 2$ **23.** $f(x) = -3x + 6$, $g(x) = -\frac{1}{3}x + 2$

24. $f(x) = \frac{1}{2}x - 4$, $g(x) = 2x + 8$ **25.** $f(x) = 4x + 1$, $g(x) = \frac{1}{4}x - \frac{1}{4}$

26. ***Temperature Conversion*** The formula to convert temperature in degrees Celsius to temperature in Kelvins is

$\quad K = C + 273.15$.

For this formula, C is the input and K is the output. Rewrite the formula so that K is the input and C is the output.

27. ***Sale Price*** A gift shop is having a store-wide 25% off sale. The sale price, S, of an item that has a regular price of R is

$\quad S = R - 0.25R$.

Rewrite this formula so that S is the input and R is the output.

In 1–5, evaluate the function for the given value of *x*.

$$f(x) = \begin{cases} x^2, & x \le 0 \\ x - 1, & x > 0 \end{cases}$$

1. $f(-1)$ **2.** $f(1)$ **3.** $f(0)$ **4.** $f(-2)$ **5.** $f(2)$

In 6–10, evaluate the function for the given value of *x*.

$$g(x) = \begin{cases} 2x + 1, & x < -1 \\ x^2 - 2, & x \ge -1 \end{cases}$$

6. $g(0)$ **7.** $g(-2)$ **8.** $g(-1)$ **9.** $g(1)$ **10.** $g(-3)$

In 11–16, sketch the graph of the compound function.

11. $f(x) = \begin{cases} x + 1, & x \le 0 \\ x^2 + 1, & x > 0 \end{cases}$

12. $g(x) = \begin{cases} x - 2, & x \le 1 \\ x^2 - 2x, & x > 1 \end{cases}$

13. $g(x) = \begin{cases} \frac{1}{2}x - 1, & x < 2 \\ x^2 - 3x + 2, & x \ge 2 \end{cases}$

14. $f(x) = \begin{cases} 3x + 4, & x < -2 \\ x^2 + 4x + 2, & x \ge -2 \end{cases}$

15. $h(x) = \begin{cases} -x^2 + 3x + 1, & x \le 3 \\ x - 4, & x > 3 \end{cases}$

16. $f(x) = \begin{cases} x - 1, & x < 1 \\ x^2 - 3x + 3, & x \ge 1 \end{cases}$

In 17–25, write the absolute value function as a compound function.

17. $f(x) = |x - 3|$

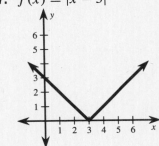

18. $f(x) = |2x - 4|$

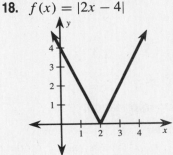

19. $f(x) = |1 - \frac{1}{2}x|$

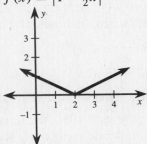

20. $f(x) = |x + 4|$

21. $f(x) = |-x + 2|$

22. $f(x) = |3x - 3|$

23. $f(x) = |4x + 12|$

24. $f(x) = |\frac{1}{2}x + 1|$

25. $f(x) = |\frac{1}{3}x - 2|$

In 26–28, sketch the graph of the step function.

26. $f(x) = \begin{cases} 2, & 0 \le x < 2 \\ 4, & 2 \le x < 4 \\ 6, & 4 \le x < 6 \\ 8, & 6 \le x < 8 \end{cases}$

27. $f(x) = \begin{cases} 9, & -3 \le x < 0 \\ 5, & 0 \le x < 3 \\ 2, & 3 \le x < 6 \\ 1, & 6 \le x < 9 \end{cases}$

28. $f(x) = \begin{cases} -4, & -2 \le x < 2 \\ -1, & 2 \le x < 6 \\ 2, & 6 \le x < 10 \\ 5, & 10 \le x < 14 \end{cases}$

29. *Band Jackets* The members of your high school band want to purchase new jackets. The silk-screen shop charges a $25 set up fee and $28 per jacket. If you order more than 48 jackets, the price per jacket is reduced to $23. Write a compound function that gives the cost, *C*, for an order of *x* jackets. Sketch the graph of the function.

Name _____

In 1–3, show how *f* and *g* are related by writing an equation of the form
$g(x) = f(\boxed{?})$ or $g(x) = f(x) + \boxed{?}$.

1. $f(x) = x^2$
  $g(x) = x^2 + 11$

2. $f(x) = |x|$
  $g(x) = |x - 2|$

3. $f(x) = x^2$
  $g(x) = (x + 3)^2$

In 4–9, describe how the graph of *g*(*x*) can be obtained from the graph of
$f(x) = x^2$.

4. $g(x) = x^2 - 1$

5. $g(x) = (x - 1)^2$

6. $g(x) = (x + 7)^2$

7. $g(x) = -x^2$

8. $g(x) = x^2 + 9$

9. $g(x) = (x + 3)^2$

In 10–12, match the function with its graph.

10. $f(x) = |x - 5| + 2$

11. $f(x) = |x - 2| + 5$

12. $f(x) = -|x - 5| + 2$

a.

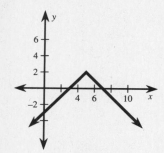

b.

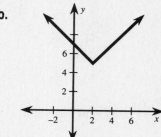

c.

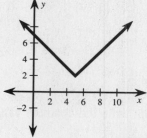

In 13–18, sketch the graph of the function.

13. $f(x) = (x + 1)^2$

14. $f(x) = (x + 1)^2 - 2$

15. $f(x) = -(x + 1)^2$

16. $f(x) = |x| - 3$

17. $f(x) = -|x|$

18. $f(x) = -|x| - 3$

School Enrollment In 19–21, use the following information.

For 1970 through 1990, the number of students, $f(t)$ (in thousands),
enrolled in public elementary schools in the United States can be modeled
by

$$f(t) = 36.7t^2 - 905.8t + 32{,}634$$

where $t = 0$ represents 1970.

19. Rewrite the model so that $t = 0$ represents 1980. Describe how this new
  model is a shift of the original model.

20. Rewrite the model so that $t = 0$ represents 1985. Describe how this new
  model is a shift of the original model.

21. Approximate the number of students enrolled in public elementary schools
  in 1983.

In 1–6, find the first five values of the recursive function.

1. $f(0) = 1$
   $f(n) = f(n-1) + 3$

2. $f(0) = 0$
   $f(n) = n + f(n-1)$

3. $f(1) = 2$
   $f(n) = 3 \cdot f(n-1)$

4. $f(1) = 10$
   $f(n) = n^2 - |f(n-1)|$

5. $f(0) = 1$
   $f(n) = [f(n-1)]^2 + 2$

6. $f(1) = 2, \ f(2) = 3$
   $f(n) = f(n-1) - f(n-2)$

In 7–9, find the first six values of the recursive function. Then use the values to find the first differences of the function.

7. $f(1) = 0$
   $f(n) = f(n-1) + 4$

8. $f(0) = -2$
   $f(n) = [f(n-1)]^2 - 3$

9. $f(0) = 1$
   $f(n) = -f(n-1) + n$

10. Which of the functions in Exercises 7–9 has a linear model?

In 11–13, find the first six values of the recursive function. Then use the values to find the second differences of the function.

11. $f(0) = 1$
   $f(n) = 2 \cdot f(n-1) + 1$

12. $f(0) = 2$
   $f(n) = n - f(n-1)$

13. $f(1) = -1$
   $f(n) = f(n-1) - 2n$

14. Which of the functions in Exercises 11–13 has a quadratic model?

In 15–17, find a linear model that has the indicated values.

15. $f(1) = 0, \ f(2) = 3$

16. $f(0) = 5, \ f(3) = 8$

17. $f(4) = 2, \ f(1) = 5$

In 18–20, find a quadratic model that has the indicated values.

18. $f(1) = -2$
   $f(2) = 2$
   $f(3) = 8$

19. $f(0) = 1$
   $f(2) = 1$
   $f(3) = 4$

20. $f(4) = -5$
   $f(1) = 4$
   $f(3) = 0$

Diagonals of a Polygon **In 21 and 22, use the following information.**

The number of diagonals, $f(n)$, from a single vertex of an n-sided polygon ($n > 3$) is given by the following function.

   $f(3) = 0$
   $f(n) = f(n-1) + 1$

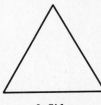 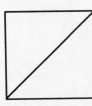 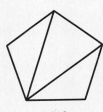 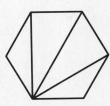 

| *3 Sides* | *4 Sides* | *5 Sides* | *6 Sides* | *7 Sides* |

21. Write the first six values of the function.

22. Write a linear model for the function.

In 1–4, use the following set of numbers.

{2, 3, 7, 1, 8, 7, 4, 5, 1, 8, 2, 6, 5, 9, 1}

1. Write the numbers in ascending order.

2. Find the mean of the numbers.

3. Find the median of the numbers.

4. Find the mode of the numbers.

In 5–7, use the following set of numbers.

{32, 23, 17, 15, 13, 27, 35, 25, 15, 12, 30, 23, 22, 14, 35, 12, 33, 28, 15, 32}

5. Write the numbers in ascending order.

6. Find the first, second, and third quartiles.

7. Construct a box-and-whisker plot for the numbers.

8. *Reading Levels* The *Pledge of Allegiance* contains 31 words. The bar graph at the right shows the number of words of different lengths in the pledge. Find the mean word length of the set of 31 words.

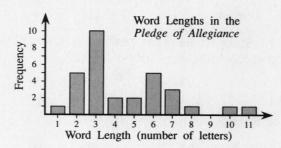

Word Lengths in the *Pledge of Allegiance*

Walking Shoes **In 9–11, use the following information.**

An important feature of walking shoes is their weight. The graph at the right shows the weight of the top-10 rated men's walking shoes.

9. Find the mean of the ten weights.

10. Find the median of the ten weights.

11. Find the mode of the ten weights.

Ranking	Weight	Ranking	Weight
1	24 oz	6	28 oz
2	22 oz	7	22 oz
3	26 oz	8	28 oz
4	28 oz	9	22 oz
5	24 oz	10	28 oz

World Series **In 12 and 13, use the following information.**

The World Series is a best-of-seven playoff between the National League champion and the American League champion. The table shows the number of games played in each World Series for 1971 through 1990.

Year	1971	1972	1973	1974	1975	1976	1977	1978	1979	1980
Games	7	7	7	5	7	4	6	6	7	6

Year	1981	1982	1983	1984	1985	1986	1987	1988	1989	1990
Games	6	7	5	5	7	7	7	5	4	4

12. Find the first, second, and third quartiles for the number of games played.

13. Construct a box-and-whisker plot for the number of games played.

Name _____

In 1–20, use properties of exponents to simplify the expression.

1. $(3^4)(3^{-2})$

2. $\dfrac{(-2)^8}{(-2)^3}$

3. $(5^2)^3$

4. $\left(\dfrac{2}{3}\right)^3$

5. $\dfrac{8^4}{8^6}$

6. $(7^6)(7^{-6})$

7. $\left(\dfrac{1}{2}\right)^{-4}$

8. $\dfrac{4 \cdot 4^3}{4^6}$

9. $x^3 \cdot x^2$

10. $\dfrac{2y^3}{y^5}$

11. $(3x)^2$

12. $\left(\dfrac{y}{2}\right)^3$

13. $(4x^3)^4$

14. $x^0 y^{-2}$

15. $\dfrac{5x^2 y}{2x^{-1} y^3}$

16. $\dfrac{-3xy}{9x^3 y^{-4}}$

17. $\dfrac{xy}{4} \cdot \dfrac{2x^2}{y^3}$

18. $\dfrac{-2x^2}{3xy^3} \cdot \dfrac{2x^{-1}}{y^{-1}}$

19. $\dfrac{x^{-4}}{y^{-2}} \cdot \dfrac{y^{-2}}{x^{-4}}$

20. $\dfrac{5x^2 y}{8} \cdot \dfrac{-2x^{-1} y}{x^3 y}$

21. *Geometry* Find an expression for the area of the triangle.

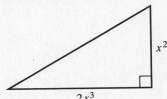

22. *Geometry* Find an expression for the area of the circle.

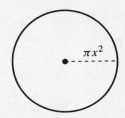

πx^2

In 23–28, use the properties of exponents to simplify the left side of the equation. Then solve the equation as demonstrated below.

$$4^{x-1} = 4^2 \implies x - 1 = 2 \implies x = 3$$

23. $2^x 2^3 = 2^5$

24. $\dfrac{3^x}{3^2} = 3^4$

25. $(5^x)^3 = 5^{12}$

26. $\dfrac{4^3}{4^x} = 4^0$

27. $\dfrac{2^{-x} y^2}{y^2} = 2^5$

28. $(-2x)^0 (3^2)(3^x) = 3^{-1}$

Class Project In 29–33, use the following information.

Your class project is to design a piece of playground equipment for an elementary school. You design a romper room that will contain small plastic balls for the children to roll around in. The room will be 10 feet by 10 feet. The plastic balls will cover the entire floor to a depth of 2 feet. A toy distributor can ship you 190 balls (each with a radius of $1\frac{3}{4}$ inches) in a cubic box, 20-inches on a side.

29. Find an expression for the volume (in cubic inches) of one ball.

30. Find an expression that represents the ratio of the volume of 190 balls to the volume of the cubic box.

31. What percent of the volume of the cubic box is filled with plastic balls?

32. Find the volume of the region in the romper room that will contain plastic balls. Give your result in cubic inches.

33. How many balls will you need to fill the romper room as described?

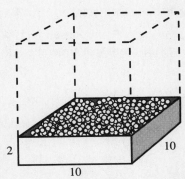

Balance in an Account In 1–5, use the following information.

You deposit $500 into a savings account for three years. The account pays 5% annual interest, compounded monthly. To calculate the balance in your account after the three years, you can use the formula $A = P\left(1 + \frac{r}{n}\right)^{nt}$

1. What is the value of P?

2. What is the value of r?

3. What is the value of n?

4. What is the value of t?

5. Use the formula to calculate the balance in your account after the three years.

6. Balance in an Account $1200 is deposited in an account that pays 6% annual interest, compounded quarterly. Find the balance after five years.

7. Balance in an Account $2000 is deposited in an account that pays 7% annual interest, compounded annually. Find the balance after ten years.

8. How Much to Deposit How much must you deposit in an account that pays 6.5% interest, compounded semi-annually, to have a balance of $5000 in 15 years?

9. Houston Astrodome The Houston Astrodome was the first baseball and football stadium to be completely enclosed. It was completed in 1965 at a cost of 45.35 million dollars. Construction costs have increased by approximately 6% each year since 1965. How much would it cost to build the Astrodome today?

In 10–13, complete the table and sketch the graph of the function. State whether the function represents exponential growth or exponential decay.

10. $y = 3(2)^x$

x	−2	−1	0	1	2
y					

11. $y = 3\left(\frac{1}{2}\right)^x$

x	−2	−1	0	1	2
y					

12. $y = \frac{1}{2}\left(\frac{3}{2}\right)^x$

x	−1	0	1	2	3
y					

13. $y = 4(0.7)^x$

x	−2	−1	0	1	2
y					

Automobile Depreciation In 14 and 15, use the following information.

A new car was purchased in 1990 for $14,000. The value of the car, V, decreased from that time according to the model

$$V = 14,000(0.84)^t$$

where $t = 0$ represents 1990.

14. Sketch the graph of this model.

15. Find the value of the car in 1993.

In 1–4, write the expression using rational exponents.

1. $\sqrt[3]{11}$ **2.** $\sqrt[4]{5}$ **3.** $\sqrt[6]{82}$ **4.** $\sqrt[5]{27}$

In 5–8, write the expression using radical notation.

5. $19^{1/3}$ **6.** $43^{1/5}$ **7.** $25^{1/4}$ **8.** $6^{1/7}$

In 9–17, use a calculator to evaluate the expression. Round the result to two decimal places.

9. $4^{1/3}$ **10.** $28^{1/4}$ **11.** $1246^{1/8}$

12. $215^{1/5}$ **13.** $(-15)^{1/3}$ **14.** $116^{1/6}$

15. $\sqrt[4]{49}$ **16.** $\sqrt[9]{19,422}$ **17.** $\sqrt[5]{-122}$

In 18–26, use the property $a^{m/n} = (a^{1/n})^m$ to rewrite the expression. Then evaluate the expression without using a calculator.

18. $8^{4/3}$ **19.** $36^{3/2}$ **20.** $16^{3/4}$

21. $81^{3/2}$ **22.** $64^{2/3}$ **23.** $32^{2/5}$

24. $4^{5/2}$ **25.** $81^{3/4}$ **26.** $243^{6/5}$

In 27–32, evaluate the expression without using a calculator.

27. $(-64)^{1/3}$ **28.** $16^{-1/4}$ **29.** $25^{-3/2}$

30. $100^{-5/2}$ **31.** $(-8)^{5/3}$ **32.** $256^{-3/4}$

33. *Geometry*   Find the length of an edge of the regular tetrahedron shown below.

34. *Geometry*   Find the radius of the sphere shown below.

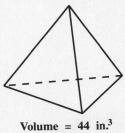

Volume = 44 in.³

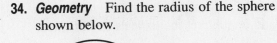

Volume = 382 cm³

Water and Ice   In 35–38, use the following information.

Water, in its liquid state, has a density of 0.9971 grams per cubic centimeter. Ice has a density of 0.9168 grams per cubic centimeter. You fill a cubical container with 510 grams of liquid water. A different cubical container is filled with 510 grams of solid water (ice).

35. Find the volume of the container filled with liquid water.

36. Find the length of the edges of the container in Exercise 35.

37. Find the volume of the container filled with ice.

38. Find the length of the edges of the container in Exercise 37.

In 1–9, use the properties of roots to simplify the expression.

1. $5^{2/3} \cdot 5^{4/3}$

2. $\dfrac{3^{1/2}}{3}$

3. $(7^{2/3})^{5/2}$

4. $3^{1/4} \cdot 4^{1/4}$

5. $\sqrt[3]{2} \cdot \sqrt[3]{4}$

6. $\dfrac{\sqrt[4]{240}}{\sqrt[4]{15}}$

7. $(3^{1/2} \cdot 5^{2/3})^{3/2}$

8. $\dfrac{\sqrt[3]{3}}{3}$

9. $\left(\dfrac{64}{125}\right)^{1/3}$

In 10–18, use the properties of roots to simplify the variable expression.

10. $\sqrt{9x^2}$

11. $\sqrt[3]{2x^3}$

12. $x^{2/3} \cdot x^{1/3}$

13. $\left(\dfrac{x}{4}\right)^{1/2}$

14. $(16x)^{1/4}$

15. $\sqrt[5]{27x} \cdot \sqrt[5]{9x^4}$

16. $\dfrac{\sqrt{12x^2}}{\sqrt{3}}$

17. $\dfrac{1}{(x^2)^{-1/3}}$

18. $\sqrt[4]{256xy^4}$

In 19–27, use the properties of roots to simplify the expression. Then use a calculator to evaluate the expression. (Round your result to two decimal places.)

19. $\sqrt[3]{2} \cdot \sqrt[3]{5}$

20. $5^{1/2} \cdot 5^{1/4}$

21. $(10^{1/3})^{1/2}$

22. $8^{2/3} \cdot 8$

23. $\dfrac{\sqrt[4]{80}}{\sqrt[4]{16}}$

24. $(3^{-2})^{2/3}$

25. $\sqrt[3]{9} \cdot \sqrt[3]{4}$

26. $(6^{1/2} \cdot 6^{3/2})^{4/3}$

27. $(2^{1/6} \cdot 2^{1/3})^{3/2}$

In 28–36, add or subtract the radicals as indicated.

28. $2\sqrt[3]{3} + \sqrt[3]{3}$

29. $5\sqrt{7} - 3\sqrt{7}$

30. $6\sqrt[5]{22} + 9\sqrt[5]{22}$

31. $-3\sqrt[4]{15} + 2\sqrt[4]{15}$

32. $3(2^{1/3}) + 5(2^{1/3})$

33. $4\sqrt{2} - \sqrt{8}$

34. $\sqrt[3]{40} + \sqrt[3]{5}$

35. $\sqrt[5]{96} - 4\sqrt[5]{3}$

36. $\sqrt{8} + \sqrt{18}$

Archery Target   **In 37–39, use the following information.**

The figure at the right shows a National Field Archers
Association official hunters' target. The area of the entire
target is approximately 490.9 square inches. The area
of the center white circle is approximately 19.6 square
inches.

37. Find the radius of the target.

38. Find the radius of the center white circle.

39. Find the ratio of the radius of the white circle to the
radius of the target.

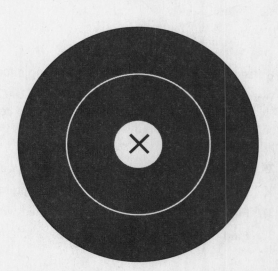

In 1–6, solve the equation by raising both sides to the appropriate power. Check for extraneous solutions.

1. $\sqrt{x} = 8$

2. $x^{1/3} = -2$

3. $\sqrt[3]{x+1} = 6$

4. $(2x)^{3/4} = 8$

5. $(x-1)^{2/3} = 4$

6. $\sqrt{2x+9} = 7$

In 7–12, isolate the radical expression and solve the equation. Check for extraneous solutions.

7. $x^{2/3} - 4 = 21$

8. $2x^{5/3} = -64$

9. $\sqrt[4]{3x} - 2 = 1$

10. $2(x+1)^{3/2} = 54$

11. $(2x+3)^{1/3} - 5 = -2$

12. $3(x-1)^{2/3} + 4 = 52$

In 13–18, solve the equation by raising both sides to the appropriate power. Check for extraneous solutions.

13. $\sqrt[3]{2x+3} = \sqrt[3]{x-1}$

14. $(4-x)^{2/3} = x^{2/3}$

15. $2\sqrt[3]{x} = \sqrt[3]{3x-5}$

16. $\sqrt{2x-5} = \sqrt{x}$

17. $\sqrt{4x} = x$

18. $\sqrt{x+7} = x+1$

19. *Geometric Mean* The geometric mean of 9 and a is 15. What is a?

20. *Geometric Mean* The geometric mean of 8 and a is $4\sqrt{2}$. What is a?

In 21–23, find the distance between the two points.

21. $(7, 6), (4, 2)$

22. $(5, 1), (3, -2)$

23. $(-1, 1), (-4, -3)$

In 24–26, find all values of x for which the distance between the given points is d.

24. $(3, 5), (0, x)$
$d = \sqrt{10}$

25. $(-1, 4), (x, 2)$
$d = \sqrt{5}$

26. $(6, x), (2, 3)$
$d = 4\sqrt{2}$

Rhode Island In 27–29, use the following information.

A grid is superimposed over the map of Rhode Island shown at the right. Each unit on the grid represents 4 miles.

27. Approximate the coordinates of the point representing Westerly.

28. Approximate the coordinates of the point representing Woonsocket.

29. Use the distance formula to approximate the distance between Westerly and Woonsocket.

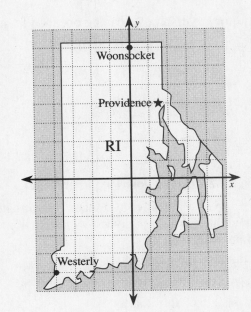

Name _____

In 1–6, match the function with its graph.

1. $f(x) = \sqrt[3]{x} + 2$

2. $f(x) = \sqrt[3]{x} - 2$

3. $f(x) = \sqrt[3]{x - 2}$

4. $f(x) = \sqrt{x + 1}$

5. $f(x) = -\sqrt{x + 1}$

6. $f(x) = \sqrt{x - 1}$

a.
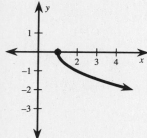

b.
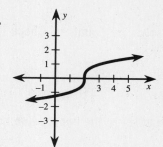

c.
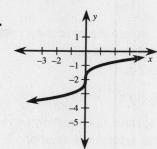

d.
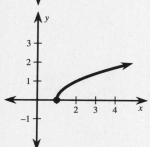

e.
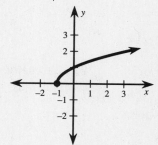

f.
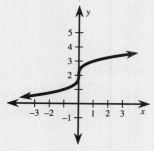

In 7–12, explain how the graph of g can be obtained from the graph of $f(x) = \sqrt{x}$.

7. $g(x) = \sqrt{x + 4}$

8. $g(x) = \sqrt{x + 4} - 2$

9. $g(x) = -\sqrt{x + 4}$

10. $g(x) = \sqrt{x - 4}$

11. $g(x) = \sqrt{x - 4} + 2$

12. $g(x) = -\sqrt{x - 4} + 2$

In 13–18, explain how the graph of g can be obtained from the graph of $f(x) = \sqrt[3]{x}$.

13. $g(x) = \sqrt[3]{x} - 1$

14. $g(x) = -\sqrt[3]{x} - 1$

15. $g(x) = -\sqrt[3]{x} + 1$

16. $g(x) = \sqrt[3]{x - 1}$

17. $g(x) = \sqrt[3]{x + 1}$

18. $g(x) = \sqrt[3]{x + 1} - 2$

In 19–24, sketch the graph of the function.

19. $f(x) = \sqrt{x - 3} + 2$

20. $g(x) = \sqrt{x + 1} - 3$

21. $f(x) = -\sqrt{x + 1} + 3$

22. $h(x) = \sqrt[3]{x + 1} + 3$

23. $f(x) = \sqrt[3]{x - 4} - 2$

24. $g(x) = -\sqrt[3]{x + 1} - 3$

Falling Object **In 25–27, use the following information.**

A stone is dropped from a height of 100 feet. The time it takes for the stone to reach a height of h feet is given by the function $t = \frac{1}{4}\sqrt{100 - h}$ where t is the time in seconds.

25. Identify the domain and range of the function.

26. Sketch the graph of the function.

27. How high is the stone after 2 seconds?

In 1–6, explain how the graph of *g* can be obtained from the graph of *f*.

1. $f(x) = \left(\frac{1}{3}\right)^x$
$g(x) = \left(\frac{1}{3}\right)^x + 2$

2. $f(x) = 2^x$
$g(x) = 2^x - 5$

3. $f(x) = \left(\frac{2}{3}\right)^x$
$g(x) = \left(\frac{2}{3}\right)^{x+1}$

4. $f(x) = 5^x$
$g(x) = 5^{x-3}$

5. $f(x) = \left(\frac{1}{2}\right)^x$
$g(x) = \left(\frac{1}{2}\right)^{x-1} + 2$

6. $f(x) = 10^x$
$g(x) = -10^{x+2}$

In 7–12, match the function with its graph.

7. $f(x) = \left(\frac{1}{3}\right)^x + 2$

8. $f(x) = \left(\frac{1}{3}\right)^{x+1} + 2$

9. $f(x) = \left(\frac{1}{3}\right)^{x+2} - 1$

10. $f(x) = 3^{x-1}$

11. $f(x) = -3^{x-1}$

12. $f(x) = -3^{x+1} + 2$

a.
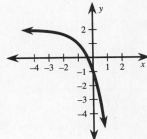

b.
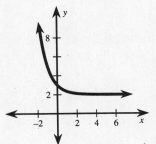

c.
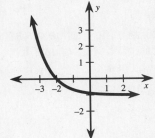

d.
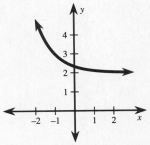

e.
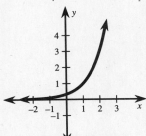

f.
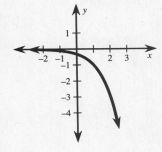

In 13–16, sketch the graph of the function.

13. $f(x) = 4^{x+2}$

14. $f(x) = -3^{x-1}$

15. $f(x) = \left(\frac{1}{2}\right)^x + 3$

16. $f(x) = 5^{x+2} - 1$

In 17–20, evaluate the expression. (Round to three decimal places.)

17. 4^{π}

18. $7^{\sqrt{5}}$

19. $15^{-\sqrt{3}}$

20. $9^{2\pi}$

Automobile Depreciation In 21–23, use the following information.

You have purchased a new car for $16,000. You expect the value of the car to decrease by 15% each year.

21. Write an exponential decay model for the value, *V*, of the car after *t* years.

22. Sketch the graph of the exponential decay model.

23. What will the car be worth after five years?

Name _____

In 1–6, write the logarithmic equation in exponential form.

1. $\log_4 16 = 2$ **2.** $\log_3 81 = 4$ **3.** $\log_2 1 = 0$

4. $\log_9 3 = \frac{1}{2}$ **5.** $\log_5 \frac{1}{5} = -1$ **6.** $\log_8 4 = \frac{2}{3}$

In 7–12, write the exponential equation in logarithmic form.

7. $2^3 = 8$ **8.** $7^2 = 49$ **9.** $10^{-2} = 0.01$

10. $5^0 = 1$ **11.** $9^{3/2} = 27$ **12.** $4^{-1/2} = \frac{1}{2}$

In 13–20, evaluate the logarithm without using a calculator.

13. $\log_2 4$ **14.** $\log_3 27$ **15.** $\log_4 1$ **16.** $\log_2 \frac{1}{2}$

17. $\log_8 2$ **18.** $\log_5 5^{2/3}$ **19.** $\log_3 3$ **20.** $\log_6 (-1)$

In 21–28, use the change of base formula to rewrite the expression. Then use a calculator to evaluate the expression. Round your result to three decimal places.

21. $\log_3 12$ **22.** $\log_6 2$ **23.** $\log_5 7$ **24.** $\log_4 0.5$

25. $\log_{0.8} 12$ **26.** $\log_{1.5} 2.8$ **27.** $\log_3 \frac{3}{2}$ **28.** $\log_{1/2} 6$

In 29–31, match the function with its graph.

29. $f(x) = \log_3 x$ **30.** $f(x) = \log_5 x$ **31.** $f(x) = \log_{1/2} x$

a.
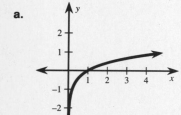

b.
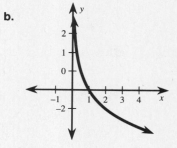

c.
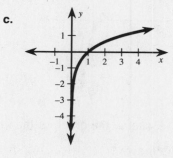

In 32–37, sketch the graph of the function.

32. $f(x) = \log_6 x$ **33.** $f(x) = 1 + \log_6 x$ **34.** $f(x) = \log_6 (x + 1)$

35. $f(x) = -\log_6 x$ **36.** $f(x) = \log_6 (2x)$ **37.** $f(x) = -1 + \log_6 x$

38. *Galloping Speed*   Four-legged animals run with two different types of motion: trotting and galloping. An animal that is trotting has at least one foot on the ground at all times. An animal that is galloping has all four feet off the ground at times. The number, s, of strides per minute at which an animal breaks from a trot to a gallop is related to the animal's weight, w (in pounds), by the model

$$s = 256.2 - 47.9 \log_{10} w.$$

Approximate the number of strides per minute for a 500-pound horse when it breaks from a trot to a gallop.

In 1–6, use the properties of logarithms to rewrite the expression in terms of $\log_{10} 3$ and $\log_{10} 4$. Then use $\log_{10} 3 \approx 0.477$ and $\log_{10} 4 \approx 0.602$ to approximate the expression.

1. $\log_{10} \frac{3}{4}$

2. $\log_{10} 12$

3. $\log_{10} 3^2$

4. $\log_{10} 16$

5. $\log_{10} 4^{-1}$

6. $\log_{10} \frac{1}{3}$

In 7–12, use the properties of logarithms to expand the expression.

7. $\log_6 3x$

8. $\log_2 \frac{x}{5}$

9. $\log_{10} xy^2$

10. $\log_4 \frac{xy}{3}$

11. $\log_3 x^{1/2} yz$

12. $\log_5 2\sqrt{x}$

In 13–18, condense the expression.

13. $\log_3 7 - \log_3 x$

14. $2\log_5 x + \log_5 3$

15. $\log_4 5 + \log_4 x + \log_4 y$

16. $\frac{1}{2} \log_{10} x - \log_{10} 4$

17. $\frac{2}{3} \log_2 x - 3 \log_2 y$

18. $\log_3 4 + 2 \log_3 x - \log_3 5$

In 19–24, condense the left side of the equation. Then solve for *x* as demonstrated below.

$3 \log_2 x = \log_2 8$ *Original equation*

$\log_2 x^3 = \log_2 8$ *Condense left side of equation.*

$x^3 = 8$ *Write in exponential form.*

$x = 2$ *Solve for x.*

19. $2 \log_4 3 = \log_4 x$

20. $\log_{10} x + \log_{10} 3 = \log_{10} 12$

21. $\log_3 5 - \log_3 x = \log_3 2$

22. $\frac{1}{2} \log_3 16 = \log_3 x$

23. $\frac{1}{3} \log_{10} x = \log_{10} 3$

24. $3 \log_5 2 + \log_5 x = \log_5 24$

Henderson-Hasselbach Formula In 25–27, use the following information.

The pH of a patient's blood can be calculated using the Henderson-Hasselbach Formula

$$pH = 6.1 + \log_{10} \frac{B}{C}$$

where B is the concentration of bicarbonate and C is the concentration of carbonic acid. The normal pH is approximately 7.4.

25. Expand the right side of the formula.

26. A patient has a bicarbonate concentration of 24 and a carbonic concentration of 1.9. Find the pH of the patient's blood.

27. A patient with a normal blood pH has a bicarbonate concentration of 24. Find the concentration of carbonic acid. (Hint: First solve the equation in Exercise 25 for $\log_{10} C$.)

8.4

Name _____

In 1–4, use a calculator to evaluate the expression. Round your result to three decimal places.

1. e^4 **2.** e^{-2} **3.** $e^{2/3}$ **4.** $e^{-1/3}$

In 5–10 simplify the expression. Then use a calculator to evaluate the expression. Round your result to three decimal places.

5. $e^3 \cdot e^2$ **6.** $\left(e^4\right)^{-2}$ **7.** $\dfrac{3e^5}{e}$

8. $\left(\dfrac{e}{2}\right)^{-1}$ **9.** $\left(4e^3\right)^2$ **10.** $-3e \cdot 4e^2$

In 11–16, decide whether the function is an example of exponential growth or exponential decay.

11. $f(x) = 2e^{3x}$ **12.** $f(x) = e^{-3x}$ **13.** $f(x) = 2e^{-3x}$

14. $f(x) = \frac{1}{2}e^{5x}$ **15.** $f(x) = \frac{1}{2}e^{-x}$ **16.** $f(x) = 4e^{5x}$

In 17–20, complete the table of values. Round your results to two decimal places.

17. $f(x) = 2e^x$

x	-2	-1.5	-1	0	1	1.5	2
$2e^x$							

18. $f(x) = 2e^{-x}$

x	-2	-1.5	-1	0	1	1.5	2
$2e^{-x}$							

19. $f(x) = e^{2x} + 3$

x	-2	-1.5	-1	0	1	1.5	2
$e^{2x} + 3$							

20. $f(x) = e^{-3x} - 2$

x	-2	-1.5	-1	0	1	1.5	2
$e^{-3x} - 2$							

In 21–26, identify the horizontal asymptote and sketch the graph of the function.

21. $f(x) = 2e^x$ **22.** $f(x) = 2e^{-x}$ **23.** $f(x) = e^x + 2$

24. $f(x) = e^{-3x} + 1$ **25.** $f(x) = \frac{1}{2}e^{2x} - 1$ **26.** $f(x) = e^{-2.5x} - 3$

Comparing Types of Compounding In 27–29, use the following information.

You deposit $1200 in an account that pays 5% interest. After 10 years, you withdraw all the money.

27. Find the balance in the account if the interest was compounded quarterly.

28. Find the balance in the account if the interest was compounded continuously.

29. Which type of compounding yielded the greatest balance?

Name _____

In 1–4, evaluate the expression without using a calculator.

1. $\ln e + 1$ **2.** $\ln e^3$ **3.** $\ln\left(\frac{1}{e}\right)$ **4.** $2\ln e^{-2}$

In 5–10, use the properties of logarithms to expand the expression.

5. $\ln 2x$ **6.** $\ln \dfrac{x}{y}$ **7.** $\ln 3x^2$

8. $\ln \dfrac{4y^2}{x}$ **9.** $\ln x^3 y^{-2}$ **10.** $\ln \sqrt{x}$

In 11–16, use the properties of logarithms to condense the expression.

11. $\ln x + \ln 4$ **12.** $\ln 2 - \ln y$ **13.** $3\ln x + 2\ln y$

14. $2\ln 3 - \ln x$ **15.** $\ln 4 - (\ln x + \ln y)$ **16.** $\ln 5 + \ln x + \frac{1}{2}\ln y$

In 17–20, complete the table of values. Round your results to three decimal places.

17. $f(x) = 2 + \ln x$

x	0.25	0.5	1	2	3
2 + ln x					

18. $f(x) = 3\ln x$

x	0.25	0.5	1	2	3
3 ln x					

19. $f(x) = \ln(x - 1)$

x	1.25	1.5	2	3	4
ln (x – 1)					

20. $f(x) = 2 - \ln(x + 1)$

x	−0.75	−0.5	0	1	2
2 – ln (x + 1)					

In 21–26, sketch the graph of the function.

21. $f(x) = 1 - \ln x$ **22.** $f(x) = 2\ln x$ **23.** $f(x) = \ln(x + 2)$

24. $f(x) = -3 + \ln(x + 1)$ **25.** $f(x) = 3\ln(x - 2)$ **26.** $f(x) = 1 - \ln(x - 3)$

Blood Alcohol Levels In 27 and 28, use the following information.

The percent risk, r, of an auto accident is related to the blood alcohol level, B, of the driver. The relation is given by

$$B = \tfrac{1}{21.4}\ln r.$$

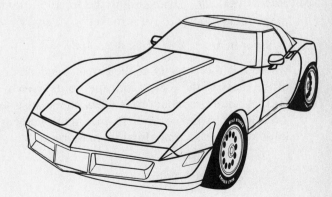

27. What is the percent risk of an auto accident if the driver's blood alcohol level is 0.14?

28. Suppose a car is certain to crash. What is the blood alcohol level of the driver?

Name _____

In 1–3, solve the exponential equation by taking the appropriate logarithm of both sides. Round your result to three decimal places.

1. $e^x = 18$

2. $10^x = 350$

3. $e^{2x} = 42$

In 4–9, isolate the exponential expression. Then solve for *x*. Round your result to three decimal places.

4. $10^x - 2 = 29$

5. $e^x + 3 = 5$

6. $2 \cdot 10^x = 150$

7. $3e^x + 1 = 85$

8. $10^{2x} - 9 = 38$

9. $\frac{1}{2}e^{3x} + 6 = 7$

In 10–12, solve the exponential equation. Use the change of base formula to approximate the solution to three decimal places.

10. $3^x = 15$

11. $2^x - 1 = 104$

12. $4^{3x} = 1500$

In 13–15, solve the logarithmic equation by exponentiating both sides. Round the result to three decimal places.

13. $\ln x = 5$

14. $\log_{10} x = -2$

15. $\log_2 x = 1.5$

In 16–21, isolate the logarithmic expression. Then solve for *x*. Round the result to three decimal places.

16. $7 + \log_{10} x = 4$

17. $7 \ln x = 21$

18. $-3 + 2 \ln x = 5$

19. $3 \log_{10} x = 12$

20. $9 \log_2 x = 15$

21. $\log_3 3x = 2$

22. *Compound Interest* You deposit $2000 in an account that pays 6% annual interest, compounded quarterly. How long will it take for the balance to reach $2500?

23. *Compound Interest* You deposit $2000 in an account that pays 6% annual interest, compounded continuously. How long will it take the balance to reach $2500?

24. *Rocket Velocity* Disregarding the force of gravity, the maximum velocity, v, of a rocket is given by

$$v = t \ln M$$

where t is the velocity of the exhaust and M is the ratio of the mass of the rocket with fuel to its mass without fuel. A solid propellant rocket has an exhaust velocity of 2.5 kilometers per second. Its maximum velocity is 7.5 kilometers per second. Find its mass ratio M.

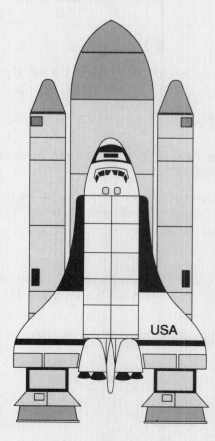

USA

In 1–6, identify the model as exponential growth, exponential decay,
logarithmic, or logistics growth.

1. $f(x) = \left(\frac{1}{2}\right)^x$

2. $f(x) = \ln 3x$

3. $f(x) = \dfrac{1}{1 + 3e^{-x}}$

4. $f(x) = e^{-2x}$

5. $f(x) = (2.5)^x$

6. $f(x) = \log_{10} 6x$

In 7–9, match the function with its graph.

7. $f(x) = \dfrac{4}{1 + 2e^{-x}}$

8. $f(x) = \dfrac{2}{1 + 2e^{-x}}$

9. $f(x) = \dfrac{4}{1 + e^{-2x}}$

a.
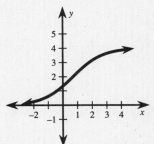

b.
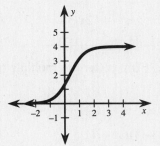

c.
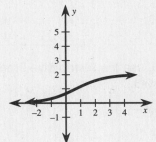

In 10–15, identify the horizontal asymptotes of the function.

10. $f(x) = \dfrac{1}{1 + 3e^{-x}}$

11. $f(x) = \dfrac{1}{1 + 4e^{-2x}}$

12. $f(x) = \dfrac{5}{1 + e^{-2x}}$

13. $f(x) = \dfrac{20}{1 + 0.4e^{-x}}$

14. $f(x) = -5 + \dfrac{1}{1 + e^{-x}}$

15. $f(x) = 10 + \dfrac{2}{1 + e^{-x}}$

In 16 and 17, complete the table of values.

16. $f(x) = \dfrac{3}{1 + 2e^{-x}}$

x	−2	−1	0	1	2
f(x)					

17. $f(x) = 4 + \dfrac{2}{1 + e^{-x}}$

x	−2	−1	0	1	2
f(x)					

In 18–20, sketch the graph of the function.

18. $f(x) = \dfrac{3}{1 + e^{-x}}$

19. $f(x) = \dfrac{1}{1 + 5e^{-x}}$

20. $f(x) = 1 + \dfrac{5}{1 + e^{-x}}$

Wildlife Management In 21–24, use the following information.

A wildlife organization releases 100 deer into
a wilderness area. The deer population, P, can
be modeled by

$$P = \frac{500}{1 + 4e^{-0.36t}}$$

where t is the time in years.

21. Sketch the graph of this model.

22. Identify the horizontal asymptotes of the graph.

23. What is the maximum number of deer the
wilderness area can support?

24. What is the population after 10 years?

Name _____

In 1–6, write the polynomial in standard form. Then identify its degree and leading coefficient.

1. $3 + x$
2. $2x^2 + 5 - x$
3. $1 - 3x + x^2 - x^3$

4. $\frac{1}{2} + \frac{2}{3}x + \frac{1}{3}x^2$
5. $4x^2 - 3x^4$
6. $3 + 2x^5 - 4x$

In 7–13, perform the indicated addition or subtraction.

7. $(x^2 + 2x + 3) + (x^2 - 5)$
8. $(3x^3 - 2x^2 + x - 1) - (x^2 + 2x + 3)$

9. $(x + 7) - (2x + 4)$
10. $(4x^2 + x - 3) - (2x^2 - 5x + 1)$

11. $\begin{array}{r} 2x^3 - 3x^2 + x - 3 \\ + \quad\quad -x^2 + 2x + 4 \\ \hline \end{array}$

12. $\begin{array}{r} x^2 - 2x + 7 \\ + \quad -5x^2 \quad\quad - 3 \\ \hline \end{array}$

13. $\begin{array}{r} 4x^3 \quad\quad - 2x \\ + \; 3x^3 - 3x^2 \quad\quad + 1 \\ \hline \end{array}$

In 14–25, use the Distributive Property or the FOIL pattern to multiply the polynomials.

14. $x(3x - 1)$
15. $2x^2(x + 3)$
16. $x(3x^2 - x + 5)$

17. $(x + 5)(x - 2)$
18. $(x + 3)(x + 1)$
19. $(x - 4)(x - 1)$

20. $(x + 1)(x^2 + x - 1)$
21. $(x - 3)(x^2 + 3x + 2)$
22. $(2x + 1)(x^2 - x - 3)$

23. $\begin{array}{r} x^2 - 2x + 1 \\ \times \quad\quad x + 3 \\ \hline \end{array}$

24. $\begin{array}{r} x^2 + 3x + 2 \\ \times \quad\quad 2x - 1 \\ \hline \end{array}$

25. $\begin{array}{r} 2x^2 + 3x - 4 \\ \times \quad\quad x + 1 \\ \hline \end{array}$

In 26–31, use one of the special product patterns to write the polynomial in standard form.

26. $(x + 1)(x - 1)$
27. $(x + 3)^2$
28. $(x - 2)^3$

29. $(2x - 1)^2$
30. $(2x + 5)(2x - 5)$
31. $(x + 3)^3$

32. *Floor Space* Find a polynomial that represents the total number of square feet for the floor plan shown at the right.

33. *Advertising* For 1980 through 1990, the amount of money, A (in millions of dollars), spent on television and newspaper advertising can by modeled by

$$A = -16.2t^3 + 153t^2 + 3609.5t + 26,265.9$$

where $t = 0$ represents 1980. The amount of money, n (in millions of dollars), spent on newspaper advertising can be modeled by

$$n = -30t^2 + 2257t + 14,761.8.$$

Write a model that represents the amount of money, v (in millions of dollars), spent on television advertising.

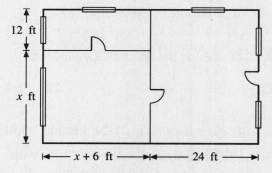

9.2

Name _____

In 1–3, state the maximum number of turns in the graph of the function.

1. $f(x) = x^4 + 2x^2 + 4$ **2.** $f(x) = -3x^3 + x^2 - x + 5$ **3.** $f(x) = 2x^6 + 1$

In 4–6, describe how the graph of g can be obtained from the graph of f.

4. $g(x) = (x - 1)^4$ **5.** $g(x) = -x^5$ **6.** $g(x) = x^3 + 4$
     $f(x) = x^4$ $f(x) = x^5$ $f(x) = x^3$

In 7–12, describe the left and right behaviors of the graph.

7. $f(x) = -2x^3 + x - 1$ **8.** $f(x) = x^4 + x^3 - 2x$ **9.** $f(x) = 3x^5 - x^2 + 4$

10. $f(x) = 0.5x^6 + 8$ **11.** $f(x) = -4x^8 + x^5 - 2x + 7$ **12.** $f(x) = -x^7 + 16$

In 13–15, match the function with its graph.

13. $f(x) = 2x^4 - 3x^2 - 2$ **14.** $f(x) = 2x^6 - 6x^4 + 4x^2 - 2$ **15.** $f(x) = -2x^4 + 3x^2 - 2$

a. 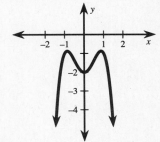   **b.** 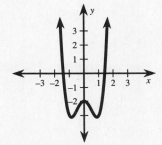   **c.**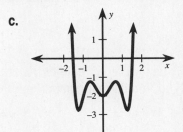

In 16–21, sketch the graph of the polynomial function.

16. $f(x) = x^5 - 2$ **17.** $f(x) = (x + 3)^4$ **18.** $f(x) = -x^3 + 5$

19. $f(x) = (x - 4)^3 + 2$ **20.** $f(x) = -x^4 - 1$ **21.** $f(x) = (x + 1)^5 - 2$

Jams and Jellies In 22–24, use the following information.

The J. M. Smucker Company is the leading maker of jams and jellies in the United States. From 1982 through 1990, its annual sales, S (in millions of dollars), can be modeled by

$$S = -0.1t^3 + 4.5t^2 - 9.2t + 202$$

where $t = 2$ represents 1982.

22. Use a calculator to complete the table of values.

t	2	3	4	5	6	7	8	9	10
S									

23. Sketch the graph of the function.

24. Use your graph to estimate the year in which the sales reached $300,000,000.

Name _____

In 1–3, factor the difference of two squares.

1. $x^2 - 4$
2. $4x^2 - 25$
3. $9x^2 - 1$

In 4–6, factor the sum or difference of two cubes.

4. $x^3 + 1$
5. $x^3 - 64$
6. $8x^3 - 1$

In 7–9, factor the polynomial by grouping.

7. $x^3 + 2x^2 + 4x + 8$
8. $2x^3 - 6x^2 + 3x - 9$
9. $3x^3 + 6x^2 - 2x - 4$

In 10–15, factor the trinomial.

10. $x^2 - 2x + 1$
11. $x^2 + x - 6$
12. $2x^2 + 3x - 2$
13. $x^2 + 4x + 3$
14. $x^2 + 4x + 4$
15. $4x^2 + 4x + 1$

In 16–21, factor the polynomial completely with respect to the integers.

16. $2x^3 - 18x$
17. $x^4 - 16$
18. $3x^3 - 3x^2 - 6x$
19. $x^4 + 2x^2 - 3$
20. $54x^3 + 2$
21. $x^4 + 2x^3 - 8x - 16$

In 22–27, factor the left side of the equation. Then use the Zero Product Property to find all real-number solutions.

22. $x^2 + 2x = 0$
23. $x^3 - 4x = 0$
24. $x^2 + 2x - 15 = 0$
25. $x^3 + 8x^2 + 16x = 0$
26. $x^4 - 13x^2 + 36 = 0$
27. $2x^3 + 4x^2 + 3x + 6 = 0$

In 28–33, collect the terms on one side of the equation and solve for x.

28. $2x^2 = 6x$
29. $x^2 - 2x = 3$
30. $x^3 = 2x^2 + 8x$
31. $3x^2 + 5x = 2$
32. $x^3 + x^2 - 25x = 25$
33. $x^3 + 3x^2 + 2x = -6$

Aquarium **In 34–37, use the following information.**

The aquarium shown at the right holds 5610 gallons
of water. Each gallon of water occupies approximately
0.13368 cubic feet.

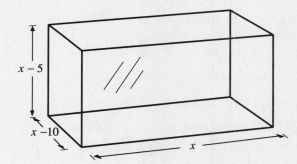

34. How many cubic feet of water does the aquarium hold?
(Round the result to the nearest cubic foot.)

35. Use the result from Exercise 34 to write an equation that
represents the volume of the aquarium.

36. Find all real solutions of the equation in Exercise 34.

37. What are the dimensions of the aquarium?

In 1–6, use long division to divide the polynomials. Write the result in fractional form.

1. $(2x^2 + x - 3) \div (x - 1)$

2. $(3x^2 + 2x - 8) \div (x + 2)$

3. $(x^3 - x^2 - x - 2) \div (x - 2)$

4. $(x^4 - 3x^3 + 3x^2 - 6x + 2) \div (x^2 + 2)$

5. $(4x^3 - 7x + 8) \div (2x - 1)$

6. $(x^3 + 5x^2 + 5x - 3) \div (x^2 + 3x - 1)$

In 7–9, write the polynomial form of the dividend, divisor, quotient, and remainder represented by the synthetic division array.

7.
$$
5 \begin{array}{|rrrr} 1 & -2 & -14 & -5 \\ & 5 & 15 & 5 \\ \hline 1 & 3 & 1 & 0 \end{array}
$$

8.
$$
-2 \begin{array}{|rrrr} 2 & 3 & 3 & 17 \\ & -4 & 2 & -10 \\ \hline 2 & -1 & 5 & 7 \end{array}
$$

9.
$$
3 \begin{array}{|rrrr} 1 & 0 & 1 & -2 \\ & 3 & 9 & 30 \\ \hline 1 & 3 & 10 & 28 \end{array}
$$

In 10–13, use synthetic division to divide the polynomials. Write the result in fractional form.

10. $(2x^3 - 7x^2 - x - 12) \div (x - 4)$

11. $(x^2 + 6x + 3) \div (x + 1)$

12. $(x^3 - 2x + 12) \div (x + 3)$

13. $(x^4 - 5x^3 + 4x - 17) \div (x - 5)$

In 14–17, use the Remainder Theorem to evaluate the function at the given value of x.

14. $f(x) = 4x^2 - 16x + 9$ at $x = 5$

15. $f(x) = 3x^3 + 8x^2 + 5x + 9$ at $x = -3$

16. $f(x) = x^4 + 5x^3 + 35x - 7$ at $x = -6$

17. $f(x) = 7x^4 - 32x^3 + 18x^2 - 32$ at $x = 4$

In 18–21, find the missing factors.

18. $x^3 + 3x^2 - 34x + 48 = (x - 3)(\,?\,)(\,?\,)$

19. $x^3 + 2x^2 - 20x + 24 = (x + 6)(\,?\,)(\,?\,)$

20. $2x^3 + 3x^2 - 3x - 2 = (x + 2)(\,?\,)(\,?\,)$

21. $3x^3 - 16x^2 + 3x + 10 = (x - 5)(\,?\,)(\,?\,)$

22. *Geometry* The volume of the box shown at the right is given by

$$V = 2x^3 - 11x^2 + 10x + 8.$$

Find an expression for the missing dimension.

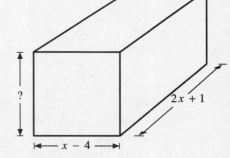

Company Profit In 23–25, use the following information.

The demand function for a type of portable radio is given by the model $p = 70 - 5x^2$, where p is measured in dollars and x is measured in millions of units. The production cost is $20 per radio.

23. Write an equation that represents the cost, C, of producing x million radios.

24. Write an equation that represents the revenue, R, generated from the sale of x million radios. Use the model $R = xp$.

25. Write an equation for the profit, P, for selling x million radios. Use the model $P = R - C$.

Name _____

In 1–3, list the possible rational zeros given by the Rational-Zero Test.

1. $f(x) = x^4 - 2x^3 + 3x - 4$

2. $g(x) = 2x^3 - x^2 + 5x + 6$

3. $h(x) = 3x^5 + 2x + 8$

In 4–8, use the Rational-Zero Test to find all rational zeros of the function.

4. $f(x) = 2x^3 - 3x^2 - 11x + 6$

5. $g(x) = 3x^3 + 8x^2 - 3x - 8$

6. $h(x) = 8x^3 - 6x^2 - 23x + 6$

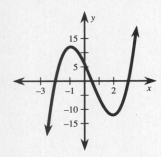
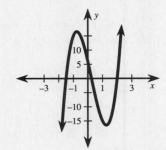

7. $f(x) = x^3 - 4x^2 - 7x + 10$

8. $g(x) = x^4 + 4x^3 + x^2 - 8x - 6$

In 9–13, find all real zeros of the function.

9. $f(x) = 2x^3 - 5x^2 - 4x + 10$

10. $g(x) = 4x^3 - 8x^2 - 15x + 9$

11. $f(x) = x^3 - 3x^2 - 3x + 9$

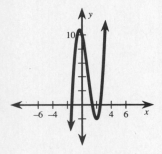
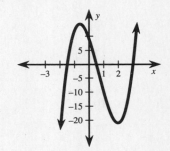
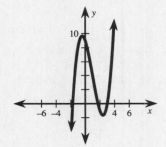

12. $h(x) = 2x^4 + 3x^3 - 6x^2 - 6x + 4$

13. $h(x) = x^4 + 2x^3 - 5x^2 - 4x + 6$

Foreign College Students **In 14–17, use the following information.**

Many students from Europe come to the United States for their college education. For 1980 through 1990, the number, S (in thousands), of European students attending a college or university in the United States can by modeled by

$$S = 0.07(t^3 - 13t^2 + 65t + 339)$$

where $t = 0$ represents 1980.

14. Write an equation (with a leading coefficient of 1) that represents the year that 31.08 thousand European students attended a U.S. college or university.

15. Use the Rational Zero Test to list all possible rational zeros of the equation in Exercise 14.

16. Which of the rational zeros listed in Exercise 15 are valid values of t?

17. In what year did 31.08 thousand European students attend a U.S. college or university?

In 1–4, determine the total number of solutions (including complex and repeated) of the polynomial equation.

1. $4x^3 - 7x^2 + 5x - 9 = 0$

2. $8x^6 - 3x^4 - 11x^3 - 2x^2 + 4 = 0$

3. $x^5 + 2x^3 - 4x^2 + 7x = 12$

4. $-3x^4 + 2x^3 + 15x^2 - x + 1 = 8$

In 5–8, decide whether the given value of *x* is a zero of the function.

5. $f(x) = x^4 + 2x^3 + 5x^2 + 8x + 4$, $x = -1$

6. $f(x) = x^4 - x^3 - 8x^2 + 2x + 12$, $x = 2$

7. $f(x) = x^3 + 4x^2 + x + 4$, $x = i$

8. $f(x) = 2x^3 - x^2 + 8x - 4$, $x = -2i$

In 9–12, identify the factors of a polynomial function that has the given zeros.

9. 3, 1, 2

10. 4, −1, −2, 0

11. −3, i, −i

12. 4 −5, $2i$, −$2i$

In 13–16, write a polynomial function that has the given zeros and has a leading coefficient of 1.

13. −1, 2, 4

14. 3, 1, 1

15. −2, i, −i

16. 0, 1, $3i$, −$3i$

In 17–20, identify the factors of a polynomial function whose graph has the given *x*-intercepts.

17. (3, 0), (1, 0)

18. (−5, 0), (7, 0)

19. (−9, 0), (−8, 0)

20. (−2, 0), (0, 0), (5, 0)

In 21–24, write a polynomial function whose graph has the given *x*-intercepts and has a leading coefficient of 1.

21. (0, 0), (2, 0)

22. (−3, 0), (1, 0)

23. (−2, 0), (−7, 0)

24. (−1, 0), (2, 0), (3, 0)

In 25–30, use synthetic division and factoring to write the polynomial as a product of linear factors.

25. $x^3 + x^2 + x + 1$

26. $2x^3 + 3x^2 - 11x - 6$

27. $x^3 + 4x^2 + 9x + 36$

28. $2x^4 + x^3 + x^2 + x - 1$

29. $x^4 - 3x^2 - 4$

30. $3x^4 + 11x^3 + 8x^2 + 44x - 16$

Room Dimension Riddle In 31–33, use the following information.

One of the bedrooms in the house shown at the right has a volume of 1144 cubic feet. The volume of the bedroom is given by $x^3 + 2x^2 - 5x - 6$, where *x* is the number of rooms in the house.

31. Factor the polynomial that represents the volume of the bedroom.

32. The factors in Exercise 31 represent the length, width, and height of the room. Which do you think represents the length, the width, and the height?

33. How many rooms does the house have?

In 1–3, find the range of the collection of numbers.

1. 3, 9, 8, 5, 2, 11, 6, 7   **2.** 1.8, 3.1, 2.4, 3.5, 1.6, 2.9   **3.** 210, 219, 231, 221, 215, 230

In 4–6, find the mean and standard deviation of the collection of numbers.
Round the results to three decimal places.

4. 1, 4, 3, 2, 1, 2, 1, 3, 1   **5.** 6.5, 7.1, 6.8, 6.6, 6.8, 7.0   **6.** 105, 106, 104, 105, 107, 106

7. *Test Scores* The bar graphs below represent three collections of test
scores. Which collection has the smallest standard deviation?

a. 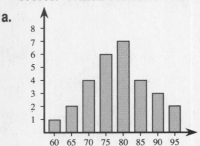 b. 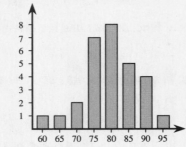 c.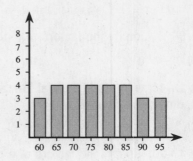

Telephones In 8–10, use the following information.

A class of 20 students took a survey of the number of telephones each
student had in his or her home. The results are shown below.

3, 1, 4, 2, 3, 2, 2, 2, 5, 1, 4, 2, 1, 3, 2, 3, 1, 2, 3, 1

8. Find the range of the results.   **9.** Find the mean of the results.

10. Find the standard deviation of the results. Round to three decimal places.

Breakfast Cereals In 11–13, use the following information.

The number of calories in a 1-ounce serving of ten popular breakfast
cereals is shown below.

Apple Jacks 116	*Froot Loops* 113	*Life* 104	*Rice Krispies* 110
Cap'n Crunch 119	*Kellogg's Corn Flakes* 101	*Lucky Charms* 106	*Trix* 110
Cheerios 106	*Kellogg's Raisin Bran* 89		

11. Find the range of this data.   **12.** Find the mean of this data.

13. Find the standard deviation of this data. Round to three decimal places.

Manufacturing Couplers In 14–16, use the following information.

A company that manufactures hydraulic couplers takes ten samples from
one machine and ten samples from another machine. The diameter of each
sample is measured with a micrometer caliper. The company's goal is to
produce couplers that have a diameter of exactly 1 inch. The results of the
measurements are shown below.

Machine #1: 1.000, 1.002, 1.001, 1.000, 1.002, 0.999, 1.000, 1.002, 1.001, 1.001

Machine #2: 0.998, 0.999, 0.999, 1.000, 0.998, 0.999, 1.000, 1.000, 1.001, 0.999

14. Find the mean diameter for each machine.   **15.** Find the standard deviation for each machine.

16. Which machine produces the more consistent diameter?

In 1–4, find the domain of the function (the values of *x* for which the denominator is not zero).

1. $f(x) = \dfrac{3}{x-5}$
2. $f(x) = \dfrac{x+4}{x+6}$
3. $f(x) = \dfrac{x}{2x-6}$
4. $f(x) = \dfrac{x-3}{x^2+3x+2}$

In 5–8, set the denominator equal to zero to find the vertical asymptote(s) of the graph of the function.

5. $f(x) = \dfrac{3}{2x-1}$
6. $f(x) = \dfrac{x}{(x+1)(x-3)}$
7. $f(x) = \dfrac{x+1}{x^2-4}$
8. $f(x) = \dfrac{x}{x^2-4x-12}$

In 9–12, compare the degree of the numerator to the degree of the denominator to find the horizontal asymptote of the graph of the function.

9. $f(x) = \dfrac{1}{x+6}$
10. $f(x) = \dfrac{2x}{x-3}$
11. $f(x) = \dfrac{x^2}{x+1}$
12. $f(x) = \dfrac{x^2+5}{2x^2-x-1}$

In 13 and 14, complete the table of values.

13. $f(x) = \dfrac{x-3}{x+1}$

14. $f(x) = \dfrac{x}{x-2}$

x	−2	−1.5	−1.25	−0.75	−0.5	0	*x*	1	1.5	1.75	2.25	2.5	3
f(x)							*f(x)*						

In 15–17, match the function with its graph.

15. $f(x) = \dfrac{2x+1}{x-1}$
16. $f(x) = \dfrac{x+1}{x-2}$
17. $f(x) = \dfrac{x-1}{x+2}$

a.
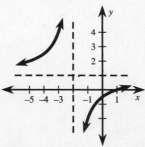

b.
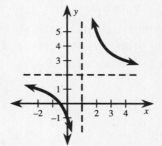

c.
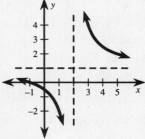

In 18–21, use asymptotes and a table of values to sketch the graph of the function.

18. $f(x) = \dfrac{x+1}{x}$
19. $f(x) = \dfrac{3}{x-2}$
20. $f(x) = \dfrac{x}{x^2-1}$
21. $f(x) = \dfrac{x^2-1}{x^2-4}$

Sports Banquet In 22–24, use the following information.

You are organizing your high school's sports banquet. The banquet hall rental is $250. In addition to this one-time charge, the meal will cost $7 per plate. Let *x* represent the number of people who attend.

22. Write an equation that represents the total cost, *C*.

23. Write an equation that represents the average cost, *A*, per person.

24. Sketch the graph of the equation in Exercise 23.

In 1–4, determine whether x and y vary directly or inversely.

1. $y = 3x$

2. $y = \dfrac{2}{x}$

3. $y = \frac{1}{2}x$

4. $xy = 0.1$

In 5–7, the variables x and y vary inversely. Find the constant of variation, k, and write an equation that relates the variables.

5. $x = 2$, $y = 4$

6. $x = \frac{1}{2}$, $y = 6$

7. $x = 3$, $y = 0.01$

In 8–10, the variable z varies jointly with the product of x and y. Find the constant of variation, k, and write an equation that relates the variables.

8. $x = 1$, $y = 2$, $z = 6$

9. $x = \frac{1}{2}$, $y = 8$, $z = 12$

10. $x = 2$, $y = 3$, $z = 4$

Boyle's Law In 11–13, use the following information.

Boyle's Law states that for a constant temperature, the pressure, P, of a gas varies inversely with its volume, V. A sample of hydrogen gas has a volume of 8.56 liters at a pressure of 1.5 atmospheres.

11. Find the constant of variation, k.

12. Write an equation that relates P and V.

13. Find the volume of the hydrogen gas if the temperature remains constant and the pressure changes to 1.2 atmospheres.

Product Demand In 14–16, use the following information.

A company has found that the monthly demand for one of its products varies inversely with the price of the product. When the price is $12.50, the demand is 12,000 units.

14. Find the constant of variation, k.

15. Write an equation that relates the demand, x, and the price, p.

16. Find the demand if the price is reduced to $12.00.

Simple Interest In 17–19, use the following information.

The simple interest, I (in dollars), for a savings account is jointly proportional to the product of the time, t (in years), and the principal, P (in dollars). After six months, the interest on a principal of $2000 is $55.

17. Find the constant of variation, k.

18. Write an equation that relates I, t, and P.

19. What will the interest be after two years?

Specific Heat In 20–22, use the following information.

The amount of heat, H (in kilocalories), necessary to change the temperature of an aluminum can is jointly proportional to the product of the mass, m (in kilograms), of the can and the temperature change desired, T (in degrees Celsius). It takes 1.54 kilocalories of heat to change the temperature of a 0.028 kilogram aluminum can 250 degrees Celsius.

20. Find the constant of variation, k.

21. Write an equation that relates H, m, and T.

22. How much heat is required to melt the can if its current temperature is 20°C? (The melting point of aluminum is approximately 660° Celsius.)

In 1–4, simplify the expression.

1. $\dfrac{x^2 - 16}{x^2 + x - 12}$

2. $\dfrac{x^2 - 2x - 15}{x^2 - 4x - 5}$

3. $\dfrac{x^2 - 8x + 12}{x^2 + 3x - 10}$

4. $\dfrac{x^2 - 2x + 1}{x^2 - 1}$

In 5–12, multiply the expressions and simplify.

5. $\dfrac{4x^2 y^3}{x^5 y^6} \cdot \dfrac{xy}{20x^3}$

6. $\dfrac{81x^9}{y^4} \cdot \dfrac{x^2}{36x^5 y}$

7. $\dfrac{16x^5 y^7}{3x} \cdot \dfrac{9xy^2}{64x^2 y}$

8. $\dfrac{21x^{10} y^5}{5x^2} \cdot \dfrac{x^3}{35y^4}$

9. $\dfrac{3x^2 - 12}{5x - 10} \cdot \dfrac{1}{2x + 4}$

10. $\dfrac{x^2 - 7x - 8}{3x^2 - 24x} \cdot \dfrac{4x^3}{x^2 - 1}$

11. $(x + 5) \cdot \dfrac{x^2 - 36}{x^2 + 11x + 30}$

12. $\dfrac{x^2 + 4x - 12}{x^4 + 9x^3 + 18x^2} \cdot 6x^2$

In 13–20, divide the expressions and simplify.

13. $\dfrac{x^2 - 3x + 2}{25x} \div \dfrac{x - 1}{5x^2}$

14. $\dfrac{5x^2 - 20}{25x^2} \div \dfrac{x^2 + 6x + 8}{x^2 + 10x + 24}$

15. $(x + 7) \div \dfrac{x^2 + 9x + 14}{x^2 + 5x + 6}$

16. $(x^2 - 5x - 36) \div \dfrac{x^2 - 10x + 9}{x - 1}$

17. $\dfrac{x^2 - 9x - 22}{x^2 + 5x - 24} \div \dfrac{x + 2}{x - 3}$

18. $\dfrac{7x^2 - 21x}{x^2 - 2x - 35} \div \dfrac{x^2}{x - 7}$

19. $\dfrac{x - 2}{x^2 + 7x - 18} \div \dfrac{x^3 - 6x^2 - 27x}{x^2 + 8x - 9}$

20. $(x^2 + 10x - 24) \div \dfrac{x^2 - 144}{3x - 36}$

In 21–24, perform the operation and simplify.

21. $\dfrac{x^2 - 3x + 2}{x + 2} \cdot \dfrac{3x}{x - 2} \cdot \dfrac{2x + 4}{5x^2 - 5x}$

22. $\dfrac{x^2 - 100}{4x^2} \cdot \dfrac{x^3 - 5x^2 - 50x}{x^4 + 10x^3} \div \dfrac{(x - 10)^2}{5x}$

23. $(x^2 + 7x - 30) \div \dfrac{x^2 + 5x - 24}{x + 2} \cdot \dfrac{x + 2}{x^2 + 3x + 2}$

24. $(x^3 + 10x^2) \div \left(\dfrac{x^2 - 9}{x + 3} \cdot \dfrac{x + 10}{x^2 + 7x + 12} \right)$

25. **CD's and Cassettes** Use the diagram below to find the ratio of the compact disc storage crate's volume to the cassette storage crate's volume.

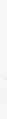
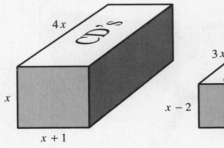
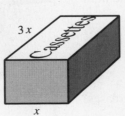

In 1–4, find the least common multiple of the expressions.

1. $x^2 - 25$, x, $x + 5$

2. $x^2 - 36$, 6, x^2

3. $2(x + 2)$, $x^2 + 4x + 4$, x

4. $x^2 - 49$, $x + 7$, $x(x - 7)$

In 5 and 6, determine whether the x-value is a solution of the equation.

5. $\dfrac{2}{x - 3} = \dfrac{3}{x + 1}$, $x = -1$

6. $\dfrac{1}{x - 3} + \dfrac{1}{x + 3} = \dfrac{10}{x^2 - 9}$, $x = 5$

In 7–12, find the zeros of the function.

7. $f(x) = \dfrac{5x}{x + 2}$

8. $f(x) = \dfrac{x - 3}{2x + 8}$

9. $f(x) = \dfrac{x + 4}{x - 4}$

10. $f(x) = \dfrac{2x + 1}{x + 1}$

11. $f(x) = \dfrac{x^2 - 7x + 12}{4x + 3}$

12. $f(x) = \dfrac{x^2 - 11x + 30}{x^2 - 1}$

In 13–20, solve the equation. Check each solution.

13. $\dfrac{100 - 4x}{3} = \dfrac{5x + 6}{4} + 6$

14. $\dfrac{15}{x} - 4 = \dfrac{6}{x} + 3$

15. $\dfrac{1}{x - 2} + \dfrac{3}{x + 3} = \dfrac{4}{x^2 + x - 6}$

16. $\dfrac{4}{x - 2} - \dfrac{3}{x + 1} = \dfrac{8}{x^2 - x - 2}$

17. $\dfrac{x}{x - 4} + 1 = \dfrac{4}{x - 4}$

18. $\dfrac{1}{x - 5} + \dfrac{1}{x + 5} = \dfrac{x + 3}{x^2 - 25}$

19. $\dfrac{2}{x - 10} - \dfrac{3}{x - 2} = \dfrac{6}{x^2 - 12x + 20}$

20. $\dfrac{2}{x^2 - 6x + 8} = \dfrac{1}{x - 4} + \dfrac{2}{x - 2}$

In 21–23, match the function with its graph.

21. $f(x) = \dfrac{8x}{x + 2}$

22. $f(x) = \dfrac{4}{x - 5}$

23. $f(x) = \dfrac{3x}{x - 7}$

a.

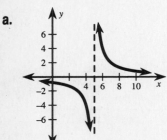

b.

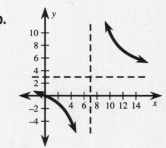

c.

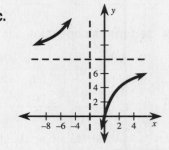

Wildlife **In 24 and 25, use the following information.**

A state game commission introduces 50 deer into newly acquired state game lands. The population, N, of the herd after t years can be modeled by

$$N = \dfrac{5000 + 3000t}{100 + 4t}.$$

24. Find the population after 5 years, 10 years, and 25 years.

25. What is the limiting size of the herd as time increases?

In 1–4, state the least common denominator of the expressions.

1. $\dfrac{5}{2x+1}$, $\dfrac{6}{4x^2-1}$

2. $\dfrac{3}{x+4}$, $\dfrac{x}{x^2-16}$, $\dfrac{x+2}{4}$

3. $\dfrac{13}{x^2-2x+1}$, $\dfrac{4}{x^2-1}$, $\dfrac{5}{x(x+1)}$

4. $\dfrac{7}{x-6}$, $\dfrac{5x}{x(x-2)}$, $\dfrac{3}{x^2-8x+12}$

In 5–13, perform the indicated operations and simplify.

5. $\dfrac{5}{x+1}+\dfrac{x}{x+1}$

6. $6-\dfrac{5}{x+3}$

7. $\dfrac{x}{x^2+x-2}+\dfrac{1}{x+2}$

8. $\dfrac{x-1}{x^2+5x+4}+\dfrac{2}{x^2-x-2}+\dfrac{10}{x^2+2x-8}$

9. $\dfrac{x}{x^2-x-30}-\dfrac{1}{x+5}$

10. $\dfrac{x+2}{x-1}-\dfrac{2}{x+6}-\dfrac{14}{x^2+5x-6}$

11. $\dfrac{4}{x}-\dfrac{2}{x^2}+\dfrac{4}{x+3}$

12. $\dfrac{5}{2(x+1)}-\dfrac{1}{2x}-\dfrac{3}{2(x+1)^2}$

13. $\dfrac{x}{x^2-9}+\dfrac{3}{x(x-3)}$

In 14–19, simplify the complex fraction.

14. $\dfrac{\left(\dfrac{1}{x}+\dfrac{1}{2x+1}\right)}{\left(\dfrac{4x}{2x+1}\right)}$

15. $\dfrac{\left(\dfrac{1}{3x}-\dfrac{4}{x+2}\right)}{\left(\dfrac{x}{x+2}+\dfrac{1}{x}\right)}$

16. $\dfrac{\left(\dfrac{4}{x^2-25}+\dfrac{2}{x+5}\right)}{\left(\dfrac{1}{x+5}+\dfrac{1}{x-5}\right)}$

17. $\dfrac{\left(\dfrac{1}{x+9}+\dfrac{1}{5}\right)}{\left(\dfrac{2}{x^2+10x+9}\right)}$

18. $\dfrac{\left(\dfrac{2}{4x+12}\right)}{\left(\dfrac{4}{2x+6}+\dfrac{1}{x+3}\right)}$

19. $\dfrac{\left(\dfrac{x}{x-4}-\dfrac{1}{4}\right)}{\left(\dfrac{9}{4x}+\dfrac{x^2}{x-4}\right)}$

In 20–22, solve the equation. Check each solution.

20. $\dfrac{\left(\dfrac{1}{x}-\dfrac{1}{x+1}\right)}{\left(\dfrac{1}{x+1}\right)}=2$

21. $\dfrac{\left(\dfrac{4}{x-3}+3\right)}{\left(\dfrac{4x-1}{x-3}+4\right)}=1$

22. $\dfrac{\left(\dfrac{7}{x+1}-\dfrac{3}{x-1}\right)}{\left(\dfrac{2}{x^2-1}\right)}=3$

Electrical Resistors **In 23 and 24, use the following information.**

When two resistors with resistance R_1 and R_2 are connected in parallel, the total resistance, R, is given by

$$R=\dfrac{1}{\left(\dfrac{1}{R_1}+\dfrac{1}{R_2}\right)}.$$

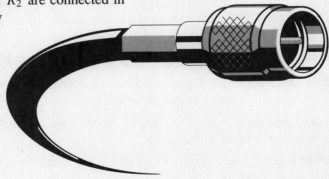

23. Simplify this complex fraction.

24. Find the total resistance (in ohms) of a 4 ohm resistor and a 2 ohm resistor that are connected in parallel.

In 1 and 2, construct an amortization table.

1. You borrow $1500 at an annual interest rate of 8% to be repaid in 9 monthly payments of $155.55 and one final payment of $155.59.

2. You borrow $2500 at an annual interest rate of 9% to be repaid in 12 monthly payments of $218.63.

Home Mortgage **In 3 and 4, find the monthly payment.**

3. A home mortgage for $120,000, with an annual interest rate of $9\frac{1}{2}\%$, is taken out for a 30-year term.

4. A small business loan for $5000, with an annual interest rate of $10\frac{1}{2}\%$, is taken out for a 5-year term.

In 5 and 6, find the total interest payment.

5. An installment loan for $12,500 is to be paid in 36 monthly payments with an annual interest rate of $8\frac{1}{4}\%$.

6. An installment loan for $3000 is to be paid in 24 monthly payments with an annual interest rate of 11%.

Home Mortgage **In 7–10, use the following information.**

A home mortgage for $75,000 is taken out with an annual interest rate of 12%.

7. What is the monthly payment for a term of 30 years?

8. What is the monthly payment for a term of 25 years?

9. Find the total payment and total interest payment for the terms in Exercises 7 and 8.

10. How much less interest is paid over the 25-year term than over the 30-year term?

11. *Car Loan* You take out a loan for a used car for $2500 with an annual interest rate of $12\frac{1}{4}\%$. You want to repay the loan as soon as possible, but you can only afford monthly payments of at most $75. Which of the following terms should you choose? Explain

   a. 24 months   **b.** 30 months   **c.** 36 months   **d.** 42 months

Mountain Bike **In 12–14, use the following information.**

You take out a personal loan for $1500 to buy a top-of-the-line mountain bike at an annual interest rate of 10% for a term of 24 months.

12. Find the monthly payment.

13. Find the total payment.

14. Suppose you can come up with $250 for a down payment. Now you only need to borrow $1250 (at the same interest rate and term). What is the monthly payment?

15. Find the total payment for the smaller loan.

16. What is one advantage of each plan?

17. *Comparing Two Repayment Plans* You borrow $5000 and have two repayment options. Which has the lesser total payment?

   a. One lending source offers the loan for 36 monthly payments at an annual interest rate of $10\frac{3}{4}\%$.

   b. Another lending source offers the loan for 30 monthly payments at an annual interest rate of 12%.

In 1–4, write the equation of the parabola in standard form.

1. $y^2 = 16x$　　　　**2.** $4x - y^2 = 0$　　　　**3.** $x^2 = \frac{9}{4}y$　　　　**4.** $8x^2 - y = 0$

In 5–8, decide whether the parabola has a vertical or horizontal axis.

5. $8x^2 = y$　　　　**6.** $3x = 4y^2$　　　　**7.** $2x + 3y^2 = 0$　　　　**8.** $x^2 = -16y$

In 9–16, find the focus and directrix of the parabola.

9. $y = 4x^2$　　　　**10.** $y = 2x^2$　　　　**11.** $x^2 + 8y = 0$　　　　**12.** $y^2 = -6x$

13. $y^2 + 12x = 0$　　　**14.** $x = 2y^2$　　　　**15.** $20y - x^2 = 0$　　　**16.** $x^2 + 32y = 0$

In 17–20, write the standard form of the equation of the parabola with vertex at the origin and the given focus.

17. $(8, 0)$　　　　**18.** $(0, -2)$　　　　**19.** $(-12, 0)$　　　　**20.** $(0, 16)$

In 21–23, match the equation with its graph.

21. $y^2 = -2x$　　　　　　**22.** $x^2 = 2y$　　　　　　**23.** $x^2 = -2y$

a. 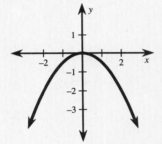　　**b.** 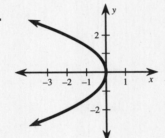　　**c.**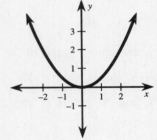

In 24–27, sketch the parabola. Label the focus and directrix.

24. $x^2 - 4y = 0$　　　**25.** $\frac{1}{2}x^2 + y = 0$　　　**26.** $x = -8y^2$　　　**27.** $x - \frac{1}{20}y^2 = 0$

28. *Sailboat Race* The course for a sailboat race includes a turnaround point marked by a stationary buoy. The sailboats must pass between the buoy and the straight shoreline. The boats follow a parabolic path past the buoy, which is 40 yards from the shoreline. Find an equation to represent the parabolic path, so that the boats remain equidistant from the buoy and the straight shoreline.

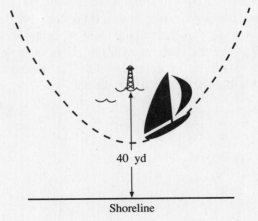

40 yd

Shoreline

In 1–4, write the standard form of the equation of the circle with the given radius and whose center is the origin.

1. 2   **2.** $\sqrt{6}$ **3.** $\frac{1}{3}$ **4.** $\frac{\sqrt{5}}{5}$

In 5–8, write the standard form of the equation of the circle that passes through the given point and whose center is the origin.

5. $(4, 6)$ **6.** $(-5, 0)$ **7.** $(-2, 4)$ **8.** $(5, -2)$

In 9–11, match the equation with its graph.

9. $x^2 + y^2 = 16$ **10.** $x^2 + y^2 = 36$ **11.** $x^2 + y^2 = 3$

a.
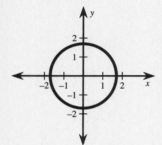

b.
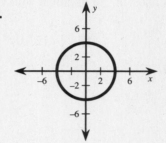

c.
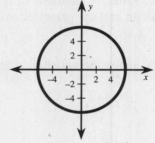

In 12–15, sketch the graph of the equation.

12. $x^2 + y^2 = 12$ **13.** $4x^2 + 4y^2 = 25$ **14.** $x^2 + y^2 = 121$ **15.** $3x^2 + 3y^2 = 21$

In 16–19, find the points of intersection, if any, of the graphs.

16. $x^2 + y^2 = 45$ **17.** $x^2 + y^2 = 25$ **18.** $x^2 + y^2 = 36$ **19.** $x^2 + y^2 = 3$
      $y = 2x$ $y = x + 1$ $x + y = 12$ $2y = x^2$

20. **Three Rivers Stadium** Three Rivers Stadium is the home of the Pittsburgh Pirates. The stadium is approximately circular with a diameter of 800 feet. Suppose a coordinate plane were superimposed over the base of the stadium with the origin at the center of the stadium. Write an equation (in standard form) for the outside boundary of the stadium.

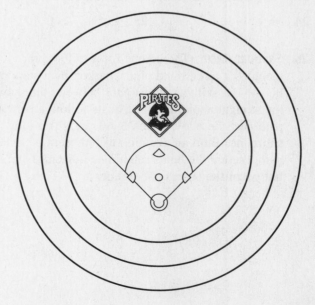

           Algebra 2

In 1–4, find the foci and vertices of the ellipse.

1. $\dfrac{x^2}{36} + \dfrac{y^2}{9} = 1$ **2.** $\dfrac{x^2}{121} + \dfrac{y^2}{100} = 1$ **3.** $\dfrac{x^2}{1} + \dfrac{y^2}{49} = 1$ **4.** $\dfrac{x^2}{64} + \dfrac{y^2}{81} = 1$

In 5–8, write the equation in standard form. Find the foci and vertices.

5. $9x^2 + 16y^2 = 144$ **6.** $25x^2 + 4y^2 = 100$ **7.** $x^2 + 4y^2 = 9$ **8.** $\dfrac{x^2}{108} + \dfrac{y^2}{75} = 3$

In 9–12, find an equation of the ellipse. The center of the ellipse is (0, 0).

9. Vertex: $(3, 0)$
   Focus: $(1, 0)$

10. Vertex: $(7, 0)$
   Co-vertex: $(0, 5)$

11. Vertex: $(0, 6)$
   Focus: $(0, 2)$

12. Vertex: $(0, \sqrt{5})$
   Co-vertex: $(\sqrt{2}, 0)$

In 13–15, match the equation with its graph.

13. $\dfrac{x^2}{36} + \dfrac{y^2}{4} = 1$ **14.** $\dfrac{x^2}{9} + \dfrac{y^2}{36} = 1$ **15.** $\dfrac{x^2}{4} + \dfrac{y^2}{16} = 1$

a.

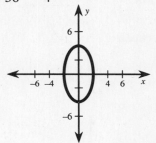

b.

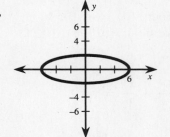

c.

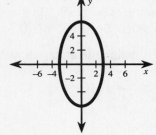

In 16–21, sketch the ellipse and find its eccentricity. (Round to three decimal places.)

16. $\dfrac{x^2}{49} + \dfrac{y^2}{16} = 1$ **17.** $\dfrac{x^2}{4} + \dfrac{y^2}{64} = 1$ **18.** $144x^2 + 36y^2 = 144$

19. $x^2 + 169y^2 = 169$ **20.** $\dfrac{x^2}{12} + \dfrac{y^2}{16} = 1$ **21.** $\dfrac{9x^2}{25} + \dfrac{9y^2}{49} = 1$

In 22 and 23, find the points of intersection of the graphs.

22. $2x^2 + 3y^2 = 4$
   $y = 2x$

23. $2x^2 + 3y^2 = 19$
   $x^2 + y^2 = 9$

24. *Archway* A semi-elliptical archway is to be formed over the entrance to an estate. The arch is to be set on pillars that are 10 feet apart. The arch has a height of 4 feet above the pillars. Where should the foci be placed in order to sketch plans for the elliptical arch?

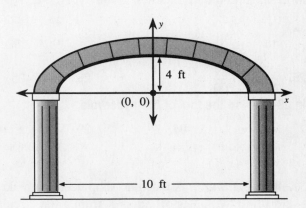

In 1–6, find the vertices and foci of the hyperbola.

1. $\dfrac{x^2}{25} - \dfrac{y^2}{16} = 1$

2. $\dfrac{y^2}{49} - \dfrac{x^2}{9} = 1$

3. $\dfrac{x^2}{36} - \dfrac{y^2}{25} = 1$

4. $\dfrac{y^2}{64} - \dfrac{x^2}{49} = 1$

5. $x^2 - \dfrac{y^2}{25} = 1$

6. $\dfrac{x^2}{16} - \dfrac{y^2}{25} = 1$

In 7–12, write the equation in standard form. Find the vertices and foci.

7. $36x^2 - y^2 = 36$

8. $9y^2 - 4x^2 = 36$

9. $49x^2 - 4y^2 = 196$

10. $y^2 - 25x^2 = 100$

11. $9x^2 - 16y^2 - 144 = 0$

12. $4y^2 - 9x^2 + 36 = 0$

In 13–18, write an equation of the hyperbola. The center of the hyperbola is (0, 0).

13. Foci: $(-3, 0)$, $(3, 0)$
    Vertices: $(-2, 0)$, $(2, 0)$

14. Foci: $(-5, 0)$, $(5, 0)$
    Vertices: $(-4, 0)$, $(4, 0)$

15. Foci: $(0, -1)$, $(0, 1)$
    Vertices: $(0, -\frac{1}{4})$, $(0, \frac{1}{4})$

16. Foci: $(-9, 0)$, $(9, 0)$
    Vertices: $(-3, 0)$, $(3, 0)$

17. Foci: $(0, -6)$, $(0, 6)$
    Vertices: $(0, -1)$, $(0, 1)$

18. Foci: $(-4, 0)$, $(4, 0)$
    Vertices: $(-1, 0)$, $(1, 0)$

In 19–21, match the equation with its graph.

19. $\dfrac{x^2}{36} - \dfrac{y^2}{4} = 1$

20. $\dfrac{y^2}{4} - \dfrac{x^2}{36} = 1$

21. $\dfrac{x^2}{4} - \dfrac{y^2}{36} = 1$

a.
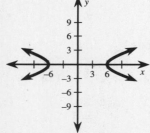

b.
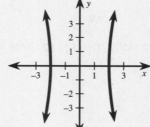

c.
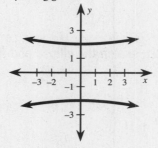

In 22–27, find the asymptotes of the hyperbola. Then sketch its graph.

22. $\dfrac{x^2}{144} - \dfrac{y^2}{36} = 1$

23. $\dfrac{y^2}{9} - \dfrac{x^2}{100} = 1$

24. $\dfrac{x^2}{81} - \dfrac{y^2}{36} = 1$

25. $\dfrac{y^2}{121} - \dfrac{x^2}{100} = 1$

26. $4x^2 - 25y^2 = 100$

27. $y^2 - 16x^2 = 64$

In 28–30, find the foci of the hyperbola.

28. Vertices: $(-2, 0)$, $(2, 0)$
    Asymptotes: $y = 4x$,
    $y = -4x$

29. Vertices: $(0, -4)$, $(0, 4)$
    Asymptotes: $y = 3x$,
    $y = -3x$

30. Vertices: $(0, -1)$, $(0, 1)$
    Asymptotes: $y = \frac{1}{2}x$,
    $y = -\frac{1}{2}x$

31. **Machine Shop** A machine shop needs to make a small engine part by drilling two holes of radius r from a flat circular piece of radius R. The area of the resulting part is 16 square inches. Write an equation that relates r and R. What is the graph of the equation?

In 1–6, match the equation with its graph.

1. $\dfrac{(x-5)^2}{25} + \dfrac{(y-4)^2}{16} = 1$

2. $\dfrac{(y+4)^2}{16} - \dfrac{(x-5)^2}{25} = 1$

3. $\dfrac{(y+5)^2}{16} + \dfrac{(x-4)^2}{25} = 1$

4. $\dfrac{(x+5)^2}{16} - \dfrac{(y+4)^2}{25} = 1$

5. $\dfrac{(y+4)^2}{25} + \dfrac{(x-5)^2}{16} = 1$

6. $\dfrac{(x-4)^2}{16} - \dfrac{(y-5)^2}{25} = 1$

a.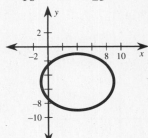

b.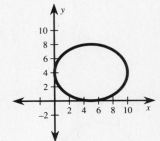

c.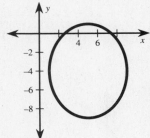

d.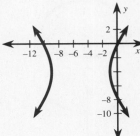

e.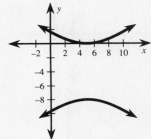

f.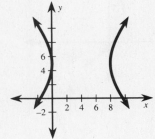

In 7–10, find an equation of the conic.

7. *Ellipse* Vertices: $(-1, 7)$, $(-1, 1)$
   Co-vertices: $(-3, 4)$, $(1, 4)$

8. *Parabola* Vertex: $(2, 2)$
   Focus: $(2, 5)$

9. *Circle* Center: $(-4, -6)$
   Radius: 7

10. *Hyperbola* Vertices: $(-5, 5)$, $(5, 5)$
    Foci: $(-7, 5)$, $(7, 5)$

In 11–18, write the equation of the conic in standard form. For circles, identify the radius and center. For parabolas, identify the vertex and focus. For ellipses and hyperbolas, identify the vertices and foci.

11. $x^2 + y^2 - 12x + 18y - 4 = 0$

12. $x^2 + y^2 + 6x - 4y + 12 = 0$

13. $x^2 + 10x - 4y + 1 = 0$

14. $y^2 - 2y + 16x - 31 = 0$

15. $x^2 + 4y^2 + 6x - 8y + 9 = 0$

16. $4x^2 + y^2 - 8x + 4y - 8 = 0$

17. $4x^2 - 3y^2 + 8x + 16 = 0$

18. $9y^2 - x^2 + 2x + 54y + 62 = 0$

19. *Sprinkler System* A sprinkler system shoots a stream of water that follows a parabolic path. The nozzle is fastened at ground level and water reaches a maximum height of 20 feet at a horizontal distance of 45 feet (from the nozzle). Find the equation that the describes the path of the water. Use the location of the nozzle as the origin.

In 1–6, classify the conic.

1. $3x^2 + y^2 - 6x - 3 = 0$ **2.** $2x^2 - y^2 + 12x + 14 = 0$ **3.** $4y^2 - 16x - 12y - 23 = 0$

4. $2x^2 + 2y^2 - 3y - 1 = 0$ **5.** $2xy + x - 3y - 6 = 0$ **6.** $2x^2 - 3y = 0$

In 7–12, match the equation with its graph.

7. $x^2 + y^2 + 2x - 2y - 2 = 0$ **8.** $2x^2 - 2y^2 + 60y - 63 = 0$

9. $4x^2 + 9y^2 - 16x + 72y + 124 = 0$ **10.** $16x^2 + 4y^2 + 64x - 12y + 57 = 0$

11. $y^2 - 4y - 5x - 1 = 0$ **12.** $25x^2 - 9y^2 + 150x + 36y - 36 = 0$

a. 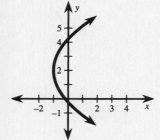   **b.** 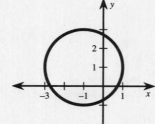   **c.**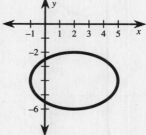

d. 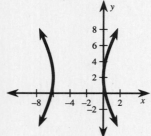   **e.** 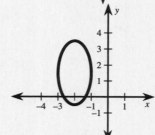   **f.**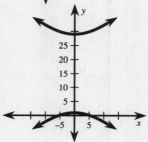

In 13–16, sketch the graph of the equation.

13. $16x^2 + 9y^2 - 96x - 18y + 9 = 0$ **14.** $25x^2 - 4y^2 + 50x + 8y + 121 = 0$

15. $x^2 - 6x - 8y + 25 = 0$ **16.** $x^2 + y^2 - 8x - 10y + 25 = 0$

In 17–20, find the points of intersection of the graphs.

17. $-2x^2 + 2y^2 - 8x - 2 = 0$ **18.** $x^2 + y^2 + x - 2y - 21 = 0$
$\quad\;\; x^2 - 5y^2 + 4x + 5 = 0$ $\qquad x^2 + y^2 + 5x - 2y - 9 = 0$

19. $x^2 + y^2 + 4x + 4y = 0$ **20.** $x^2 + 8y^2 - 4x - 16y + 4 = 0$
$\quad\;\; 2x^2 - y^2 + 6x - 4y = 0$ $\qquad\; x^2 - 4x + 16y + 4 = 0$

21. *Geometry* The circle $x^2 + y^2 + 4x - 5 = 0$ passes through the ends
of the minor axis and the foci of an ellipse. The major axis of the ellipse
lies on the x-axis. Find the points of intersection of the graphs. Write the
equation of the ellipse.

In 1–8, write the first five terms of the sequence. Begin with $n = 1$.

1. $a_n = 2n^2$

2. $a_n = \dfrac{n+4}{n}$

3. $a_n = \dfrac{n^2}{n+1}$

4. $a_n = 2n + 3$

5. $a_n = n! + 2$

6. $a_n = (n+2)!$

7. $a_n = \dfrac{1}{2n}$

8. $a_n = \dfrac{n+1}{n!}$

In 9 and 10, the sequence is defined recursively. Write the first six terms of the sequence. Begin with $n = 0$.

9. $a_0 = 1$
$a_n = (a_{n-1})^2 + 1$

10. $a_0 = 1$
$a_1 = 1$
$a_n = 2a_{n-1} + a_{n-2}$

In 11–18, write the terms of the series. Then evaluate the sum.

11. $\displaystyle\sum_{n=0}^{5} (n+1)^2$

12. $\displaystyle\sum_{j=2}^{6} j(j-1)$

13. $\displaystyle\sum_{m=1}^{5} (-m^2)$

14. $\displaystyle\sum_{k=0}^{4} (2k)!$

15. $\displaystyle\sum_{n=1}^{5} n^2(n-1)$

16. $\displaystyle\sum_{j=0}^{4} (j^2 + 5)$

17. $\displaystyle\sum_{i=2}^{5} (i-1)!$

18. $\displaystyle\sum_{k=3}^{6} (k! + k)$

In 19 and 20, use summation notation to represent the sum. Use i as the index and begin with $i = 1$.

19. $3 + 9 + 19 + 33 + 51 + 73$

20. $1 + 2 + 4 + 8 + 16 + 32$

In 21–24, use a formula to evaluate the sum.

21. $\displaystyle\sum_{i=1}^{25} i$

22. $\displaystyle\sum_{i=1}^{40} i^2$

23. $\displaystyle\sum_{i=1}^{36} 1$

24. $\displaystyle\sum_{i=1}^{60} i$

25. *Marching Band* To begin the half-time performance, a high school band marches onto the football field in a pyramid formation. The drum major leads the band alone in the first row. There are two band members in the second row, three in the third row, four in the fourth row, and so on. The pyramid formation has 15 rows. How many members does the band have?

In 1–6, decide whether the sequence is arithmetic.

1. 4, 7, 10, 13, 16, ...

2. $\frac{1}{2}$, $\frac{3}{2}$, $\frac{9}{2}$, $\frac{27}{2}$, $\frac{81}{2}$, ...

3. 2, 9, 16, 23, 30, 37, ...

4. 3, 6, 12, 24, 48, ...

5. 2, 5, 8, 11, 14, ...

6. 7, 12, 17, 22, 27, ...

In 7–9, find the common difference of the arithmetic sequence. Then write the next term.

7. 3, 7, 11, 15, 19, ...

8. $\frac{9}{2}$, 5, $\frac{11}{2}$, 6, $\frac{13}{2}$, ...

9. 1, −4, −9, −14, −19, ...

In 10–12, find a formula for the *n*th term of the arithmetic sequence.

10. Common difference: −2
First term: 2

11. Common difference: 5
First term: $\frac{1}{2}$

12. Common difference: 4
First term: −3

In 13–15, answer the question about the arithmetic sequence.

13. Common difference: 2
Sixth term: 15
What is the 9th term?

14. Common difference: $-\frac{1}{2}$
First term: −5
What is the 10th term?

15. Common difference: 4
Eighth term: 36
What are the 1st 4 terms?

In 16–18, match the sequence with its graph.

16. $a_n = \frac{1}{2}n - 2$

17. $a_n = 5n - 2$

18. $a_n = 3n + 2$

a.

b.

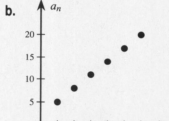

c.

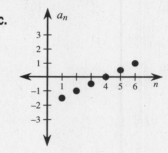

In 19–21, find the sum of the first *n* terms of the arithmetic sequence. Begin with n = 1.

19. $a_n = 15 - 3n$; $n = 10$

20. $a_n = -5 + 7n$; $n = 25$

21. $a_n = -\frac{7}{2} + 4n$; $n = 20$

In 22–24, evaluate the sum.

22. $\displaystyle\sum_{i=1}^{25} (4i + 1)$

23. $\displaystyle\sum_{i=1}^{40} (5i - 1)$

24. $\displaystyle\sum_{i=1}^{50} (2i + 5)$

25. *Baling Hay*   As a farmer bales a field of hay, each trip around the field gets shorter. On the first trip around the field, there were 267 bales of hay. On the second trip, there were 253. The number of bales on each succeeding trip decreases arithmetically. The total number of trips is 13. How many bales of hay does the farmer get from the field?

In 1–6, decide whether the sequence is arithmetic, geometric, or neither.

1. $5, \frac{5}{2}, \frac{5}{4}, \frac{5}{8}, \frac{5}{16}, \ldots$

2. $2, \frac{9}{2}, 7, \frac{19}{2}, 12, \frac{29}{2}, \ldots$

3. $2, 5, 10, 13, 26, 29, 58, \ldots$

4. $1, -4, 16, -64, 256, \ldots$

5. $-5, 5, 7, -7, -5, 5, 7, -7, \ldots$

6. $-3, \frac{3}{4}, -\frac{3}{16}, \frac{3}{64}, -\frac{3}{256}, \ldots$

In 7–12, find the common ratio of the geometric sequence. Then, write the next term.

7. $6, 18, 54, 162, 486, \ldots$

8. $2, -8, 32, -128, 512, \ldots$

9. $5, 15, 45, 135, 405, \ldots$

10. $\frac{1}{3}, \frac{2}{9}, \frac{4}{27}, \frac{8}{81}, \frac{16}{243}, \ldots$

11. $-2, \frac{1}{2}, -\frac{1}{8}, \frac{1}{32}, -\frac{1}{128}, \ldots$

12. $7, \frac{21}{4}, \frac{63}{16}, \frac{189}{64}, \frac{567}{256}, \ldots$

In 13–18, write the first five terms of the geometric sequence.

13. $a_1 = 6, r = \frac{1}{2}$

14. $a_1 = 1, r = \frac{3}{5}$

15. $a_1 = \frac{2}{9}, r = -6$

16. $a_1 = 7, r = 3$

17. $a_1 = 15, r = \frac{2}{3}$

18. $a_1 = 1, r = \frac{1}{6}$

In 19–24, find the indicated term of the geometric sequence.

19. $a_1 = 4, r = \frac{1}{8}, a_3 = \boxed{?}$

20. $a_1 = 10, r = \frac{1}{5}, a_5 = \boxed{?}$

21. $a_1 = 2, r = 3, a_{12} = \boxed{?}$

22. $a_1 = 4, r = \frac{2}{5}, a_6 = \boxed{?}$

23. $a_1 = 100, r = 4, a_4 = \boxed{?}$

24. $a_1 = \frac{1}{2}, r = \frac{1}{2}, a_{20} = \boxed{?}$

In 25–27, write a formula for the *n*th term of the geometric sequence.

25. $1, \frac{4}{9}, \frac{16}{81}, \frac{64}{729}, \frac{256}{6561}, \ldots$

26. $100, 5, \frac{1}{4}, \frac{1}{80}, \frac{1}{1600}, \ldots$

27. $-5, 10, -20, 40, -80, \ldots$

In 28–30, write the missing information about the geometric sequence.

28. Common ratio: $\frac{1}{4}$
First term: 1024
Sixth term: $\boxed{?}$

29. Third term: 180
Sixth term: 38,880
Common ratio: $\boxed{?}$

30. Fifth term: 768
Seventh term: 12,288
Formula for a_n: $\boxed{?}$

In 31–33, evaluate the sum.

31. $\displaystyle\sum_{i=1}^{15} 4(\frac{1}{2})^{i-1}$

32. $\displaystyle\sum_{i=1}^{10} \frac{1}{2}(6^{i-1})$

33. $\displaystyle\sum_{n=0}^{11} 6(\frac{1}{2})^n$

34. *Salary Plan* Suppose you go to work at a company that pays $0.01 for the first day, $0.02 for the second day, $0.04 for the third day, and so on. (Each day your wage doubles.) What would your total income be if you worked for 10 days? 20 days? 30 days?

12.4 Name _____

In 1–6, decide whether the infinite series has a sum.

1. $\sum_{n=1}^{\infty} 3(\frac{7}{2})^{n-1}$

2. $\sum_{n=1}^{\infty} -4(\frac{1}{6})^{n-1}$

3. $\sum_{n=1}^{\infty} 10(2)^{n-1}$

4. $\sum_{n=1}^{\infty} 5(-\frac{2}{5})^{n-1}$

5. $\sum_{n=0}^{\infty} 3(\frac{4}{5})^n$

6. $\sum_{n=1}^{\infty} (\frac{8}{7})^{n-1}$

In 7–15, find the sum of the series (if it has one).

7. $\sum_{n=1}^{\infty} 2(\frac{2}{3})^{n-1}$

8. $\sum_{n=0}^{\infty} 12(\frac{1}{4})^n$

9. $\sum_{n=1}^{\infty} 5(\frac{4}{9})^{n-1}$

10. $\sum_{n=1}^{\infty} \frac{1}{8}(8)^{n-1}$

11. $\sum_{n=1}^{\infty} 10(-\frac{1}{2})^{n-1}$

12. $\sum_{n=0}^{\infty} -5(0.1)^n$

13. $\sum_{n=1}^{\infty} 2(0.05)^{n-1}$

14. $\sum_{n=1}^{\infty} -\frac{1}{4}(-\frac{1}{3})^{n-1}$

15. $\sum_{n=0}^{\infty} (-0.25)^n$

In 16–18, find the fraction that is equal to the given repeating decimal. For example, use the fact that $0.5555\ldots = 0.5 + 0.05 + 0.005 + 0.0005 + \cdots$

16. $0.5555\ldots$

17. $0.40404040\ldots$

18. $0.18181818\ldots$

19. *Geometry*   A square has sides of 10 inches each. A second square is inscribed in the original square by joining the midpoints of the sides, as shown below. A third square is then inscribed inside the second square by joining the midpoints of the sides of the second square. This process is continued endlessly. What is the sum of the areas of the infinite sequence of squares?

 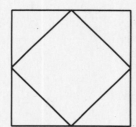 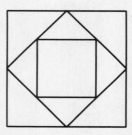

20. *Compact Disk*   In coming to rest, suppose that a CD makes one half as many revolutions in a second as in the previous second. How many revolutions does the CD make in coming to rest if it makes 4 revolutions in the first second after the stop function is activated?

In 1–6, evaluate the binomial coefficient.

1. $\dbinom{5}{2}$ **2.** $\dbinom{8}{1}$ **3.** $\dbinom{7}{3}$

4. $\dbinom{12}{6}$ **5.** $\dbinom{14}{10}$ **6.** $\dbinom{10}{5}$

In 7–12, use the Binomial Theorem to expand the binomial.

7. $(x - 4)^3$ **8.** $(x + 3)^5$ **9.** $(2x + 3)^4$

10. $(x + 2y)^6$ **11.** $(3x - 2)^5$ **12.** $(x + y)^4$

13. Find the coefficient of x^7 in the expansion of $(x + 4)^9$.

14. Find the coefficient of x^5 in the expansion of $(x - 3)^7$.

15. Complete the following grid with the first 7 rows of Pascal's Triangle.

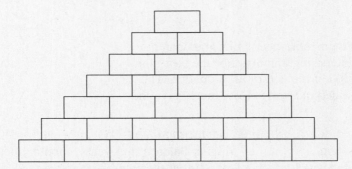

In 16–19, use Pascal's Triangle to find the binomial coefficient.

16. $\dbinom{7}{2}$ **17.** $\dbinom{5}{2}$ **18.** $\dbinom{6}{4}$ **19.** $\dbinom{4}{1}$

In 20–25, use Pascal's Triangle to expand the binomial.

20. $(2x + y)^5$ **21.** $(x - 3y)^4$ **22.** $(x + 4)^6$

23. $(2x - 3z)^3$ **24.** $(4x + 1)^5$ **25.** $(x - 3)^6$

26. *Jet Ski* You have bought a new jet ski for $2500. It depreciates at a rate of r each year. Its value V after n years is given by

$$V = 2500(1 - r)^n.$$

Expand this expression for $n = 4$.

In 1 and 2, construct an annuity table showing the deposits and balances for the given savings plan.

1. At the end of every two months for one year, $350 is invested in an increasing annuity. The annuity pays 8% annual interest, compounded bimonthly.

2. At the end of each month for one year, $50 is invested in an increasing annuity. The annuity pays 9% annual interest, compounded monthly.

In 3–6, find the balance of the increasing annuity.

	Periodic Deposit	Number of Deposits per Year	Number of Years	Annual Interest Rate	Compounding Period
3.	$25	12	5	10%	Monthly
4.	$100	24	2	8%	Semimonthly
5.	$5	52	1	$6\frac{1}{2}\%$	Weekly
6.	$150	26	3	6%	Biweekly

7. **Retirement Plan** In preparing for their retirement, your grandparents have been putting money into an increasing annuity. For the past nine years, their deposits have been $1000 at the end of each quarter. The annual interest rate is 8%, compounded quarterly. How much have they accumulated to date?

8. **Audio-Video System** You want to buy a new audio-video system. The system costs $4500. How much must be deposited each month into an annuity paying $8\frac{1}{4}\%$, compounded monthly, to attain a balance of $4500 after 1 year?

9. **Comparing Plans** Which would produce a higher balance in 5 years: monthly deposits of $100 at 6% interest, compounded monthly, or monthly deposits of $80 at 8% interest, compounded monthly?

10. **Savings Plan** You deposit $150 each month into an increasing annuity that pays an annual interest rate of $10\frac{1}{2}\%$, compounded monthly. What is the balance after 20 years? How much of the balance is interest?

11. **Comparing Plans** You want to save $30,000. Which plan would require a smaller total deposit: monthly payments with $8\frac{1}{2}\%$ interest, compounded monthly for ten years, or monthly payments with $6\frac{1}{2}\%$ interest, compounded monthly for eight years?

12. **Pickup Truck** An eleven-year-old starts saving so that by the time she gets her driver's license, she will have enough money to buy a used pickup truck. She deposits $5 each week into an increasing annuity that pays 12%, compounded weekly. How much will she have saved in 5 years?

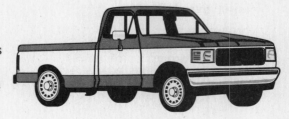

In 1–6, evaluate the six trigonometric functions of θ.

1.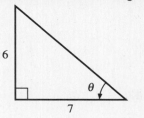

2.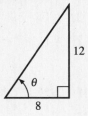

3.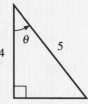

4.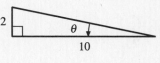

5.

6.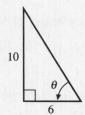

In 7–15, sketch a right triangle that has θ as one of its acute angles. Then find the values of the five trigonometric functions that are not given.

7. $\cos\theta = \frac{2}{5}$

8. $\sec\theta = 4$

9. $\cot\theta = \frac{12}{13}$

10. $\tan\theta = 2$

11. $\csc\theta = 2$

12. $\cos\theta = \frac{5}{6}$

13. $\sin\theta = \frac{3}{4}$

14. $\sin\theta = \frac{2}{7}$

15. $\tan\theta = 5$

16. Given $\sin\theta = \frac{2}{3}$, find $\cos\theta$.

17. Given $\cos\theta = \frac{1}{2}$, find $\tan\theta$.

18. Given $\tan\theta = 3$, find $\csc\theta$.

19. Given $\csc\theta = 5$, find $\cos\theta$.

20. Given $\cot\theta = \frac{5}{4}$, find $\sin\theta$.

21. Given $\sec\theta = 4$, find $\tan\theta$.

22. Given $\csc\theta = 2$, find $\sec\theta$.

23. Given $\csc\theta = 2$, find $\tan\theta$.

In 24–29, use a calculator to approximate the value of the trigonometric function. Round your result to three decimal places.

24. $\sin 15°$

25. $\cos 47°$

26. $\tan 65°$

27. $\csc 18°$

28. $\sec 25°$

29. $\cot 62°$

30. *Baseball Diamond* A baseball diamond is laid out so that the bases are 90 feet apart and at right angles as shown at the right. The distance from home plate to the pitcher's mound is 60 feet 6 inches. Find the distance from the pitcher's mound to second base. (Hint: The mound is not exactly half-way between home plate and second base.)

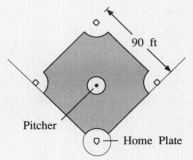

In 1–8, decide whether the angles are coterminal.

1. $\frac{13\pi}{6}$, $\frac{\pi}{6}$ **2.** $\frac{3\pi}{4}$, $-\frac{5\pi}{4}$ **3.** 280°, 80°   **4.** $-\frac{2\pi}{3}$, $\frac{4\pi}{3}$

5. 135°, −225°   **6.** 315°, 45°   **7.** $\frac{4\pi}{5}$, $\frac{14\pi}{5}$ **8.** 270°, −90°

In 9–16, find the complement of the angle.

9. 60°   **10.** 15°   **11.** 72°   **12.** $\frac{\pi}{8}$

13. $\frac{3\pi}{7}$ **14.** $\frac{\pi}{4}$ **15.** $\frac{3\pi}{20}$ **16.** $\frac{2\pi}{13}$

In 17–24, find the supplement of the angle.

17. 105°   **18.** 175°   **19.** 60°   **20.** 35°

21. $\frac{5\pi}{6}$ **22.** $\frac{3\pi}{4}$ **23.** $\frac{2\pi}{5}$ **24.** $\frac{4\pi}{15}$

In 25–32, find two angles, one with positive measure and the other with negative measure, that are coterminal with the given angle.

25. 225°   **26.** 340°   **27.** 540°   **28.** 60°

29. $\frac{12\pi}{5}$ **30.** $\frac{15\pi}{2}$ **31.** $\frac{20\pi}{3}$ **32.** $\frac{16\pi}{5}$

In 33–38, rewrite the degree measure in radians.

33. 135°   **34.** 40°   **35.** 260°

36. 215°   **37.** −340°   **38.** 210°

In 39–44, rewrite the radian measure in degrees.

39. $\frac{7\pi}{12}$ **40.** $-\frac{5\pi}{6}$ **41.** $\frac{2\pi}{3}$

42. $\frac{13\pi}{4}$ **43.** $\frac{8\pi}{3}$ **44.** $\frac{\pi}{6}$

In 45–47, match the measure with the angle.

45. $\frac{12\pi}{5}$ **46.** $\frac{6\pi}{5}$ **47.** $\frac{7\pi}{4}$

a.   **b.**   **c.**

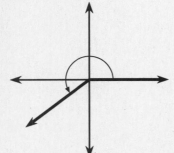 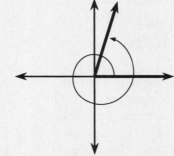 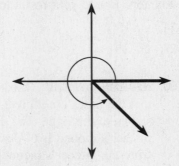

48. *Earth* Assuming that Earth is a sphere of radius 4000 miles, what is the difference in latitude of two cities, one of which is 325 miles due north of the other?

In 1–9, you are given a point on the terminal side of an angle. Find the sine, cosine, and tangent of the angle.

1.

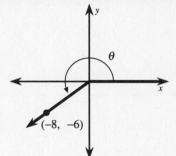

2.

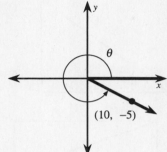

3.

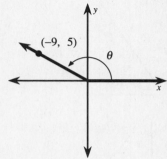

4. $(5, 8)$ **5.** $(-4, 4)$ **6.** $(3, 7)$

7. $(-10, -2)$ **8.** $(4, -9)$ **9.** $(-4, 5)$

In 10–21, sketch the angle. Then find its reference angle. (Note: The angle measure in Exercises 14–21 is radians.)

10. $-225°$ **11.** $315°$ **12.** $-150°$ **13.** $65°$

14. $\frac{7\pi}{4}$ **15.** $-\frac{2\pi}{3}$ **16.** $\frac{13\pi}{4}$ **17.** $\frac{7\pi}{3}$

18. 5.2 **19.** 1.0 **20.** -3.2 **21.** 2.7

In 22–27, without using a calculator, decide whether the equation is true or false. Then use a calculator to verify your decision.

22. $\sin 152° = \sin 28°$ **23.** $\cos 225° = -\cos 45°$ **24.** $\tan 325° = -\tan 35°$

25. $\cos \frac{5\pi}{4} = \cos \frac{\pi}{4}$ **26.** $\tan \frac{12\pi}{5} = -\tan \frac{2\pi}{5}$ **27.** $\sin \frac{7\pi}{9} = \sin \frac{2\pi}{9}$

In 28–35, evaluate the function without using a calculator.

28. $\sin 300°$ **29.** $\csc 225°$ **30.** $\cot(-\frac{7\pi}{6})$ **31.** $\sec \frac{5\pi}{4}$

32. $\cos(-750°)$ **33.** $\tan \frac{17\pi}{3}$ **34.** $\csc \frac{11\pi}{4}$ **35.** $\sin(-\frac{2\pi}{3})$

In 36–41, use a calculator to evaluate the function. Round your result to four decimal places.

36. $\sin 435°$ **37.** $\cos \frac{17\pi}{4}$ **38.** $\sec 3.1$

39. $\cot \frac{7\pi}{3}$ **40.** $\tan \frac{11\pi}{13}$ **41.** $\csc(-222°)$

42. *Driving Golf Balls*   You and friend are driving golf balls at a driving range. If the angle of elevation is $30°$ and the ball travels 625 feet horizontally, what is the initial velocity of the ball? Suppose you used the same initial velocity, but hit the ball at an angle of $45°$. How far would it travel?

In 1–6, write the measure of the angle in degrees and in radians. Round to three decimal places.

1.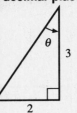

2.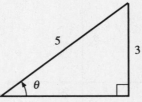

3.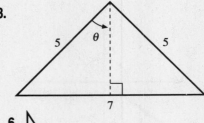

4.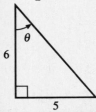

5.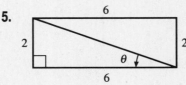

6.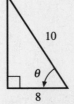

In 7–14, evaluate the expression without using a calculator. Write the result in degrees and in radians.

7. $\arcsin(-\frac{1}{2})$

8. $\arctan(-\frac{\sqrt{3}}{3})$

9. $\arccos(1)$

10. $\arcsin(\frac{\sqrt{3}}{2})$

11. $\arcsin(-\frac{\sqrt{2}}{2})$

12. $\arctan(1)$

13. $\arccos(\frac{\sqrt{3}}{2})$

14. $\arccos(-\frac{1}{2})$

In 15–22, use a calculator to approximate the value. Write the result in degrees and in radians. Round to three decimal places.

15. $\arcsin(0.6)$

16. $\arccos(-0.75)$

17. $\arctan(4.5)$

18. $\arccos(-0.25)$

19. $\arccos(0.1)$

20. $\arctan(-2.5)$

21. $\arcsin(0.9)$

22. $\arcsin(-0.4)$

23. *Basketball Backboard* The height of an outdoor basketball backboard is $12\frac{1}{2}$ feet, and the backboard casts a shadow $17\frac{1}{3}$ feet long, as shown at the right. Find the angle of elevation of the sun. List the angle in degrees and in radians.

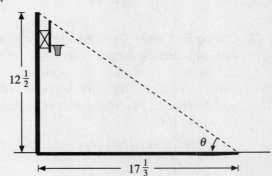

In 1–11, solve the triangle. Some of the "triangles" have no solution and some have two solutions.

1.
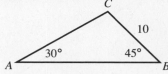

2.
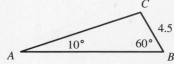

3.
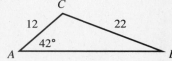

4. $A = 36°$, $a = 8$, $b = 5$

5. $A = 150°$, $C = 20°$, $a = 200$

6. $B = 15.5°$, $a = 4.5$, $b = 6.8$

7. $C = 145°$, $b = 4$, $c = 14$

8. $A = 58°$, $a = 4.5$, $b = 12.8$

9. $A = 58°$, $a = 4.5$, $b = 5$

10. $A = 65°$, $B = 49°$, $a = 45.7$

11. $B = 48.13°$, $a = 5.24$, $b = 4.44$

In 12–17, decide whether there are no solutions, exactly one solution, or two solutions. (You do not need to solve the triangle.)

12. $A = 63°$, $a = 42$, $b = 120$

13. $B = 47°$, $A = 60°$, $a = 45$

14. $B = 30°$, $b = 40$, $a = 60$

15. $A = 60°$, $B = 40°$, $c = 6$

16. $A = 76.4°$, $a = 176$, $b = 189$

17. $A = 48.2°$, $a = 15$, $b = 20$

In 18–20, find the area of the triangle.

18.
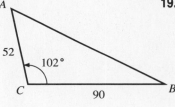

19.
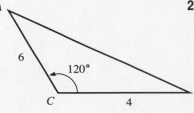

20.
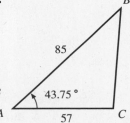

21. *Surveying* A surveyor wants to find the width of a narrow, deep gorge from a point on the edge. To do this, the surveyor takes measurements as shown in the figure at the right. How wide is the gorge?

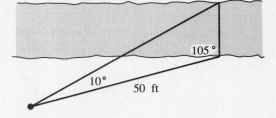

In 1–11, solve the triangle.

1.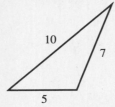

2.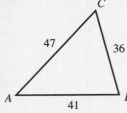

3.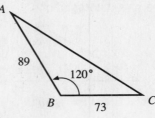

4. $C = 45°$, $a = 13\sqrt{2}$, $b = 23$

5. $C = 46°$, $a = 113$, $b = 137$

6. $C = 51°$, $a = 307$, $b = 345$

7. $A = 117.5°$, $b = 7.5$, $c = 3.9$

8. $a = 4.3$, $b = 5.2$, $c = 8.2$

9. $a = 20.1$, $b = 30.4$, $c = 25.7$

10. $C = 39.4°$, $a = 126$, $b = 80.1$

11. $a = 21.46$, $b = 12.85$, $c = 9.179$

In 12–20, find the area of the triangle.

12.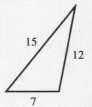

13.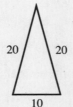

14.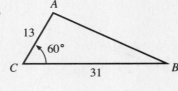

15. $a = 2.5$, $b = 10.2$, $c = 9$

16. $a = 75.4$, $b = 52$, $c = 52$

17. $a = 4.25$, $b = 1.55$, $c = 3$

18. $a = 3$, $b = 4$, $c = 5$

19. $a = 9$, $b = 12$, $c = 15$

20. $a = 1.42$, $b = 0.75$, $c = 1.25$

21. **Boat Race** A boat race occurs along a triangular course marked by buoys A, B, and C. The race starts with the boats going 8000 feet due north. The other two sides of the course lie to the east of the first side, and their lengths are 3500 feet and 6500 feet as shown at the right. Find the bearings for the last two legs of the course.

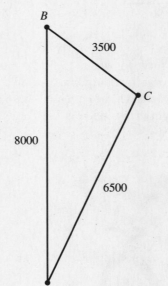

In 1–8, find the amplitude and period of the graph.

1.

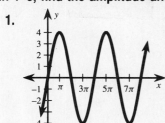

2.

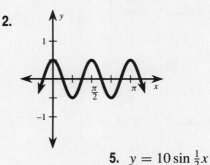

3. $y = \sin 8x$

4. $y = \frac{1}{3}\cos 2x$

5. $y = 10\sin\frac{1}{2}x$

6. $y = 6\cos 3\pi x$

7. $y = \frac{1}{2}\sin\frac{1}{2}\pi x$

8. $y = 4\cos 4\pi x$

In 9–11, match the equation with its graph.

9. $y = 4\cos 4x$

10. $y = 4\sin\frac{1}{4}x$

11. $y = 4\sin 4x$

a.

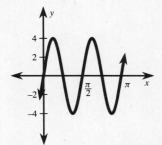

b.

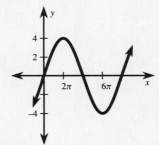

c.

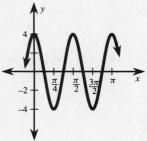

In 12–17, sketch two cycles of the graph of the equation.

12. $y = \frac{1}{3}\cos 3x$

13. $y = 3\cos 2x$

14. $y = \frac{1}{2}\sin 2\pi x$

15. $y = 10\sin\pi x$

16. $y = 4\cos\frac{\pi}{8}x$

17. $y = \frac{1}{6}\sin 6\pi x$

In 18–20, write an equation of the indicated function. (Use $a > 0$ and $b > 0$.)

18. $y = a\sin bx$
Amplitude = 2
Period = 4

19. $y = a\sin bx$
Amplitude = $\frac{1}{8}$
Period = 8π

20. $y = a\cos bx$
Amplitude = 4
Period = $\frac{\pi}{2}$

In 21 and 22, write two x-values at which the function has a minimum and two x-values at which the function has a maximum.

21. $y = 5\sin 2x$

22. $y = \frac{1}{4}\cos\frac{1}{2}\pi x$

23. After exercising for a few minutes, a person has a respiratory cycle for which the velocity, v (in liters per second), of air flow is approximated by
$$v = 1.75\sin\frac{\pi}{2}t$$
where t is time in seconds. Inhalation occurs when $v > 0$ and exhalation occurs when $v < 0$.

a. Find the time for one full respiratory cycle.
b. Find the number of cycles per minute.
c. Sketch the graph of the velocity function.

In 1–6, describe how the graphs of $y = \sin x$ or $y = \cos x$ can be shifted to produce the graph of the function.

1. $y = 5 + \sin x$

2. $y = \sin(x + \pi)$

3. $y = -4 + \cos(x - \frac{\pi}{4})$

4. $y = 2 + \sin(x + \frac{\pi}{2})$

5. $y = -2 + \cos(x - \pi)$

6. $y = \cos(x + \frac{\pi}{4})$

In 7–9, match the equation to its graph.

7. $y = -2\sin(2x + \pi)$

8. $y = 2 + \sin(x + \pi)$

9. $y = 2\sin(x - \pi)$

a.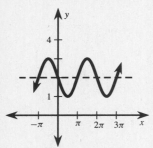

b.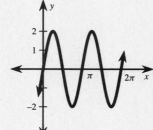

c.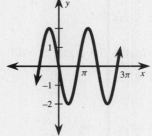

10. The graph of $y = 3\sin\frac{1}{2}x$ is drawn, then shifted down $\frac{1}{2}$ unit. Write an equation of the resulting graph.

11. The graph of $y = 3\cos(x)$ is drawn, then shifted π units to the left and 2 units up. Write an equation of the resulting graph.

In 12–16, sketch the graph of the function.

12. $y = 3 + \cos(x - \frac{\pi}{2})$

13. $y = 4 - \frac{1}{2}\cos(x)$

14. $y = 1 - \sin\frac{1}{2}\pi x$

15. $y = -2 + \sin(2x + \frac{\pi}{2})$

16. $y = 2 + 2\cos(x - \pi)$

17. What are the minimum and maximum values of $y = 3 - 2\cos 2x$? Write two x-values at which the minimum occurs. Write two x-values at which the maximum occurs.

18. Write an equation of the graph below.

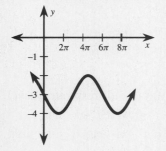

19. Suppose that the brightness of a distant star is given by

$$y = 10.5 + 5.2\cos\left(\frac{\pi t}{20} + 40\right)$$

where t is given in days. Sketch the graph for $0 \le t \le 80$. Which day(s) is the brightness the greatest? Which day(s) is the brightness the least?

In 1–9, simplify the expression.

1. $\cot x \sin x$

2. $\dfrac{\cos^2 x}{\sin x} + \sin x$

3. $\dfrac{1 - \cos^2 x}{\cos^2 x}$

4. $\cos x + \sin x \tan x$

5. $\sin^3 x + \cos(\frac{\pi}{2} - x)\cos^2 x$

6. $\sin^2 x + \tan^2 x + \cos^2 x$

7. $\dfrac{\sin(\frac{\pi}{2} - x)}{\cos(\frac{\pi}{2} - x)}$

8. $\dfrac{\sin(-x)}{\cos(-x)}$

9. $\cot(\frac{\pi}{2} - x)\cos x$

In 10–19, verify the identity.

10. $\sin^2 x - \sin^4 x = \cos^2 x - \cos^4 x$

11. $\dfrac{1}{\sin x} - \sin x = \cot x \cos x$

12. $\dfrac{1}{\tan x} + \dfrac{1}{\cot x} = \tan x + \cot x$

13. $(1 + \sin x)(1 + \sin(-x)) = \cos^2 x$

14. $2\sec^2 x - 2\sec^2 x \sin^2 x - \sin^2 x - \cos^2 x = 1$

15. $2 + \cos^2 x - 3\cos^4 x = \sin^2 x(2 + 3\cos^2 x)$

16. $\dfrac{1 + \sec(-x)}{\sin(-x) + \tan(-x)} = -\csc x$

17. $\dfrac{\tan^3 x - 1}{\tan x - 1} = \tan^2 x + \tan x + 1$

18. $\cos(\frac{\pi}{2} - x) + \cos x \tan(\frac{\pi}{2} - x) = \csc x$

19. $\dfrac{1 - \tan^2 x}{1 + \tan^2 x} = 1 - 2\sin^2 x$

20. Sketch the curve represented by $x = 3\cos t$, $y = 4\sin t$. Then use a trigonometric identity to verify that the graph is a circle, an ellipse, or a hyperbola.

21. While drawing the plans for the plumbing of your new home, the contractor finds it necessary for two water pipes to be joined at right angles. The expression

$$(r \cos x)^2 + (R - r)(R + r)$$

is used. Show that this expression can be written as $R^2 - r^2 \sin^2 x$.

In 1–6, verify that the given values of x are solutions of the equation.

1. $3\tan^2 2x - 1 = 0$, $x = \frac{5\pi}{12}$

2. $2\sin^2 x - \sin x - 1 = 0$, $x = \frac{\pi}{2}$

3. $\sec^4 x - 4\sec^2 x = 0$, $x = \frac{5\pi}{3}$

4. $2\sin^2 x - \sin x = 0$, $x = 0$

5. $2\cos^2 x - 1 = 0$, $x = \frac{5\pi}{4}$

6. $\sec^2 x - 2\tan x = 4$, $x = \frac{7\pi}{4}$

In 7–18, solve the equation for $0 \le x < 2\pi$.

7. $\sqrt{3}\csc x - 2 = 0$

8. $2\sin^2 x - 1 = 0$

9. $3\sec^2 x - 4 = 0$

10. $\sin^2 x + \sin x = 0$

11. $2\cos^2 x = -\cos x$

12. $2\sin^2 x = 2 + \cos x$

13. $2\sec^2 x + \tan^2 x - 3 = 0$

14. $2\sin^2 x + 5\cos x + 1 = 0$

15. $1 - 2\sin^2 x = 0$

16. $4\cos^2 x = 1$

17. $2\cos^2 x + \sin x - 1 = 0$

18. $2\cos x - 4\cos^2 x = 0$

19. Find the x-intercepts of the graph of $y = 3\sin x + 3$ for $0 \le x < 2\pi$.

20. Find the intersection points of the two graphs in the interval $0 \le x < 2\pi$.

$$y = \sin x + 1$$
$$y = 2\sin^2 x + 1$$

21. In calculus, it can be shown that the function $y = 2\sin x - \cos 2x$ has minimum or maximum values when

$$2\cos x + 4\cos x \sin x = 0.$$

Find all solutions of $2\cos x + 4\cos x \sin x = 0$ in the interval $0 \le x < 2\pi$.
Verify your solutions with a graphing calculator or a computer.

14.5 Name _____

In 1–6, find the exact value of the expression.

1. $\sin 165°$

2. $\cos \frac{7\pi}{12}$

3. $\tan 255°$

4. $\cot \frac{11\pi}{12}$

5. $\sec 195°$

6. $\csc \left(-\frac{\pi}{12}\right)$

In 7–10, simplify the given expression. Do not evaluate it.

7. $\sin 40° \cos 32° + \cos 40° \sin 32°$

8. $\cos \frac{\pi}{6} \cos \frac{2\pi}{7} + \sin \frac{\pi}{6} \sin \frac{2\pi}{7}$

9. $\dfrac{\tan 135° + \tan 40°}{1 - \tan 135° \tan 40°}$

10. $\sin 4.5 \cos 2.7 - \cos 4.5 \sin 2.7$

In 11-14, evaluate the expression.

11. $\sin \frac{\pi}{3} \cos \frac{4\pi}{3} - \sin \frac{4\pi}{3} \cos \frac{\pi}{3}$

12. $\cos \frac{\pi}{6} \cos \frac{\pi}{4} - \sin \frac{\pi}{6} \sin \frac{\pi}{4}$

13. $\dfrac{\tan 135° - \tan 45°}{1 + \tan 135° \tan 45°}$

14. $\sin 315° \cos 30° + \cos 315° \sin 30°$

In 15 and 16, verify the identity.

15. $\sin(\frac{\pi}{2} + x) = \cos x$

16. $\cos(\frac{3\pi}{2} - x) = -\sin x$

In 17 and 18, evaluate the expression.

Use the fact that $\sin u = -\frac{3}{5}$, $\frac{3\pi}{2} < u < 2\pi$ and $\cos v = \frac{7}{25}$, $0 < v < \frac{\pi}{2}$.

17. $\sin(u + v)$

18. $\cos(v - u)$

In 19–22, solve the equation for $0 \le x < 2\pi$.

19. $\cos(x + \frac{\pi}{4}) - \cos(x - \frac{\pi}{4}) = 1$

20. $\sin(x + \frac{\pi}{6}) - \sin(x - \frac{\pi}{6}) = \frac{1}{2}$

21. $\tan(x + \pi) + \cos(x - \frac{\pi}{2}) = 0$

22. $\sin(x + \pi) + \sin(x - \pi) = 2$

23. Show that
$$\sin(x + y + z) = \sin x \cos y \cos z + \sin y \cos x \cos z + \sin z \cos x \cos y - \sin x \sin y \sin z.$$
(Hint: Group $(x + y + z)$ as $[(x + y) + z]$.)

24. Use the result of Exercise 23 to find $\sin(\frac{31\pi}{12})$ using
$$\frac{31\pi}{12} = \frac{3\pi}{4} + \frac{2\pi}{3} + \frac{7\pi}{6}.$$

14.6 Name _____

In 1–6, rewrite each expression without double angles. Simplify the expression.

1. $\sin 4x$

2. $\dfrac{\cos 2x}{\cos x}$

3. $\dfrac{\sin 2x}{2 \sin x}$

4. $2 \csc 2x$

5. $\cos 2x + \sin x$

6. $\cos 2x + \cos x$

In 7–12, solve the equation for $0 \le x < 2\pi$.

7. $\cos 2x = -\sin x$

8. $\cos 2x + \cos x = 0$

9. $\sec 2x = 2$

10. $\cos 2x = \cos x$

11. $\sin 2x \sin x = \cos x$

12. $\sin 2x + \sqrt{2} \sin x = 0$

In 13–18, find the exact value of the expression.

13. $\sin \frac{\pi}{8}$

14. $\cos \frac{7\pi}{12}$

15. $\tan \frac{11\pi}{12}$

16. $\cos(67.5°)$

17. $\tan(-112.5°)$

18. $\sin \frac{5\pi}{8}$

In 19–22, find the exact value of the sine, cosine, and tangent of $\frac{1}{2} u$.

19. $\cos u = \frac{4}{5}, \ \frac{3\pi}{2} \le u < 2\pi$

20. $\sin u = \frac{7}{25}, \ \frac{\pi}{2} \le u < \pi$

21. $\tan u = \frac{3}{4}, \ \pi \le u < \frac{3\pi}{2}$

22. $\sin u = -\frac{5}{13}, \ \frac{3\pi}{2} \le u < 2\pi$

23. A batted baseball leaves the bat at an angle of θ with the horizontal, with a velocity of $v_0 = 100$ feet per second, and is caught by an outfielder. If $\sin \theta = 0.60$, first find the distance the ball was hit and then check your answer by finding θ. Remember that

$$r = \tfrac{1}{32} v_0^2 \sin 2\theta,$$

where r is the horizontal distance traveled.

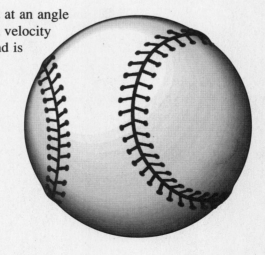

In 1–4, use the following sample space to find the probability of the event.

{1, 2, 3, 4, 5, 6, 7, 8, 9, 10, 11, 12}

1. An even number is chosen.

2. A prime number is chosen.

3. A multiple of 3 is chosen.

4. A two-digit number is chosen.

Hitting a Star **In 5–7, use the following information.**

You are throwing a dart at the square shown at the right. Assume that the dart is equally likely to land at any point in the square. The square is 2 inches by 2 inches. Each star has an area of 0.01 square inch.

5. The dart has landed inside the square. What is the probability that it hit a star?

6. The dart has landed inside the square. What is the probability that it hit a star in the top three rows?

7. The dart has landed inside the square. What is the probability that it hit one of the four corner stars?

Starting Smoking **In 8–10, use the following information.**

Of all smokers in the United States, 24% began smoking when they were younger than 16, 28% began smoking at the ages of 16 and 17, 35% began smoking at the ages of 18, 19, or 20, and the others began smoking at the age of 21 or older. (*Source: Centers for Disease Control*)

8. If an American smoker is chosen at random, what is the probability that he or she began smoking at the age of 16 or 17?

9. If an American smoker is chosen at random, what is the probability that he or she began smoking at the age of 16, 17, 18, 19, or 20?

10. If an American smoker is chosen at random, what is the probability that he or she began smoking at the age of 21 or older?

Farm Animals **In 11–13, use the following information.**

Your cousin lives on a small farm. She is a member of the 4-H club and is showing the nine animals at the right at the county fair. Two of her animals won a blue ribbon (1st place), one won a red ribbon (2nd place), and three won white ribbons (3rd place). You don't know which animals won which prizes.

11. If you choose one of your cousin's animals at random, what is the probability that the animal won a 1st place ribbon?

12. If you choose one of your cousin's animals at random, what is the probability that the animal won a ribbon?

13. If you choose one of your cousin's animals at random, what is the probability that the animal won a red or white ribbon?

In 1–4, find the number of permutations of the given digits. (For example, the digits 1, 2, and 3 can be permuted in six ways: 123, 132, 213, 231, 312, and 321.)

1. 3, 4, 6 **2.** 1, 5, 7, 8 **3.** 2, 4, 6, 8, 9 **4.** 1, 3, 4, 5, 7, 9

5. *Stacking Books* Five books are taken from a shelf and laid in a stack on a table. In how many different orders can the books be stacked?

6. *Committee Meeting* Six people are having a meeting. In how many orders can the people leave the meeting room? (They leave one at a time.)

7. *Decorating a Room* You are choosing curtains, paint, and carpet for your room. You have 12 choices of curtains, 8 choices of paint color, and 20 choices of carpeting. How many different ways can you choose curtains, paint, and carpeting?

8. *Naming a Dog* You are choosing a name for your registered beagle. Your dog's "grandparent's" names are Willow-Sutton, Carolina-Downing, Hollybrook-Loner, and Starfire-Wolf. You want your dog's first name to be the same as one of its grandparent's first names, and its second name to be the same as one of its grandparent's second names, but it can't have exactly the same name as one of its grandparents. How many names do you have to choose from?

9. *Coins* You have 8 pennies in your pocket—dated 1972, 1978, 1979, 1985, 1989, 1990, 1991, and 1992. You take the coins out of your pocket one at a time. What is the probability that they are taken out in order by date?

10. *More Coins* In Exercise 9, you have chosen the first two coins—the first is 1972 and the second is 1978. What is the probability that you will choose the remaining coins in order by date?

11. *Women Directors* In 1991, the number of women on the corporate boards of the 1000 *Fortune's* Industrial 500 and Service 500 were as follows: 481 boards had no women, 386 had one woman, 113 had two women, 15 had three women, 3 had four women, and 2 had five women. You are asked to interview five of these women: one from a board with only one woman, one from a board with two women, and so on. How many different groups of five women can you choose? (*Source: Catalyst*).

In 1–4, how many combinations of two letters can be chosen from the given letters?

1. A, B, C   **2.** A, B, C, D   **3.** A, B, C, D, E   **4.** A, B, C, D, E, F

In 5–8, how many combinations of three letters can be chosen from the given letters?

5. A, B, C   **6.** A, B, C, D   **7.** A, B, C, D, E   **8.** A, B, C, D, E, F

9. *State Flags*   The flags of Arizona, Colorado, New Mexico, and Texas are shown below. You are choosing two of the flags to draw with a computer "paint program." How many different pairs of flags can you choose?

 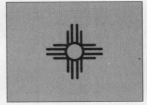 

10. *Bowling Team*   Nine people in your class want to be on a 5-person bowling team to represent the class. How many different teams can be chosen?

11. *Pizza Toppings*   A pizza shop offers twelve toppings. How many different "three-topping pizzas" can be formed with the twelve toppings? (Assume no topping is used twice.)

12. *Geometry*   How many different rectangles occur in the grid shown below? (*Hint:* A rectangle is formed by choosing two of the vertical lines in the grid and two of the horizontal lines in the grid.)

13. *Geometry*   How many different rectangles occur in the grid shown below? (*Hint:* A rectangle is formed by choosing two of the vertical lines in the grid and two of the horizontal lines in the grid.)

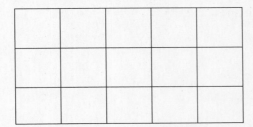 

14. *Choosing a Card*   You are dealing a 3-card hand from a standard deck of playing cards like that shown on page 797 of the text. What is the probability that the hand contains the following?

a. All red cards.

b. All aces.

c. All face cards.

In 1–6, find the indicated probability. State whether *A* and *B* are mutually exclusive.

1. $P(A) = 0.45$
$P(B) = 0.15$
$P(A \cup B) = 0.60$
$P(A \cap B) = \boxed{?}$

2. $P(A) = 0.50$
$P(B) = 0.20$
$P(A \cup B) = 0.60$
$P(A \cap B) = \boxed{?}$

3. $P(A) = 0.80$
$P(B) = 0.10$
$P(A \cup B) = \boxed{?}$
$P(A \cap B) = 0.10$

4. $P(A) = 0.50$
$P(B) = 0.40$
$P(A \cup B) = \boxed{?}$
$P(A \cap B) = 0.10$

5. $P(A) = \boxed{?}$
$P(B) = 0.40$
$P(A \cup B) = 0.80$
$P(A \cap B) = 0.30$

6. $P(A) = 0.75$
$P(B) = \boxed{?}$
$P(A \cup B) = 0.85$
$P(A \cap B) = 0.25$

7. If $P(A) = 0.32$, what is $P(A')$?

8. If $P(A) = 0.81$, what is $P(A')$?

9. Find $P(A')$ using the figure below. (The sample space has 70 outcomes.)

10. Find $P(A \cup B)$ using the figure below. (The sample space has 650 outcomes.)

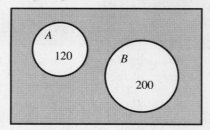

11. **Exercising** In a survey conducted by *USA Today*, men and women were asked how often they exercise on business trips. Of those surveyed, 579 said occasionally, 284 said often, 148 said always, and 125 said never. If you chose one of the respondents at random, what is the probability that the person answered "always" or "never?"

12. **Probability of Snow** The probability that it will snow today is 0.3, and the probability that it will snow tomorrow is 0.5. The probability that it will snow both days is 0.2. What is the probability that it will snow today or tomorrow?

Married or Single In 13 and 14, use the following information.

In 1970, 32% of American women (18 or older) were single and 22% of American men (18 or older) were single. In 1990, 40% of American women (18 or older) were single and 36% of American men (18 or older) were single. (*Source: U.S. Bureau of Census*)

13. In 1970, a group of 100 women and 100 men were asked whether they were married or single. The percent of married and single people was the same as in the general population. If one of the people in the group was chosen at random, what was the probability that the person was single? What was the probability that the person was married?

14. In 1990, a group of 100 women and 100 men were asked whether they were married or single. The percent of married and single people was the same as in the general population. If one of the people in the group was chosen at random, what was the probability that the person was single? What was the probability that the person was married?

15.5 Name _____

In 1–4, state whether the events A and B are independent or dependent

1. A single coin is tossed twice. Event A is having the coin land heads up on the first toss. Event B is having the coin land tails up on the second toss.

2. Two cards are drawn from a deck. The first card *is not* placed back in the deck before the second card is drawn. Event A is drawing a queen for the first card. Event B is drawing a king for the second card.

3. Two cards are drawn from a deck. The first card *is* placed back in the deck before the second card is drawn. Event A is drawing a queen for the first card. Event B is drawing a king for the second card.

4. You buy one state lottery ticket this week and one next week. Event A is winning the lottery this week. Event B is winning the lottery next week.

In 5–10, A and B are independent events. Find the indicated probability.

5. $P(A) = \frac{1}{2}$
   $P(B) = \frac{2}{3}$
   $P(A \cap B) = \boxed{?}$

6. $P(A) = 0.40$
   $P(B) = 0.20$
   $P(A \cap B) = \boxed{?}$

7. $P(A) = 0.80$
   $P(B) = \boxed{?}$
   $P(A \cap B) = 0.64$

8. $P(A) = 0.50$
   $P(B) = \boxed{?}$
   $P(A \cap B) = 0.40$

9. $P(A) = \boxed{?}$
   $P(B) = 0.70$
   $P(A \cap B) = 0.35$

10. $P(A) = 0.60$
    $P(B) = \boxed{?}$
    $P(A \cap B) = 0.60$

File Cabinet **In 11–13, use the following information.**

Each drawer in the file cabinet shown at the right has 100 folders. You are hunting for some information that is in one of the folders, but you don't know which folder has the information.

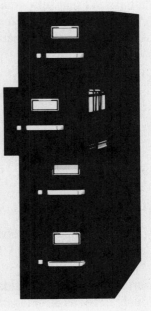

11. What is the probability that the information is in the first drawer you choose?

12. What is the probability that the information is *not* in the first folder you choose?

13. What is the probability that the information is *not* in the first six folders you choose?

Marbles in a Jar **In 14–16, use the following information.**

A jar contains 12 red marbles, 16 blue marbles and 18 white marbles.

14. Three marbles are chosen from the jar without replacement. What is the probability that none are white?

15. Four marbles are chosen from the jar without replacement. What is the probability that all are white?

16. Three marbles are chosen from the jar without replacement. What is the probability that at least one is white?

In 1 and 2, find the expected value of the sample space. Is the game fair?

1.

Outcome	A	B
Probability	$\frac{1}{4}$	$\frac{3}{4}$
Payoff	$3	−$1

2.

Outcome	A	B
Probability	$\frac{1}{2}$	$\frac{1}{2}$
Payoff	$3	−$1

In 3 and 4, find the expected value of the sample space. Is the game fair?

3.

Outcome	A	B	C
Probability	$\frac{1}{2}$	$\frac{3}{8}$	$\frac{1}{8}$
Payoff	$2	−$1	$1

4.

Outcome	A	B	C
Probability	$\frac{1}{2}$	$\frac{3}{8}$	$\frac{1}{8}$
Payoff	$2	−$1	−$5

In 5 and 6, find the expected value of the sample space. Is the game fair?

5.

Outcome	A	B	C	D
Probability	$\frac{1}{5}$	$\frac{2}{5}$	$\frac{1}{5}$	$\frac{1}{5}$
Payoff	$7	−$5	$1	$2

6.

Outcome	A	B	C	D
Probability	$\frac{1}{7}$	$\frac{3}{7}$	$\frac{2}{7}$	$\frac{1}{7}$
Payoff	$7	−$5	$1	$2

Aircraft Sales In 7 and 8, use the following information.

You own a business that sells small aircraft. You currently have 6 potential customers. The list below shows the price per aircraft, the number of aircraft, and the probability of getting the sale.

Customer	Price	Number of Aircraft	Probability
A	$40,000	2	0.80
B	$60,000	1	0.60
C	$80,000	3	0.30
D	$50,000	1	0.90
E	$60,000	2	0.90
F	$30,000	5	0.70

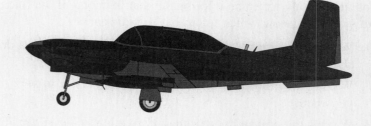

7. What is your expected income from these six customers?

8. You just learned that the probability that customer **C** will make the purchase has increased to 0.90. What is your expected income now?

Game Theory In 9 and 10, consider a game in which each of two people simultaneously chooses an integer: 1 or 2. Find the expected value for player *A* and the expected value for player *B*. Is each game fair?

9. If the numbers are the same, then player *A* wins 1 point from player *B*. If the numbers are different, then player *B* wins 1 point from player *A*.

10. If the numbers are the same, then player *A* wins 2 points from player *B*. If the numbers are different, then player *B* wins 1 point from player *A*.

Answers to Exercises

Lesson 1.1

1. < **2.** > **3.** >
4. < **5.** < **6.** >

7.

8.

9.

10.

11. $-\frac{25}{2}$ $-\frac{14}{5}$

12. $-\sqrt{2}$ $-\frac{2}{5}$

13. Associative Property of Addition
14. Inverse Property of Addition
15. Commutative Property of Multiplication
16. Commutative Property of Addition
17. Inverse Property of Multiplication
18. Left Distributive Property
19. Identity Property of Addition
20. Identity Property of Multiplication
21. Associative Property of Multiplication
22. 10 **23.** 7 **24.** -7 **25.** 10
26. 20 **27.** -72 **28.** 3 **29.** -6
30. 22 in. **31.** 3

Lesson 1.2

1. -3 **2.** 18 **3.** 15 **4.** 7
5. 9 **6.** $-\frac{5}{2}$ **7.** 2^3 **8.** 5^6
9. $(3x)^2$ **10.** $(-9)^4$ **11.** a^5 **12.** $(-x)^3$
13. $(2y)^3 + 7$ **14.** $(4b)^2 + (2a)^2$ **15.** $x^3 y^2$
16. $2y(x + y)$ **17.** $(x + 3y)^2$
18. 30 **19.** 121 **20.** -7 **21.** 15
22. 42 **23.** 5 **24.** 8 **25.** 24
26. 15 **27.** 112 **28.** $-\frac{1}{2}$
29. $270 **30.** $415

Lesson 1.3

1. -3 **2.** 9 **3.** -1 **4.** 24
5. 3 **6.** 8 **7.** 4 **8.** -3
9. 18 **10.** -6 **11.** $-\frac{1}{3}$ **12.** $\frac{1}{3}$
13. 2 **14.** 3 **15.** 2 **16.** -5
17. $\frac{5}{2}$ **18.** -3 **19.** $\frac{1}{7}$ **20.** -13
21. $\frac{4}{7}$ **22.** 0 **23.** $-\frac{1}{8}$ **24.** -2
25. $2x - 3 = 11$ ft, $3x - 5 = 16$ ft, $15 - x = 8$ ft
26. 9 ft by 10 ft **27.** 47.5 hr **28.** 2.75 hr

Lesson 1.4

1. Total cost = $120
Price per case = $7.50
Num. of cases = x
2. $120 = 7.50x$
3. $x = 16$
4. 16 cases
5. Distance = 168 miles
Rate = r mph
Time = 3.5 hr
6. $168 = r(3.5)$
7. $r = 48$
8. 48 mph

9.
Total cost	=	Price per sq yd	·	Num. of sq yd

10. Total cost = $450
Price per sq yd = p
Num. of sq yd = 30
11. $450 = p(30)$
12. $p = 15$
13. $15

14.
Distance friend drove
Friend's speed	·	Friend's time	+

Distance you drove
Your speed	·	Your time	=	Total distance

15. Friend's speed = 52 mph
Friend's time = 3 hr
Your speed = x mph
Your time = 3 hr
Total distance = 300 mi

16. $52(3) + x(3) = 300$ **17.** $x = 48$
18. 48 mph

Lesson 1.5

1. $t = \frac{d}{r}$ **2.** $r = \frac{I}{Pt}$ **3.** $s = \frac{2h}{\sqrt{3}}$
4. $h = \frac{3V}{\pi r^2}$ **5.** $b_1 = \frac{2A}{h} - b_2$
6. $R = \frac{S}{\pi s} - r$ **7.** $h = \frac{V}{\pi r^2}$
8. $w = \frac{2S}{h_1 + h_2}$ **9.** ≈ 4.5 feet
10. 23 in. **11.** $r^3 = \frac{3V}{4\pi}$, $r = 4$ m
12. 8 m **13.** ≈ 201 sq m

Lesson 1.6

1. e. **2.** c. **3.** b. **4.** f.
5. a. **6.** d. **7.** $x < -2$ **8.** $x \geq 7$
9. $x \geq -3$ **10.** $x > 3$ **11.** $x \leq 10$
12. $x > -3$ **13.** $x > -2$ **14.** $x < 2$
15. $x \geq 1$ **16.** $x \leq 6$ **17.** $x > 9$
18. $x \leq -\frac{1}{3}$ **19.** $x > 1$ **20.** $x \leq -1$
21. $x \geq 2$ **22.** $x < 2$ **23.** $x > -\frac{5}{9}$
24. $x \leq 0$

■ **Lesson 1.6 (continued)**

25. $x \le 3$

26. $x < 1$

27. $x \ge -\frac{1}{2}$

28. $12 \le x \le 18$

29. $\frac{3}{2} < x < 4$

30. $-4 < x < 6$

31. $x \le 6$ or $x \ge 8$

32. $x < -2$ or $x > 1$

33. $x \ge 2$ or $x \le -2$

34. $0.4 \le x \le 8$

■ **Lesson 1.7**

1. $x + 2 = 7$
$x + 2 = -7$

2. $2x - 1 = 5$
$2x - 1 = -5$

3. $5x + 11 = 6$
$5x + 11 = -6$

4. $\frac{1}{2}t - 3 = 1$
$\frac{1}{2}t - 3 = -1$

5. $5 - t = 3$
$5 - t = -3$

6. $1 - 4t = 9$
$1 - 4t = -9$

7. $x = 2$ or $x = -8$

8. $x = \frac{10}{3}$ or $x = -2$

9. $x = 4$ or $x = -10$

10. $t = 10$ or $t = 6$

11. $t = 3$ or $t = \frac{13}{3}$

12. $t = \frac{1}{7}$ or $t = -1$

13. $-3 < x + 7 < 3$

14. $-10 \le 2x - 4 \le 10$

15. $-7 < 5 - 3x < 7$

16. $x - 4 > 5$ or $x - 4 < -5$

17. $5x + 1 \ge 4$ or $5x + 1 \le -4$

18. $2 - x > 9$ or $2 - x < -9$

19. $4 < x < 6$

20. $-3 \le x \le \frac{5}{3}$

21. $-1 < x < 9$

22. $x \le -11$ or $x \ge -5$

23. $x < -2$ or $x > 3$

24. $x < \frac{7}{3}$ or $x > 5$

25. $|x| \le 27$

26. $|x - 58| \le 15$

27. $|x - 12.25| \le 8.75$

■ **Lesson 1.8**

1. Most likely that team hit 1 home run.

2.

Number	Tally	Frequency
3					3
4			1
5						4
6				2
7			1
8				2

2. (continued)

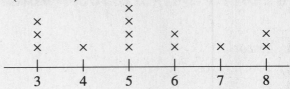

3.

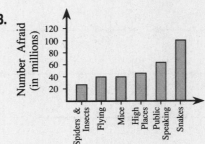

4. Snakes $\approx 31.8\%$, Speaking $\approx 20.2\%$
Heights $\approx 14.7\%$, Mice $\approx 12.4\%$
Flying $\approx 12.4\%$, Spiders $\approx 8.5\%$

5.

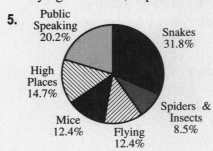

■ **Lesson 2.1**

1. $A = (3, 3)$, Quad. I
$B = (-2, 1)$, Quad. II

2. $A = (-4, 2)$, Quad. II
$B = (1, -3)$, Quad. IV

3. $A = (1, 1)$, Quad. I
$B = (-5, -4)$, Quad. III

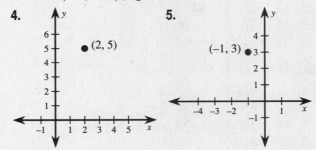

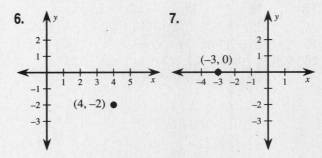

100 *ALGEBRA 2 Extra Practice Answers*

ⓒ D.C. Heath and Company

8.

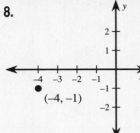

9.

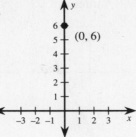

(0, 6)

10.

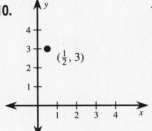

$(\frac{1}{2}, 3)$

11.

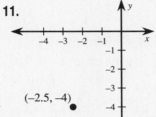

(−2.5, −4)

12.

x	−2	−1	0	1	2
y	−1	1	3	5	7

13.

x	−2	−1	0	1	2
y	5	4.5	4	3.5	3

14. Tables may vary.

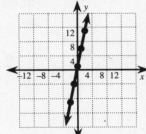

x	y
−2	−9
−1	−4
0	1
1	6
2	11

15. Tables may vary.

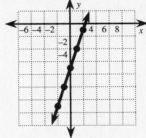

x	y
−2	−13
−1	−10
0	−7
1	−4
2	−1

16. Tables may vary.

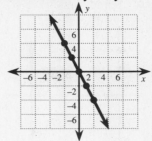

x	y
−2	4
−1	2
0	0
1	−2
2	−4

17. Tables may vary.

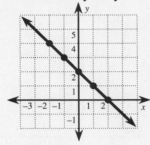

x	y
−2	4
−1	3
0	2
1	1
2	0

18. Tables may vary.

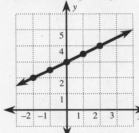

x	y
−2	2
−1	2.5
0	3
1	3.5
2	4

19. Tables may vary.

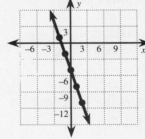

x	y
−2	1
−1	−2
0	−5
1	−8
2	−11

20. (3, 3).

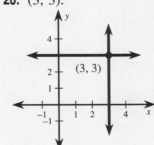

(3, 3)

21. (−5, 2)

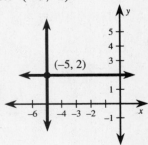

(−5, 2)

■ Lesson 2.1 (continued)

22. $(1, -3)$

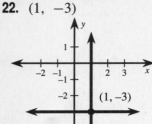

23. $(6, 0)$

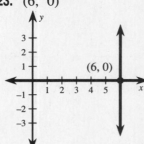

24. $(-4, -1)$

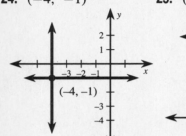

25. $(0, 5)$

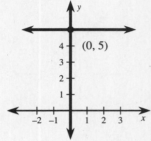

26. $x = -6$, $x = 6$, $y = 0$, $y = 11$

■ Lesson 2.2

1. 2 **2.** 0 **3.** $-\frac{3}{4}$ **4.** 2 **5.** -3

6. 8 **7.** $-\frac{1}{2}$ **8.** $-\frac{1}{3}$ **9.** $\frac{4}{3}$

10. Line 1: $m = 1$, Line 2 (steeper): $m = 4$

11. Line 1: $m = -2$, Line 2 (steeper): $m = -3$

12. Line 1: $m = -\frac{1}{2}$, Line 2 (steeper): $m = -1$

13. Line 1 (steeper): $m = \frac{1}{3}$, Line 2: $m = \frac{1}{8}$

14. Rises to the right   **15.** Horizontal

16. Falls to the right   **17.** Vertical

18. Falls to the right   **19.** Horizontal

20. Rises to the right   **21.** Vertical

22. Falls to the right

23. The slopes of parallel lines are the same.

24. The slopes of perpendicular lines are negative reciprocals of each other.

25. 12.5 quarts per hour

26. Pillar: $m = \pm\frac{500}{10.5} \approx \pm 47.6$

Pyramid: $m = \pm\frac{55}{17} \approx \pm 3.2$

■ Lesson 2.3

1. 4   **2.** -4 **3.** $-\frac{1}{2}$ **4.** $\frac{12}{7}$

5. -6 **6.** $\frac{1}{4}$ **7.** 3   **8.** $-\frac{7}{5}$

9. -1 **10.** $-\frac{1}{4}$ **11.** $-\frac{3}{2}$ **12.** 3

13. x-intercept: 2
y-intercept: -4

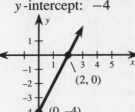

14. x-intercept: -4
y-intercept: 3

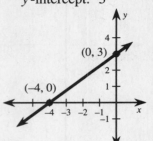

15. x-intercept: $-\frac{8}{5}$
y-intercept: -4

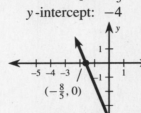

16. x-intercept: 3
y-intercept: $\frac{1}{2}$

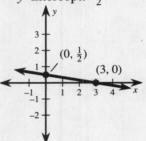

17. x-intercept: $-\frac{6}{7}$
y-intercept: 3

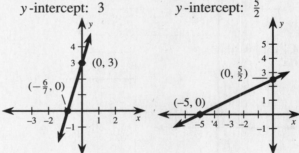

18. x-intercept: -5
y-intercept: $\frac{5}{2}$

19. $y = 7x - 1$ **20.** $y = -2x + \frac{3}{2}$

21. $y = \frac{3}{5}x + 3$ **22.** $y = \frac{2}{3}x + 2$

23. $y = 2x - 2$ **24.** $y = 4x - 3$

25. $m = 3$
y-intercept: -1

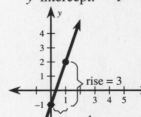

26. $m = -1$
y-intercept: 6

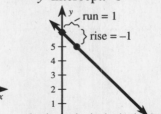

Lesson 2.3 (continued)

27. $m = \frac{2}{3}$
y-intercept: 2

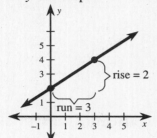

28. $m = -\frac{1}{4}$
y-intercept: 3

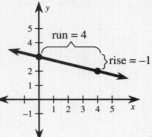

29. $m = \frac{5}{3}$
y-intercept: -4

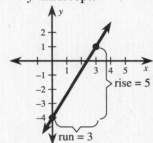

30. $m = -\frac{7}{2}$
y-intercept: -3

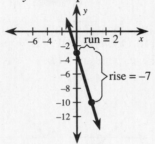

31. $0.10x + 0.25y = 50$, x dimes, y quarters

32. $0.03x + 0.04y = 250$
x sale price (\$), y regular price (\$)

33. $\frac{2}{7}$ **34.** 2 **35.** $y = \frac{2}{7}x + 2$

Lesson 2.4

1. $y = x - 3$ **2.** $y = -5x + 2$
3. $y = -\frac{1}{2}x - 4$ **4.** $y = \frac{4}{3}x + 6$
5. $y = 8x$ **6.** $y = 5$ **7.** $y = -2x + 5$
8. $y = 5x + 23$ **9.** $y = x - 12$
10. $y = 3x - 7$ **11.** $y = -8x + 8$
12. $y = -4x + \frac{8}{3}$ **13.** $y = \frac{3}{4}x + \frac{5}{2}$
14. $y = -2x + 1$ **15.** $y = \frac{1}{2}x + \frac{1}{2}$
16. $k = 3$, $y = 3x$ **17.** $k = -5$, $y = -5x$
18. $k = -\frac{5}{2}$, $y = -\frac{5}{2}x$ **19.** $k = 0.25$, $y = 0.25x$
20. $k = -\frac{1}{4}$, $y = -\frac{1}{4}x$ **21.** $k = 3$, $y = 3x$
22. $y = \frac{103}{64}x$, where x = speed (mph),
and y = speed (km/h)

23. Your speed $\approx$ 89 km/h. You are speeding.
24. $y = \frac{10.1}{6}t + 31.85$ **25.** 57.1 pounds

Lesson 2.5

1. $(0, -1)$ is not a solution, $(3, 2)$ is.
2. $(2, 1)$ is not a solution, $(-3, 6)$ is.
3. $(-3, 6)$ is not a solution, $(2, -5)$ is.
4. $(6, 3)$ is a solution, $(-4, -2)$ is not.
5. $x = -3$ **6.** $y = 7$ **7.** $y = -2x$

8. $\frac{1}{2}x = 5$ or $x = 10$
9. $2x + y = 5$ or $y = -2x + 5$
10. $6x + 2y = 1$ or $y = -3x + \frac{1}{2}$
11. $3x - 4y = -8$ or $y = \frac{3}{4}x + 2$
12. $-5x - 3y = 3$ or $y = -\frac{5}{3}x - 1$

13. $x = 1$ **14.** $x = -\frac{1}{2}$

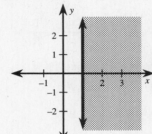
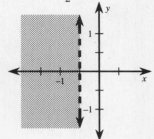

15. $x = 3$ **16.** $x = -5$

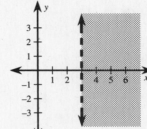
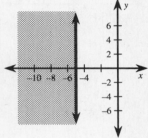

17. $y = 4$ **18.** $y = -5$

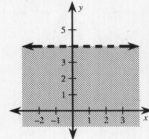
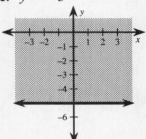

19. $y = -6$ **20.** $y = 7$

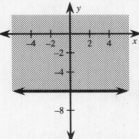
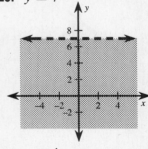

21. $y = 2x - 1$ **22.** $y = \frac{1}{2}x + 5$

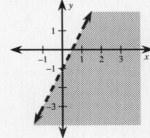
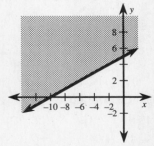

23. $y = -4x - 2$

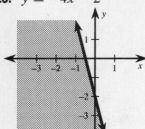

24. $y = -\frac{1}{2}x + 2$

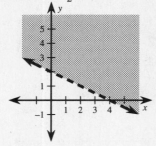

25. $y = x + \frac{1}{5}$

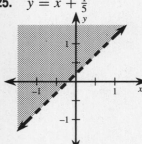

26. $y = 3x - 7$

27. $y = \frac{1}{2}x - 2$

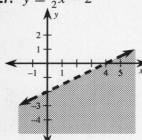

28. $y = 2x + \frac{1}{3}$

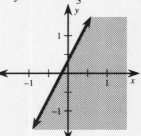

29.

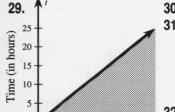

Number of Pounds

30. $(p, t) = (2.5, 12)$

31. Yes, the roast could completely defrost because (2.5, 12) is a solution of $t \le 5p$.

32. $3x + 5y \le 800$

33.

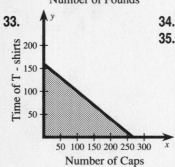

Number of Caps

34. (50, 150)

35. No, (50, 150) is not a solution of $3x + 5y \le 800$.

■ **Lesson 2.6**

1. $(0, -3)$ **2.** $(1, 2)$ **3.** $\left(-\frac{3}{2}, -5\right)$
4. $(3, 4)$ **5.** $(-6, -6)$ **6.** $(2, 1)$

7.

x	−3	−2	−1	0	1	2	3
y	11	9	7	5	7	9	11

8.

x	−7	−5	−3	−1	1	3	5
y	3	1	−1	−3	−1	1	3

9.

x	−5	−3	−1	$\frac{1}{2}$	2	4	6
y	9	5	1	−2	1	5	9

10.

x	−5	−3	−1	$-\frac{1}{3}$	1	3	5
y	−24	−12	0	4	−4	−16	−28

11. Opens down **12.** Opens up **13.** Opens up
14. Opens up **15.** Opens down **16.** Opens up

17.

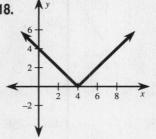

18.

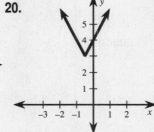

19.

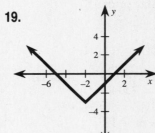

20.

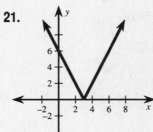

21.

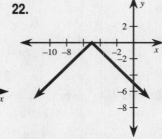

22.

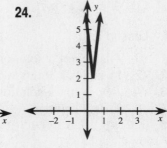

23.

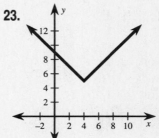

24.

25.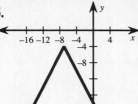

26.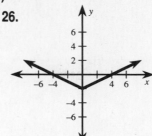

27.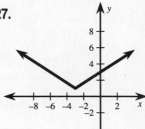

28.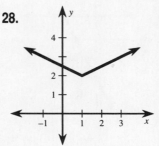

29. (0, 22) **30.** The home is 22 feet high.

31.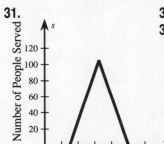

32. (6.5, 105)
33. The restaurant serves the greatest number of people, 105, at 6:30 P.M.

■ **Lesson 2.7**

1. Positive correlation

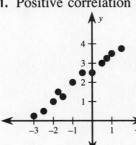

2. No correlation

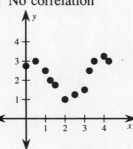

3. Negative correlation

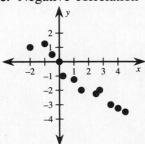

(In 4–7, answers may vary.)
4. $y = -\frac{3}{4}x + \frac{7}{2}$
5. $y = \frac{1}{4}x + \frac{3}{2}$
6. $y = -\frac{2}{5}x + \frac{11}{4}$
7. $y = -\frac{7}{30}x + \frac{206}{3}$

8.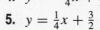

Year (0 ↔ 1980)

9. $y = 0.3x + 1.5$ (Answers may vary.)

10. Approximately 6 pounds (Answers may vary.)

■ **Lesson 3.1**

1. No solution **2.** One solution
3. Many solutions
4. (1, 5) is not a solution.
5. (−2, 3) is a solution.
6. (−3, −4) is a solution.

7. (3, 0) **8.** (4, 2)

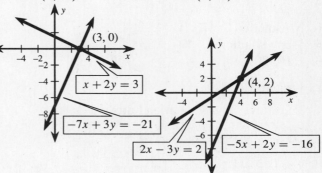

9. (−3, −1) **10.** (2, −5)

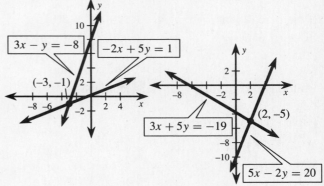

11. (−2, 2) **12.** (0, 4)

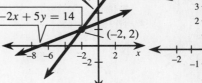

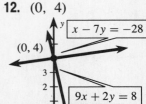

13. 16 adults and 26 children
14. $R = 5600t$ **15.** $C = 3800t + 110,000$

Lesson 3.1 (continued)

16.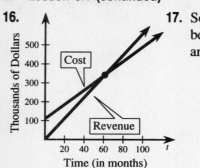

17. Somewhere between 61 and 62 months

Lesson 3.2

1. $(2, -1)$ **2.** $(-3, -2)$ **3.** $\left(\frac{1}{2}, 4\right)$
4. $(5, 3)$ **5.** $(-6, 9)$ **6.** $\left(\frac{5}{2}, \frac{1}{2}\right)$
7. $(2, -4)$ **8.** $\left(\frac{1}{2}, -1\right)$ **9.** $(-3, 7)$
10. $(2, 2)$ **11.** $\left(-\frac{2}{3}, -\frac{7}{2}\right)$ **12.** $(-1, 5)$
13. $\left(-2, -\frac{2}{7}\right)$ **14.** $(-4, 0)$ **15.** $(3, -18)$
16. No solution **17.** $\left(\frac{5}{3}, \frac{1}{2}\right)$
18. Many solutions **19.** 1983
20. $(110, 90)$

Lesson 3.3

1. You drove 3 hr, your friend drove 2 hr.

2. $10 \cdot \boxed{\begin{array}{c}\text{Price of}\\\text{balloons}\end{array}} + 6 \cdot \boxed{\begin{array}{c}\text{Price of}\\\text{paper}\end{array}} = \$20.10$

$4 \cdot \boxed{\begin{array}{c}\text{Price of}\\\text{balloons}\end{array}} + 8 \cdot \boxed{\begin{array}{c}\text{Price of}\\\text{paper}\end{array}} = \$12.80$

3. Price of balloons $= b$ **4.** $10b + 6c = 20.10$
Price of paper $= c$ $\quad\quad 4b + 8c = 12.80$

5. $(b, c) = (1.50, 0.85)$ **6.** 40 full-size bags
Balloons: \$1.50 per 84 collapsible bags
bag
Paper: \$0.85 per roll

7. $W = -0.65t + 17$ **8.** $L = 0.60t + 9.2$
9. 1987

Lesson 3.4

1. b. **2. a.** **3. c.**

4. 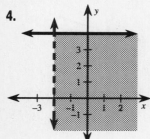 **5.**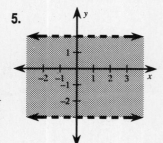

6. 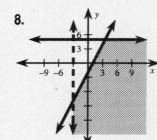 **7.**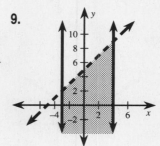

8. 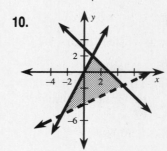 **9.**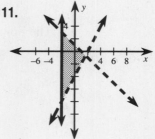

10. 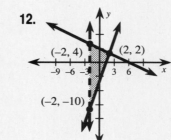 **11.**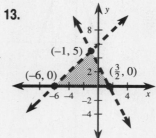

12. 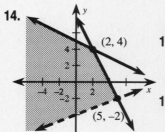 **13.**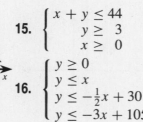

14. **15.** $\begin{cases} x + y \le 44 \\ \quad\quad y \ge 3 \\ \quad\quad x \ge 0 \end{cases}$

16. $\begin{cases} y \ge 0 \\ y \le x \\ y \le -\frac{1}{2}x + 30 \\ y \le -3x + 105 \end{cases}$

Lesson 3.5

1. Minimum C: -6, Maximum C: 5
2. Minimum C: -4, Maximum C: 10
3. Minimum C: -15, Maximum C: 5

■ Lesson 3.5 (continued)

4. Minimum C: -6
Maximum C: 9

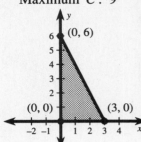

Vertices: (0, 6), (0, 0), (3, 0)

5. Minimum C: 6
Maximum C: 26

Vertices: (3, 5), (0, 3), (3, 0)

6. Minimum C: -2
Maximum C: 20

Vertices: (0, 4), (2, 1), (−2, 0)

7. Minimum C: -9
Maximum C: 20

Vertices: (5, 5), (0, 3), (0, 0), (5, 0)

8. Minimum C: 8
Maximum C: None

Vertices: (0, 6), (1, 2), (3, 1)

9. Minimum C: 6
Maximum C: 30

Vertices: (4, 5), (0, 3), (4, 2), (1, 1)

10. $P = 40x + 55y$

11. $\begin{cases} 2x + 6y \le 150 \\ 5x + 4y \le 155 \\ x \ge 0 \\ y \ge 0 \end{cases}$

12.

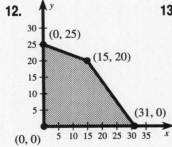

Vertices: (0, 25), (15, 20), (31, 0), (0, 0)

13. 15 cases of peanuts and 20 cases of pretzels

■ Lesson 3.6

1. (3, 2, −1)   **2.** (4, −1, 3)   **3.** (3, −5, −4)

4. $\begin{cases} x - 3y + z = -1 \\ 2y + 4z = 6 \\ 3y + 5z = 7 \end{cases}$ **5.** $\begin{cases} x - 3y + z = -1 \\ y + 2z = 3 \\ 3y + 5z = 7 \end{cases}$

6. $\begin{cases} x - 3y + z = -1 \\ y + 2z = 3 \\ -z = -2 \end{cases}$

7. $\begin{cases} x - 3y + z = -1 \\ y + 2z = 3 \\ z = 2 \end{cases}$

8. $\begin{cases} x - 3y + 2z = 15 \\ y - 5z = 4 \\ z = -3 \end{cases}$ **9.** $\begin{cases} x + 2y - z = 4 \\ y + z = 3 \\ z = 2 \end{cases}$

10. $\begin{cases} x + y + z = 8 \\ y - 2z = -5 \\ z = 4 \end{cases}$

11. (−2, −8, −1)
12. (3, 5, 2)
13. (1, 0, −2)

14. (2, −3, 5)
15. (1, 1, −2)
16. (−6, 5, 3)

17. 1st: 1200 pounds;
2nd: 800 pounds;
3rd: 1300 pounds

■ Lesson 4.1

1. 4×3 **2.** 3×2 **3.** 2×1

4. 3×4 **5.** $\begin{bmatrix} 5 & 12 \\ 5 & 6 \\ 0 & 10 \end{bmatrix}$ **6.** $\begin{bmatrix} 6 & 1 \\ -5 & 3 \end{bmatrix}$

7. $\begin{bmatrix} 3 & 1 & -7 \\ -3 & 6 & 1 \\ -4 & 0 & -3 \end{bmatrix}$ **8.** $[\,13 \quad 3 \quad -2 \quad 10\,]$

9. $\begin{bmatrix} 3 & 12 \\ -9 & 6 \end{bmatrix}$ **10.** $\begin{bmatrix} 1 & 0 & -4 \\ -6 & -8 & 2 \\ 4 & -3 & -10 \end{bmatrix}$

11. $\begin{bmatrix} 2 \\ 13 \\ 5 \end{bmatrix}$ **12.** $\begin{bmatrix} -5 & -20 & 10 & -15 \\ 0 & 25 & -5 & -20 \end{bmatrix}$

13. $\begin{bmatrix} 6 & 11 \\ 1 & 3 \end{bmatrix}$ **14.** $\begin{bmatrix} -1 & -2 \\ -2 & 0 \\ 3 & 2 \end{bmatrix}$

15. $\begin{bmatrix} 8 & 10 & 2 \\ 10 & 20 & 0 \end{bmatrix}$ **16.** $\begin{bmatrix} 0 & -17 \\ -1 & -23 \end{bmatrix}$

17. $1704   **18.** $1752

■ Lesson 4.2

1. A: 3×2, B: 1×3, AB is not defined.
2. A: 2×3, B: 3×3, AB: 2×3
3. A: 4×1, B: 1×2, AB: 4×2
4. A: 4×2, B: 3×4, AB is not defined.

5. $4(2) + (-2)(\ 3)$
$4(1) + (-2)(-2)$
$4(0) + (-2)(\ 4)$
$\begin{bmatrix} 9 & 1 & 4 \\ 2 & 8 & -8 \end{bmatrix}$

6. $-2(-4)$, $-2(6)$
$3(-4)$, $3(6)$
$\begin{bmatrix} -4 & 6 \\ 8 & -12 \\ -12 & 18 \end{bmatrix}$

7. $\begin{bmatrix} -7 & -3 \\ 38 & 14 \end{bmatrix}$ **8.** $\begin{bmatrix} -4 & -6 & 5 \\ 7 & -5 & -1 \\ 0 & -16 & 4 \end{bmatrix}$

Lesson 4.2 (continued)

9. $\begin{bmatrix} -7 & -3 & 11 \\ -2 & 6 & 18 \end{bmatrix}$ 10. $[6]$

11. $\begin{bmatrix} 0 & -1 & -6 & 8 \\ 6 & -3 & 12 & 6 \\ 8 & -2 & 28 & -8 \end{bmatrix}$ 12. $\begin{bmatrix} 10 \\ 4 \\ 11 \\ 14 \end{bmatrix}$

13. $\begin{bmatrix} -22 & -18 \\ 33 & 27 \end{bmatrix}$ 14. $\begin{bmatrix} 11 & -2 \\ -4 & -14 \end{bmatrix}$

15. $\begin{bmatrix} 20 & -6 \\ 45 & 42 \\ -10 & 15 \end{bmatrix}$ 16. $\begin{bmatrix} 20 & 20 \\ 16 & 16 \\ 4 & 4 \end{bmatrix}$

17. $\begin{bmatrix} 420 & 300 \\ 400 & 450 \\ 510 & 475 \end{bmatrix}\begin{bmatrix} 3.50 \\ 2.50 \end{bmatrix} = \begin{bmatrix} 2220 \\ 2525 \\ 2972.5 \end{bmatrix}$

$2220.00 on opening night
$2525.00 on the second night
$2972.50 on the final night

Lesson 4.3

1. 20   2. -19 3. 0   4. 7
5. -18 6. 10   7. 28   8. -48
9. 41   10. 0   11. -13 12. -40
13. 73   14. 4   15. 8.5   16. 11
17. 9712.5 square miles; actual area is about 9297 square miles which differs from this answer by 415.5 square miles.

Lesson 4.4

1. Yes   2. No   3. Yes
4. Yes   5. No   6. $\begin{bmatrix} 9 & -5 \\ -7 & 4 \end{bmatrix}$

7. $\begin{bmatrix} 3 & -4 \\ 2 & -3 \end{bmatrix}$ 8. $\begin{bmatrix} 1 & 0 \\ 0 & \frac{1}{2} \end{bmatrix}$ 9. $\begin{bmatrix} -1 & -1 \\ -\frac{5}{3} & -2 \end{bmatrix}$

10. $A^{-1} = \begin{bmatrix} -3 & 2 \\ 2 & -1 \end{bmatrix}$, $X = \begin{bmatrix} -2 & 7 \\ 3 & -4 \end{bmatrix}$

11. $A^{-1} = \begin{bmatrix} 9 & 4 \\ 11 & 5 \end{bmatrix}$, $X = \begin{bmatrix} 3 & 8 \\ 4 & 10 \end{bmatrix}$

12. $A^{-1} = \begin{bmatrix} 6 & -7 \\ -5 & 6 \end{bmatrix}$, $X = \begin{bmatrix} -15 & -7 & -40 \\ 13 & 6 & 34 \end{bmatrix}$

13. $A^{-1} = \begin{bmatrix} 3 & -2 \\ 2 & -\frac{3}{2} \end{bmatrix}$, $X = \begin{bmatrix} 7 & -9 & 0 \\ 5 & -6 & -1 \end{bmatrix}$

14. $[13 \quad 5][5 \quad 20][0 \quad 13][5 \quad 0][1 \quad 20]$
$[0 \quad 19][21 \quad 14][19 \quad 5][20 \quad 0]$

15. $[75 \quad -44][65 \quad -35][26 \quad -13]$
$[25 \quad -15][45 \quad -23][38 \quad -19]$
$[133 \quad -77][105 \quad -62][100 \quad -60]$

16. 75, -44, 65, -35, 26, -13, 25, -15, 45, -23, 38, -19, 133, -77, 105, -62, 100, -60
17. IT IS NOT A MAN
18. SHE WEARS GLASSES
19. SHE HAS LONG HAIR   20. Miss Behave

Lesson 4.5

1. $\begin{bmatrix} 1 & -1 \\ -2 & 1 \end{bmatrix}\begin{bmatrix} x \\ y \end{bmatrix} = \begin{bmatrix} 3 \\ 4 \end{bmatrix}$ 2. $\begin{bmatrix} 3 & -1 \\ 4 & 1 \end{bmatrix}\begin{bmatrix} x \\ y \end{bmatrix} = \begin{bmatrix} -1 \\ 15 \end{bmatrix}$

3. $\begin{bmatrix} 6 & -3 \\ 5 & 9 \end{bmatrix}\begin{bmatrix} x \\ y \end{bmatrix} = \begin{bmatrix} 39 \\ -25 \end{bmatrix}$

4. $\begin{bmatrix} 1 & -1 & 1 \\ 2 & 0 & 3 \\ 0 & 3 & -1 \end{bmatrix}\begin{bmatrix} x \\ y \\ z \end{bmatrix} = \begin{bmatrix} -2 \\ 4 \\ 7 \end{bmatrix}$

5. $\begin{bmatrix} 3 & 1 & -2 \\ 1 & -2 & 1 \\ 1 & 4 & 0 \end{bmatrix}\begin{bmatrix} x \\ y \\ z \end{bmatrix} = \begin{bmatrix} 1 \\ 12 \\ -18 \end{bmatrix}$

6. $\begin{bmatrix} 5 & -3 & 1 \\ 2 & 2 & 3 \\ 1 & -5 & -4 \end{bmatrix}\begin{bmatrix} x \\ y \\ z \end{bmatrix} = \begin{bmatrix} 6 \\ -1 \\ 9 \end{bmatrix}$

7. $\underbrace{\begin{bmatrix} 1 & 1 \\ 2 & 1 \end{bmatrix}}_{A}\underbrace{\begin{bmatrix} x \\ y \end{bmatrix}}_{X} = \underbrace{\begin{bmatrix} 2 \\ -1 \end{bmatrix}}_{B}, \begin{bmatrix} -3 \\ 5 \end{bmatrix}$

8. $\underbrace{\begin{bmatrix} 3 & -2 \\ 4 & -3 \end{bmatrix}}_{A}\underbrace{\begin{bmatrix} x \\ y \end{bmatrix}}_{X} = \underbrace{\begin{bmatrix} 8 \\ 10 \end{bmatrix}}_{B}, \begin{bmatrix} 4 \\ 2 \end{bmatrix}$

9. $\underbrace{\begin{bmatrix} 5 & -2 \\ -7 & 3 \end{bmatrix}}_{A}\underbrace{\begin{bmatrix} x \\ y \end{bmatrix}}_{X} = \underbrace{\begin{bmatrix} -9 \\ 14 \end{bmatrix}}_{B}, \begin{bmatrix} 1 \\ 7 \end{bmatrix}$

10. $\underbrace{\begin{bmatrix} 2 & 1 & -1 \\ 3 & 0 & 1 \\ 5 & 2 & -2 \end{bmatrix}}_{A}\underbrace{\begin{bmatrix} x \\ y \\ z \end{bmatrix}}_{X} = \underbrace{\begin{bmatrix} 3 \\ -5 \\ 5 \end{bmatrix}}_{B}, \begin{bmatrix} -1 \\ 3 \\ -2 \end{bmatrix}$

11. $\underbrace{\begin{bmatrix} 1 & 1 & -1 \\ 9 & 6 & -7 \\ -6 & -4 & 5 \end{bmatrix}}_{A}\underbrace{\begin{bmatrix} x \\ y \\ z \end{bmatrix}}_{X} = \underbrace{\begin{bmatrix} 2 \\ 24 \\ -15 \end{bmatrix}}_{B}, \begin{bmatrix} 5 \\ 0 \\ 3 \end{bmatrix}$

12. $\underbrace{\begin{bmatrix} 1 & 1 & -2 \\ 2 & 1 & 1 \\ -1 & -2 & 6 \end{bmatrix}}_{A}\underbrace{\begin{bmatrix} x \\ y \\ z \end{bmatrix}}_{X} = \underbrace{\begin{bmatrix} -9 \\ 0 \\ 21 \end{bmatrix}}_{B}, \begin{bmatrix} -9 \\ 12 \\ 6 \end{bmatrix}$

13. $\begin{cases} x + y + z = 10{,}000 \\ 0.06x + 0.08y + 0.12z = 850 \\ x + y - 3z = 0 \end{cases}$

14. $\underbrace{\begin{bmatrix} 1 & 1 & 1 \\ 0.06 & 0.08 & 0.12 \\ 1 & 1 & -3 \end{bmatrix}}_{A}\underbrace{\begin{bmatrix} x \\ y \\ z \end{bmatrix}}_{X} = \underbrace{\begin{bmatrix} 10{,}000 \\ 850 \\ 0 \end{bmatrix}}_{B}$

■ **Lesson 4.5 (continued)**

15. $A^{-1}B = \begin{bmatrix} 2500 \\ 5000 \\ 2500 \end{bmatrix}$ **16.** $2500 in Stock X
$5000 in Stock Y
$2500 in Stock Z

$x = 2500$
$y = 5000$
$z = 2500$

■ **Lesson 4.6**

1. $\begin{bmatrix} 2 & 1 & -1 & \vdots & 4 \\ 3 & 2 & 1 & \vdots & 6 \\ -1 & 1 & 3 & \vdots & -1 \end{bmatrix}$

2. $\begin{bmatrix} 1 & -2 & 3 & \vdots & 10 \\ 1 & 0 & -1 & \vdots & 2 \\ 1 & 3 & -4 & \vdots & -9 \end{bmatrix}$

3. $\begin{bmatrix} 3 & -2 & -7 & \vdots & 3 \\ 0 & 3 & -1 & \vdots & -6 \\ 1 & -2 & -5 & \vdots & -15 \end{bmatrix}$

4. $\begin{cases} x - y + 4z = 3 \\ y + 4z = 5 \\ z = -2 \end{cases}$

5. $\begin{cases} 2x - 3y = 11 \\ y + 4z = -1 \\ z = 6 \end{cases}$

6. $\begin{cases} x - 2y + 7z = -21 \\ 3y = 15 \\ z = -4 \end{cases}$

7. $\begin{bmatrix} 1 & 2 & -1 & \vdots & 12 \\ 1 & 3 & -1 & \vdots & -6 \\ 0 & 2 & 1 & \vdots & 5 \end{bmatrix}, \begin{bmatrix} 89 \\ -18 \\ 41 \end{bmatrix}$

8. $\begin{bmatrix} 2 & -3 & -5 & \vdots & 1 \\ 1 & -2 & 0 & \vdots & 12 \\ -4 & 6 & 7 & \vdots & -23 \end{bmatrix}, \begin{bmatrix} 36 \\ 12 \\ 7 \end{bmatrix}$

9. $\begin{bmatrix} 1 & -1 & 1 & \vdots & -8 \\ 2 & 3 & -3 & \vdots & 4 \\ 1 & 2 & 7 & \vdots & 13 \end{bmatrix}, \begin{bmatrix} -4 \\ 5 \\ 1 \end{bmatrix}$

10. $\begin{bmatrix} 3 & 2 & -4 & \vdots & 0 \\ 1 & -1 & 2 & \vdots & 10 \\ 2 & -3 & 5 & \vdots & 14 \end{bmatrix}, \begin{bmatrix} 4 \\ 18 \\ 12 \end{bmatrix}$

11. $\begin{bmatrix} 1 & 0 & -2 & \vdots & 7 \\ 1 & 3 & 4 & \vdots & -5 \\ 5 & -1 & 3 & \vdots & 9 \end{bmatrix}, \begin{bmatrix} 3 \\ 0 \\ -2 \end{bmatrix}$

12. $\begin{bmatrix} 5 & 2 & 3 & \vdots & 20 \\ 2 & -3 & 4 & \vdots & -2 \\ 1 & -2 & 3 & \vdots & 16 \end{bmatrix}, \begin{bmatrix} -23 \\ 24 \\ 29 \end{bmatrix}$

13. $\begin{cases} x + y + z = 246 \\ x - 2y = 0 \\ z = 123 \end{cases}$

14. $\begin{bmatrix} 1 & 1 & 1 & \vdots & 246 \\ 1 & -2 & 0 & \vdots & 0 \\ 0 & 0 & 1 & \vdots & 123 \end{bmatrix}$

15. $x = 82, \; y = 41, \; z = 123$

16. 300 pounds of Alloy X, 700 pounds of Alloy Y, 400 pounds of Alloy Z

■ **Lesson 4.7**

1. 1   **2.** 2   **3.** 10   **4.** −1
5. 1   **6.** 4   **7.** (−2, 1)
8. (6, −2)   **9.** (11, 6)   **10.** (5, 0, 3)
11. (1, 3, −1)   **12.** (6, −4, 4)
13. *Winnie-the-Pooh*: 1926
The House at Pooh Corner: 1928

14. $x + y + z = 6.047$ **15.** $x - y = 0.908$
16. $y - z = 1.935$
17. $\begin{cases} x + y + z = 6.047 \\ x - y = 0.908 \\ y - z = 1.935 \end{cases}$

$x = 3.266, \; y = 2.358, \; z = 0.423$

■ **Lesson 5.1**

1. $x^2 = 1, \pm 1$ **2.** $x^2 = 9, \pm 3$
3. $x^2 = 64, \pm 8$ **4.** $x^2 = 4, \pm 2$
5. $x^2 = 5, \pm\sqrt{5}$ **6.** $x^2 = 25, \pm 5$
7. $x^2 = 2, \pm\sqrt{2}$ **8.** $x^2 = 81, \pm 9$
9. $x^2 = 36, \pm 6$ **10.** $x^2 = 16, \pm 4$
11. $x^2 = 7, \pm\sqrt{7}$ **12.** $x^2 = 1, \pm 1$
13. 8.06   **14.** 7.21   **15.** ≈ 2.24 sec
16. ≈ 3.16 sec   **17.** ≈ 4.47 sec
18. No, when the object dropped from $2s$ feet has fallen s feet, it is accelerating. Therefore, it takes less time to fall the remaining s feet.

19. 1986   **20.** 7   **21.** 49 ft   **22.** 14 ft

■ **Lesson 5.2**

1. $y = 2x^2 + x - 1, \; a = 2,$ up
2. $y = -x^2 - x + 3, \; a = -1,$ down
3. $y = -5x^2 + 3x + 4, \; a = -5,$ down
4. $y = x^2 - 2x + 1, \; a = 1,$ up
5. $y = -3x^2 + 4, \; a = -3,$ down
6. $y = 9x^2 + x, \; a = 9,$ up
7. $(-1, -2), \; x = -1$ **8.** $(2, -5), \; x = 2$
9. $(-3, 17), \; x = -3$ **10.** $\left(\frac{1}{2}, \frac{15}{4}\right), \; x = \frac{1}{2}$
11. $(0, 4), \; x = 0$ **12.** $(-1, -2), \; x = -1$

13.

x	−2	−1	0	1	2	3	4
y	9	4	1	0	1	4	9

14.

x	−1	0	1	2	3	4	5
y	−13	−3	3	5	3	−3	−13

■ Lesson 5.2 (continued)

15.

x	−3	−2	−1	0	1	2	3
y	13	8	5	4	5	8	13

16.

x	0	1	2	3	4	5	6
y	0	−5	−8	−9	−8	−5	0

17.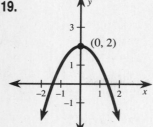

18.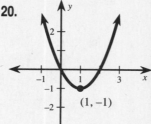

19.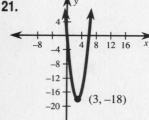

20.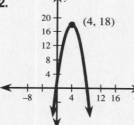

21.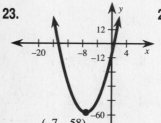

22.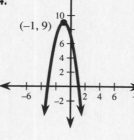

23.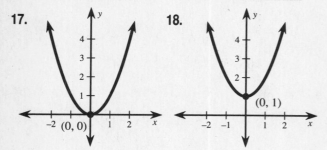

24.

25.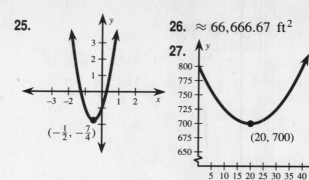

26. $\approx 66{,}666.67 \text{ ft}^2$

27.

28. \$700 **29.** 20

■ Lesson 5.3

1. $(x + 1)^2$ **2.** $(x - 2)^2$ **3.** $(x - 8)^2$

4. $\left(x + \frac{3}{2}\right)^2$ **5.** $\left(x - \frac{1}{4}\right)^2$ **6.** $\left(x + \frac{5}{2}\right)^2$

7. 9 **8.** 49 **9.** 16 **10.** $\frac{1}{4}$

11. 121 **12.** $\frac{49}{4}$ **13.** $x^2 - 2x = 2,\ 1 \pm \sqrt{3}$

14. $x^2 + 4x = 1,\ -2 \pm \sqrt{5}$

15. $x^2 - 6x = -2,\ 3 \pm \sqrt{7}$

16. $x^2 + 12x = -3,\ -6 \pm \sqrt{33}$

17. $x^2 + x = 2,\ 1,\ -2$

18. $x^2 - x = 1,\ \frac{1}{2} \pm \frac{\sqrt{5}}{2}$

19. $2x^2 - 2x = 4,\ 2,\ -1$

20. $3x^2 + 9x = 12,\ 1,\ -4$

21. $2x^2 - 4x = 10,\ 1 \pm \sqrt{6}$

22. $-5x^2 + 10x = -20,\ 1 \pm \sqrt{5}$

23. $4x^2 - 4x = 2,\ \frac{1}{2} \pm \frac{\sqrt{3}}{2}$

24. $3x^2 - 12x = -1,\ 2 \pm \sqrt{\frac{11}{3}}$

25. $10.675 \text{ ft} \times 16.675 \text{ ft}$

26. $4.490 \text{ cm} \times 10.245 \text{ cm}$

27. $x^2 + (2x + 7)^2 = 44^2$

28. ≈ 16.8 **29.** $\approx 33.7 \text{ in.}$ **30.** $\approx 40.7 \text{ in.}$

■ Lesson 5.4

(In 1–6, answers may vary by multiple of −1.)

1. $2x^2 - x - 5 = 0,\ a = 2,\ b = -1,\ c = -5$

2. $x^2 - 5x + 6 = 0,\ a = 1,\ b = -5,\ c = 6$

3. $3x^2 + 3x - 7 = 0,\ a = 3,\ b = 3,\ c = -7$

4. $2x^2 + 4x + 5 = 0,\ a = 2,\ b = 4,\ c = 5$

5. $x^2 - 9x + 2 = 0,\ a = 1,\ b = -9,\ c = 2$

6. $6x^2 - 3 = 0,\ a = 6,\ b = 0,\ c = -3$

7. −11 **8.** 0 **9.** 25 **10.** 0

11. −76 **12.** 49 **13.** 16, 2 solutions

14. 17, 2 real solutions   **15.** -11, no real solution

16. 0, 1 real solution   **17.** -8, no real solution

18. -31, no real solution   **19.** $\frac{1}{2} \pm \frac{\sqrt{5}}{2}$

20. $2, -\frac{1}{2}$ **21.** $-\frac{1}{4} \pm \frac{\sqrt{33}}{4}$ **22.** $2, \frac{1}{4}$

23. $-\frac{1}{10} \pm \frac{\sqrt{204}}{20}$ **24.** $\frac{7}{16} \pm \frac{\sqrt{113}}{16}$

25. $x^2 - 4x - 2 = 0, \ 2 \pm \frac{\sqrt{24}}{2}$

26. $x^2 - 2x - 4 = 0, \ 1 \pm \frac{\sqrt{20}}{2}$

27. $2x^2 + x - 7 = 0, \ -\frac{1}{4} \pm \frac{\sqrt{57}}{4}$

28. $3x^2 + 3x - 5 = 0, \ -\frac{1}{2} \pm \frac{\sqrt{69}}{6}$

29. $2x^2 - 5x - 1 = 0, \ \frac{5}{4} \pm \frac{\sqrt{33}}{4}$

30. $4x^2 + 3x - 2 = 0, \ -\frac{3}{8} \pm \frac{\sqrt{41}}{8}$

31. 7.477 in. $\times$ 3.277 in.

32. 5.379 cm $\times$ 11.879 cm   **33.** ≈ 10.2 sec

34. $h = -16t^2 + 27t + 6$ **35.** ≈ 1.9 sec

■ **Lesson 5.5**

1. $4i$ **2.** $6i$ **3.** $11i$ **4.** $-8i$

5. $i\sqrt{6}$ **6.** $i\sqrt{7}$ **7.** $i\sqrt{11}$ **8.** $-i\sqrt{15}$

9. -3 **10.** -9 **11.** 5 **12.** -25

13. -4 **14.** -49 **15.** -13 **16.** -11

17. $\pm 4i$ **18.** $\pm 9i$ **19.** $\pm 12i$ **20.** $\pm i$

21. $\pm 2i$ **22.** $\pm 2i$ **23.** $7 + 7i$

24. $4 - i$ **25.** $4 - i$ **26.** $2 + 9i$

27. $11 - 4i$ **28.** $-2 - 2i$ **29.** $-1 + 4i$

30. $-6 - 3i$ **31.** $-28 - 12i$ **32.** $4 + 2i$

33. $3 - 11i$ **34.** $-6 + 17i$

35. $A = 2 + 3i, \ B = -4 + i, \ C = 1 - 3i$

36. $A = 4i, \ B = -3 - 3i, \ C = 3 - i$

37. $A = -2 + 4i, \ B = -2i, \ C = 4$

38. A sandwich in a box.

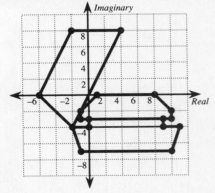

■ **Lesson 5.6**

1. Solution   **2.** Not a solution

3. Solution   **4.** Solution

5. Not a solution   **6.** Solution

7. $1 \pm i$ **8.** $6 \pm i$ **9.** $-4 \pm i$

10. $1 \pm 3i$ **11.** $\frac{1}{2} \pm i$ **12.** $2 \pm \frac{1}{3}i$

13. $\frac{4}{3} \pm \frac{1}{3}i$ **14.** $\frac{1}{2} \pm \frac{3}{2}i$ **15.** $\frac{7}{2} \pm \frac{\sqrt{3}}{2}i$

16. 1.14, -6.14 **17.** 5.54, -0.54

18. 3.24, -1.24 **19.** 2.63, -0.83

20. 1.34, -3.74 **21.** 1.49, -1.42

22. Yes, the equation $x(40 - x) = 350$ has real solutions.

23. No, the equation $x(8 - x) = 20$ has no real solution.

24. There is no income level (between \$5000 and \$100,000) at which Americans give 1%. The equation $0.0014x^2 - 0.1529x + 5.855 = 1$ has no real solution.

■ **Lesson 5.7**

1. Solution   **2.** Not a solution

3. Not a solution   **4.** Solution

5. b   **6.** a   **7.** c

8.
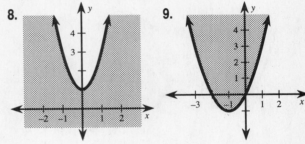

9.

10.
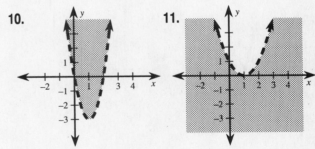

11.

12.
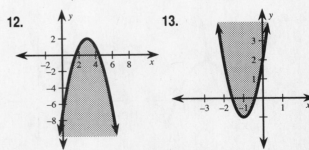

13.

14.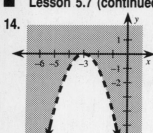

15.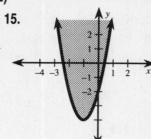

16.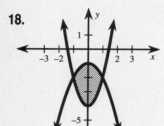

17.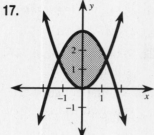

18.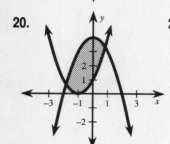

19.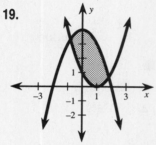

20.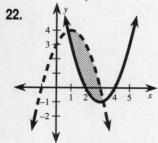

21.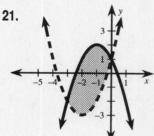

22.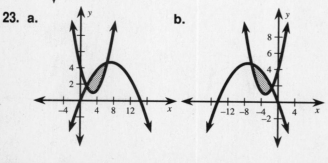

23. a.

b.

24. b   25. a

26. $y \geq 0.33x^2 - 2x + 4, \ y \geq 0.33x^2 + 2x + 4$

■ **Lesson 6.1**

1. Domain: $\{1, 2, 3, 4, 5\}$
Range: $\{-4, -3, -2, -1, 0\}$

2. Domain: $\{0, 1, 2, 3, 4\}$, Range: $\{-3, -1, 1, 2\}$

3. $\{(1, \ 0), \ (2, \ -1), \ (3, \ -2)\}$

4. $\{(1, \ 0), \ (2, \ 0), \ (2, \ -1), \ (3, \ -1), \ (3, \ -2)\}$

5. $\{(1, \ -1), \ (2, \ -1), \ (3, \ -1)\}$

6.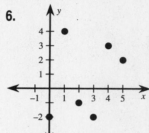

7.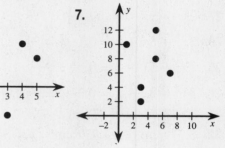

8.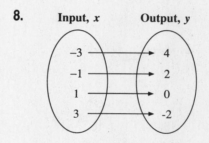

9.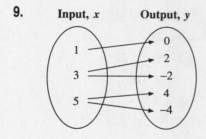

10.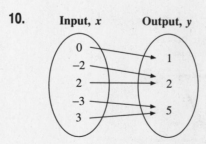

11. 6   **12.** 8, 10   **13.** Is a function.

14. Is not a function.   **15.** 1   **16.** 3

17. 6   **18.** 0   **19.** 1   **20.** −46   **21.** Yes

Lesson 6.2

1. All real numbers   **2.** All real numbers

3. $x \neq 0$ **4.** $x \geq 0$ **5.** $x \neq 1$

6. $x \geq -2$ **7.** $3x + 1$ **8.** $x^2 + 2x + 2$

9. $2x^2 - 2x + 2$ **10.** $2x^2 - x - 1$

11. $x - 3$ **12.** $-x + 2$ **13.** $x^2 - x - 2$

14. $x^2 - 4x + 4$ **15.** $6x - 3$

16. $3x^2 + x - 2$ **17.** $2x^3 + 2x^2 - 2x$

18. $-x^3 + x^2 + 4x + 2$ **19.** $\dfrac{3x}{x + 2}$

20. $\dfrac{x^2 + 1}{x - 2}$ **21.** $\dfrac{x - 2}{x^2 + x - 4}$ **22.** $\dfrac{3x^2 - x + 1}{x + 3}$

23. $f(g(x)) = 6x + 3$, $g(f(x)) = 6x + 1$

24. $f(g(x)) = 3x - 1$, $g(f(x)) = 3x + 1$

25. $f(g(x)) = x^2 - 4x + 5$, $g(f(x)) = x^2 - 1$

26. $f(g(x)) = x^2 + 3x - 1$, $g(f(x)) = x^2 + x - 2$

27. $x - 100$ **28.** $0.75x$ **29.** $0.75x - 75$

30. $0.75x - 100$ **31.** Discount

Lesson 6.3

1. $\{(3, 1), (-2, 4), (0, -1), (1, 2), (-4, -3)\}$

2. $\{(1, 0), (-2, 1), (4, 2), (-1, 3), (0, 4)\}$

3. $\{(5, -3), (4, -5), (7, 2), (-2, -1), (1, 4)\}$

4. $\{(6, \frac{1}{2}), (4, 0), (2, -\frac{2}{3}), (1, -1), (0, 3)\}$

5. $x = 2y$ **6.** $x = -y + 5$ **7.** $x = 3y + 1$

8. $x = 4y - 9$ **9.** $x = \frac{1}{2}y + 6$ **10.** $x = y^2 + 3$

11. $g(x) = \frac{1}{4}x - \frac{3}{4}$ **12.** $g(x) = 2x + 2$

    g is a function of x. g is a function of x.

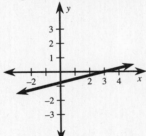 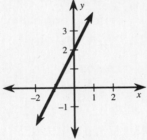

13. $x = y^2 + 2$, Inverse   **14.** Inverse is
    is not a function.   a function.

    15. Inverse is not
    a function.

    16. Inverse is not
    a function.

17. Inverse is not a function.

18. Inverse is a function.

19. Inverse is a function.

20. $f(g(x)) = 2\left(\frac{x}{2}\right) = x$, $g(f(x)) = \frac{2x}{2} = x$

21. $f(g(x)) = 1 - (1 - x) = x$
    $g(f(x)) = 1 - (1 - x) = x$

22. $f(g(x)) = (x + 2) - 2 = x$
    $g(f(x)) = (x - 2) + 2 = x$

23. $f(g(x)) = -3\left(-\frac{1}{3}x + 2\right) + 6 = x$
    $g(f(x)) = -\frac{1}{3}(-3x + 6) + 2 = x$

24. $f(g(x)) = \frac{1}{2}(2x + 8) - 4 = x$
    $g(f(x)) = 2\left(\frac{1}{2}x - 4\right) + 8 = x$

25. $f(g(x)) = 4\left(\frac{1}{4}x - \frac{1}{4}\right) + 1 = x$
    $g(f(x)) = \frac{1}{4}(4x + 1) - \frac{1}{4} = x$

26. $C = K - 273.15$ **27.** $R = \frac{1}{0.75}S$

Lesson 6.4

1. 1   **2.** 0   **3.** 0   **4.** 4   **5.** 1

6. -2 **7.** -3 **8.** -1 **9.** -1 **10.** -5

11. 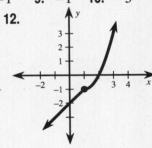   **12.**

13. 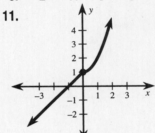   **14.**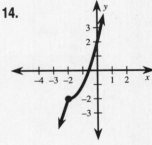

15. 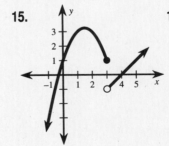   **16.**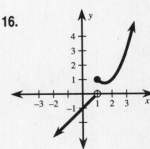

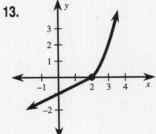

■ Lesson 6.4 (continued)

17. $f(x) = \begin{cases} -(x-3), & x < 3 \\ x-3, & x \geq 3 \end{cases}$

18. $f(x) = \begin{cases} -(2x-4), & x < 2 \\ 2x-4, & x \geq 2 \end{cases}$

19. $f(x) = \begin{cases} 1 - \frac{1}{2}x, & x < 2 \\ -(1 - \frac{1}{2}x), & x \geq 2 \end{cases}$

20. $f(x) = \begin{cases} -(x+4), & x < -4 \\ x+4, & x \geq -4 \end{cases}$

21. $f(x) = \begin{cases} -x+2, & x < 2 \\ -(-x+2), & x \geq 2 \end{cases}$

22. $f(x) = \begin{cases} -(3x-3), & x < 1 \\ 3x-3, & x \geq 1 \end{cases}$

23. $f(x) = \begin{cases} -(4x+12), & x < -3 \\ 4x+12, & x \geq -3 \end{cases}$

24. $f(x) = \begin{cases} -(\frac{1}{2}x+1), & x < -2 \\ \frac{1}{2}x+1, & x \geq -2 \end{cases}$

25. $f(x) = \begin{cases} -(\frac{1}{3}x-2), & x < 6 \\ \frac{1}{3}x-2, & x \geq 6 \end{cases}$

26. **27.**

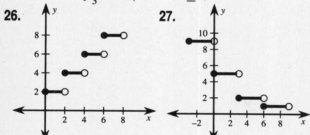

28. **29.**

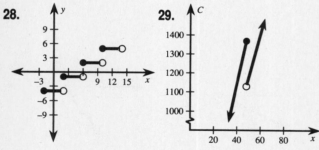

$C = \begin{cases} 28x + 25, & x \leq 48 \\ 23x + 25, & x > 48 \end{cases}$

■ Lesson 6.5

1. $g(x) = f(x) + 11$ **2.** $g(x) = f(x-2)$

3. $g(x) = f(x+3)$

4. Shift graph of f 1 unit down.

5. Shift graph of f 1 unit to right.

6. Shift graph of f 7 units to left.

7. Reflect graph of f in x-axis.

8. Shift graph of f 9 units up.

9. Shift graph of f 3 units to left.

10. c **11. b** **12. a**

13. **14.**

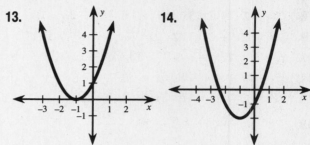

15. **16.**

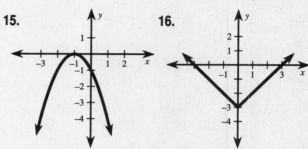

17. **18.**

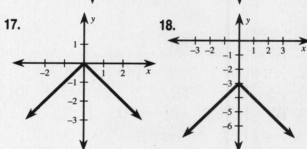

19. $f(t) = 36.7(t+10)^2 - 905.8(t+10) + 32,634$, shift the original graph 10 units to left.

20. $f(t) = 36.7(t+15)^2 - 905.8(t+15) + 32,634$, shift the original graph 15 units to left.

21. 27,060,900

■ Lesson 6.6

1. 1, 4, 7, 10, 13 **2.** 0, 1, 3, 6, 10

3. 2, 6, 18, 54, 162 **4.** 10, −6, 3, 13, 12

5. 1, 3, 11, 123, 15131 **6.** 2, 3, 1, −2, −3

7. 0, 4, 8, 12, 16, 20; 1st differences: 4, 4, 4, 4, 4

8. −2, 1, −2, 1, −2, 1;
1st differences: 3, −3, 3, −3, 3

9. 1, 0, 2, 1, 3, 2;
1st differences: −1, 2, −1, 2, −1

10. 7

11. 1, 3, 7, 15, 31, 63;
2nd differences: 2, 4, 8, 16

12. 2, −1, 3, 0, 4, 1;
2nd differences: 7, −7, 7, −7

Lesson 6.6 (continued)

13. $-1, -5, -11, -19, -29, -41;$
    2nd differences: $-2, -2, -2, -2$

14. 13   15. $f(n) = 3n - 3$

16. $f(n) = n + 5$ 17. $f(n) = -n + 6$

18. $f(n) = n^2 + n - 4$ 19. $f(n) = n^2 - 2n + 1$

20. $f(n) = -n^2 + 2n + 3$

21. 0, 1, 2, 3, 4, 5   22. $f(n) = n - 3$

Lesson 6.7

1. {1, 1, 1, 2, 2, 3, 4, 5, 5, 6, 7, 7, 8, 8, 9}

2. 4.6   3. 5   4. 1

5. {12, 12, 13, 14, 15, 15, 15, 17, 22, 23, 23, 25, 27, 28, 30, 32, 32, 33, 35, 35}

6. 1st Quartile: 15, 2nd Quartile: 23
   3rd Quartile: 31

7.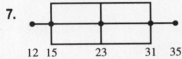
   12 15   23   31 35

8. ≈ 4.5 9. 25.2 oz   10. 25 oz   11. 28 oz

12. 1st Quartile: 5, 2nd Quartile: 6
    3rd Quartile: 7

13.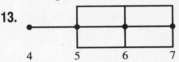
    4   5   6   7

Lesson 7.1

1. 9   2. -32 3. 15,625   4. $\frac{8}{27}$

5. $\frac{1}{64}$ 6. 1   7. 16   8. $\frac{1}{16}$

9. x^5 10. $\frac{2}{y^2}$ 11. $9x^2$ 12. $\frac{y^3}{8}$

13. $256x^{12}$ 14. $\frac{1}{y^2}$ 15. $\frac{5x^3}{2y^2}$ 16. $-\frac{y^5}{3x^2}$

17. $\frac{x^3}{2y^2}$ 18. $-\frac{4}{3y^2}$ 19. 1   20. $-\frac{5y}{4x^2}$

21. x^5 22. $\pi^3 x^4$ 23. $2^{x+3} = 2^5$, $x = 2$

24. $3^{x-2} = 3^4$, $x = 6$ 25. $5^{3x} = 5^{12}$, $x = 4$

26. $4^{3-x} = 4^0$, $x = 3$ 27. $2^{-x} = 2^5$, $x = -5$

28. $3^{2+x} = 3^{-1}$, $x = -3$ 29. $\frac{4}{3}\pi \left(\frac{7}{4}\right)^3$ in.^{3}

30. $\dfrac{190 \cdot \frac{4}{3}\pi \left(\frac{7}{4}\right)^3}{(20)^3}$ 31. $\approx 53.3\%$

32. 345,600 in^3 33. ≈ 8205

Lesson 7.2

1. $500   2. 0.05   3. 12   4. 3

5. $580.74   6. $1616.23

7. $3934.30   8. $1915.44

9. Answer depends upon present year.

10. Growth

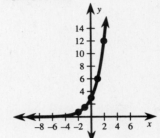

x	y
-2	$\frac{3}{4}$
-1	$\frac{3}{2}$
0	3
1	6
2	12

11. Decay

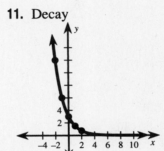

x	y
-2	12
-1	6
0	3
1	$\frac{3}{2}$
2	$\frac{3}{4}$

12. Growth

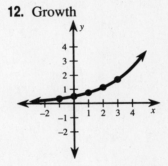

x	y
-1	$\frac{1}{3}$
0	$\frac{1}{2}$
1	$\frac{3}{4}$
2	$\frac{9}{8}$
3	$\frac{27}{16}$

13. Decay

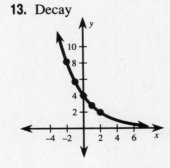

x	y
-2	8.16
-1	5.71
0	4
1	2.8
2	1.96

Lesson 7.2 (continued)

14.

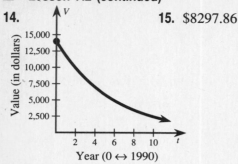

Year (0 ↔ 1990)

15. $8297.86

Lesson 7.3

1. $11^{1/3}$　**2.** $5^{1/4}$　**3.** $82^{1/6}$　**4.** $27^{1/5}$

5. $\sqrt[3]{19}$　**6.** $\sqrt[5]{43}$　**7.** $\sqrt[4]{25}$　**8.** $\sqrt[7]{6}$

9. 1.59　**10.** 2.30　**11.** 2.44　**12.** 2.93

13. -2.47　**14.** 2.21　**15.** 2.65　**16.** 3.00

17. -2.61　**18.** $(8^{1/3})^4 = 16$

19. $(36^{1/2})^3 = 216$　**20.** $(16^{1/4})^3 = 8$

21. $(81^{1/2})^3 = 729$　**22.** $(64^{1/3})^2 = 16$

23. $(32^{1/5})^2 = 4$　**24.** $(4^{1/2})^5 = 32$

25. $(81^{1/4})^3 = 27$　**26.** $(243^{1/5})^6 = 729$

27. -4　**28.** $\frac{1}{2}$　**29.** $\frac{1}{125}$　**30.** $\frac{1}{100,000}$

31. -32　**32.** $\frac{1}{64}$　**33.** ≈ 7.2 in.

34. ≈ 4.5 cm　**35.** ≈ 511.48 cm^3　**36.** ≈ 8 cm

37. ≈ 556.28 cm^3　**38.** ≈ 8.22 cm

Lesson 7.4

1. 25　**2.** $\dfrac{1}{3^{1/2}}$　**3.** $7^{5/3}$　**4.** $12^{1/4}$

5. 2　**6.** 2　**7.** $5 \cdot 3^{3/4}$　**8.** $\dfrac{1}{3^{2/3}}$

9. $\frac{4}{5}$　**10.** $3|x|$　**11.** $\sqrt[3]{2}x$　**12.** x

13. $\dfrac{x^{1/2}}{2}$　**14.** $2x^{1/4}$　**15.** $3x$　**16.** $2|x|$

17. $x^{2/3}$　**18.** $4|y|\sqrt[4]{x}$　**19.** $\sqrt[3]{10} \approx 2.15$

20. $5^{3/4} \approx 3.34$　**21.** $10^{1/6} \approx 1.47$

22. $8^{5/3} = 32$　**23.** $\sqrt[4]{5} \approx 1.50$

24. $3^{-4/3} \approx 0.23$　**25.** $\sqrt[3]{36} \approx 3.30$

26. $36^{4/3} \approx 118.87$　**27.** $2^{3/4} \approx 1.68$

28. $3\sqrt[3]{3}$　**29.** $2\sqrt{7}$　**30.** $15\sqrt[5]{22}$

31. $-\sqrt[4]{15}$　**32.** $8(2^{1/3})$　**33.** $2\sqrt{2}$

34. $3\sqrt[3]{5}$　**35.** $-2\sqrt[5]{3}$　**36.** $5\sqrt{2}$

37. 12.5 in.　**38.** 2.5 in.　**39.** 0.2 or 20%

Lesson 7.5

1. 64　**2.** -8　**3.** 215　**4.** 8

5. 9, -7　**6.** 20　**7.** ±125　**8.** -8

9. 27　**10.** 8　**11.** 12　**12.** 65

13. -4　**14.** 2　**15.** -1　**16.** 5

17. 0, 4　**18.** 2　**19.** 25　**20.** 4

21. 5　**22.** $\sqrt{13}$　**23.** 5　**24.** 4, 6

25. 0, -2　**26.** -1, 7　**27.** $(-16, -20)$

28. $(0, 28)$　**29.** ≈ 50.6 mi

Lesson 7.6

1. f　**2.** c　**3.** b　**4.** d　**5.** a　**6.** e

7. Shift graph of f 4 units to left.

8. Shift graph of f 4 units to left and 2 units down.

9. Shift graph of f 4 units to left and reflect in x-axis.

10. Shift graph of f 4 units to right.

11. Shift graph of f 4 units to right and 2 units up.

12. Shift graph of f 4 units to right, reflect in x-axis, and shift 2 units up.

13. Shift graph of f 1 unit down.

14. Reflect graph of f in x-axis and shift 1 unit down.

15. Reflect graph of f in x-axis and shift 1 unit up.

16. Shift graph of f 1 unit to right.

17. Shift graph of f 1 unit to left.

18. Shift graph of f 1 unit to left and 2 units down.

19.　**20.**

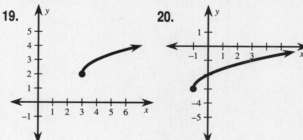

21.　**22.**

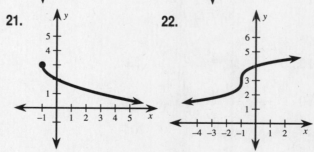

■ Lesson 7.6 (continued)

23.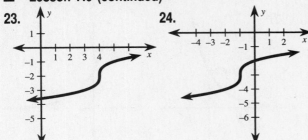

24.

22.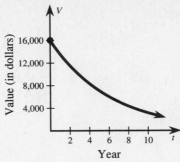

23. $7099.29

25. Domain: $0 \le h \le 100$, Range: $0 \le t \le \frac{5}{2}$

26.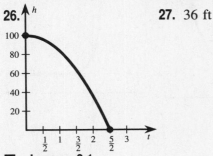

27. 36 ft

■ Lesson 8.2

1. $4^2 = 16$ **2.** $3^4 = 81$ **3.** $2^0 = 1$

4. $9^{1/2} = 3$ **5.** $5^{-1} = \frac{1}{5}$ **6.** $8^{2/3} = 4$

7. $\log_2 8 = 3$ **8.** $\log_7 49 = 2$

9. $\log_{10} 0.01 = -2$ **10.** $\log_5 1 = 0$

11. $\log_9 27 = \frac{3}{2}$ **12.** $\log_4 \frac{1}{2} = -\frac{1}{2}$

13. $\log_2 4 = 2$ **14.** $\log_3 27 = 3$ **15.** $\log_4 1 = 0$

16. $\log_2 \frac{1}{2} = -1$ **17.** $\log_8 2 = \frac{1}{3}$

18. $\log_5 5^{2/3} = \frac{2}{3}$ **19.** $\log_3 3 = 1$

20. Undefined   **21.** ≈ 2.262 **22.** ≈ 0.387

23. ≈ 1.209 **24.** -0.500 **25.** ≈ -11.136

26. ≈ 2.539 **27.** ≈ 0.369 **28.** ≈ -2.585

29. c **30. a** **31. b**

■ Lesson 8.1

1. Shift graph of f 2 units up.

2. Shift graph of f 5 units down.

3. Shift graph of f 1 unit to left.

4. Shift graph of f 3 units to right.

5. Shift graph of f 1 unit to right and 2 units up.

6. Reflect graph of f in x-axis and shift 2 units to left.

7. b   **8. a**   **9. c**   **10. e**   **11. f**   **12. d**

13.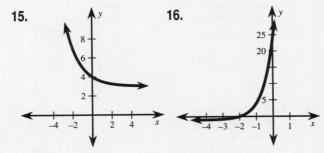

14.

15.

16.

32.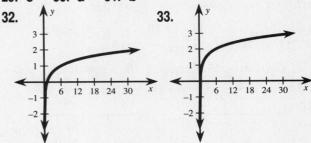

33.

34.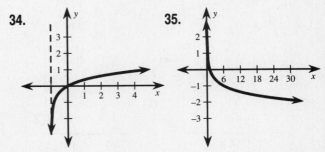

35.

36.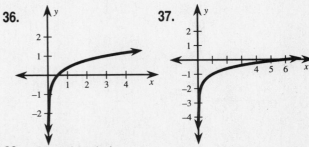

37.

17. ≈ 77.880 **18.** ≈ 77.571 **19.** ≈ 0.009

20. $\approx 990,107.875$ **21.** $V = 16,000(0.85)^t$

38. 127 strides/min

■ Lesson 8.3

1. $\log_{10} 3 - \log_{10} 4 \approx -0.125$
2. $\log_{10} 3 + \log_{10} 4 \approx 1.079$
3. $2 \log_{10} 3 \approx 0.954$ 4. $2 \log_{10} 4 = 1.204$
5. $- \log_{10} 4 \approx -0.602$
6. $- \log_{10} 3 \approx -0.477$
7. $\log_6 3 + \log_6 x$ 8. $\log_2 x - \log_2 5$
9. $\log_{10} x + 2 \log_{10} y$
10. $\log_4 x + \log_4 y - \log_4 3$
11. $\frac{1}{2} \log_3 x + \log_3 y + \log_3 z$
12. $\log_5 2 + \frac{1}{2} \log_5 x$
13. $\log_3 \frac{7}{x}$ 14. $\log_5 3x^2$ 15. $\log_4 5xy$
16. $\log_{10} \frac{\sqrt{x}}{4}$ 17. $\log_2 \frac{\sqrt[3]{x^2}}{y^3}$ 18. $\log_3 \frac{4x^2}{5}$
19. 9   20. 4   21. $\frac{5}{2}$ 22. 4   23. 27
24. 3   25. $6.1 + \log_{10} B - \log_{10} C$
26. ≈ 7.201 27. ≈ 1.203

■ Lesson 8.4

1. ≈ 54.598 2. ≈ 0.135 3. ≈ 1.948
4. ≈ 0.717 5. $e^5 \approx 148.413$ 6. $e^{-8} \approx 0.000$
7. $3e^4 \approx 163.794$ 8. $\frac{2}{e} \approx 0.736$
9. $16e^6 \approx 6454.861$ 10. $-12e^3 \approx -241.026$
11. Growth   12. Decay   13. Decay
14. Growth   15. Decay   16. Growth

17.

x	$2e^x$
-2	0.27
-1.5	0.45
-1	0.74
0	2
1	5.44
1.5	8.96
2	14.78

18.

x	$2e^{-x}$
-2	14.78
-1.5	8.96
-1	5.44
0	2
1	0.74
1.5	0.45
2	0.27

19.

x	$e^{2x} + 3$
-2	3.02
-1.5	3.05
-1	3.14
0	4
1	10.39
1.5	23.09
2	57.60

20.

x	$e^{-3x} - 2$
-2	401.43
-1.5	88.02
-1	18.09
0	-1
1	-1.95
1.5	-1.99
2	-2.00

21. $y = 0$
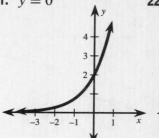

22. $y = 0$
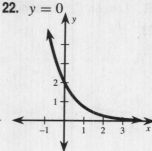

23. $y = 2$ 24. $y = 1$
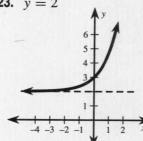
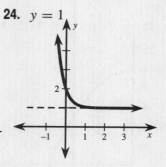

25. $y = -1$ 26. $y = -3$
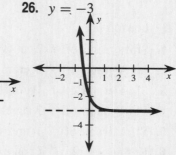

27. $1972.34   28. $1978.47   29. Continuous

■ Lesson 8.5

1. 2   2. 3   3. -1   4. -4
5. $\ln 2 + \ln x$ 6. $\ln x - \ln y$ 7. $\ln 3 + 2 \ln x$
8. $\ln 4 + 2 \ln y - \ln x$ 9. $3 \ln x - 2 \ln y$
10. $\frac{1}{2} \ln x$ 11. $\ln 4x$ 12. $\ln \frac{2}{y}$ 13. $\ln x^3 y^2$
14. $\ln \frac{9}{x}$ 15. $\ln \frac{4}{x+y}$ 16. $\ln 5x \sqrt{y}$

17.

x	$2 + \ln x$
0.25	0.614
0.5	1.307
1	2
2	2.693
3	3.099

18.

x	$3 \ln x$
0.25	-4.159
0.5	-2.079
1	0
2	2.079
3	3.296

19.

x	$\ln(x-1)$
1.25	-1.386
1.5	-0.693
2	0
3	0.693
4	1.099

20.

x	$2 - \ln(x+1)$
-0.75	3.386
-0.5	2.693
0	2
1	1.307
2	0.901

Lesson 8.5 (continued)

21.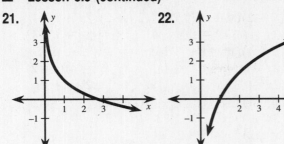

22.

23.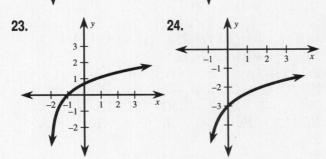

24.

25.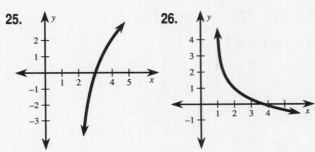

26.

27. 20.01% **28.** 0.215

Lesson 8.6

1. ≈ 2.890 **2.** ≈ 2.544 **3.** ≈ 1.869
4. ≈ 1.491 **5.** ≈ 0.693 **6.** ≈ 1.875
7. ≈ 3.332 **8.** ≈ 0.836 **9.** ≈ 0.231
10. ≈ 2.465 **11.** ≈ 6.714 **12.** ≈ 1.758
13. ≈ 148.413 **14.** ≈ 0.01 **15.** ≈ 2.828
16. ≈ 0.001 **17.** ≈ 20.086 **18.** ≈ 54.598
19. 10,000 **20.** ≈ 3.175
21. 3 **22.** 45 months
23. ≈ 3.719 years **24.** ≈ 20.086

Lesson 8.7

1. Exponential decay **2.** Logarithmic
3. Logistics growth **4.** Exponential decay
5. Exponential growth **6.** Logarthmic
7. a **8. c** **9. b**
10. $y = 0$, $y = 1$ **11.** $y = 0$, $y = 1$
12. $y = 0$, $y = 5$ **13.** $y = 0$, $y = 20$
14. $y = -5$, $y = -4$ **15.** $y = 10$, $y = 12$

16.

x	−2	−1	0	1	2
f(x)	0.190	0.466	1	1.728	2.361

17.

x	−2	−1	0	1	2
f(x)	4.238	4.538	5	5.462	5.762

18.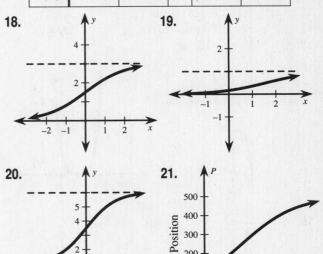

19.

20.

21.

22. $y = 0$, $y = 500$ **23.** 500 **24.** ≈ 451

Lesson 9.1

1. $x + 3$, 1, 1 **2.** $2x^2 - x + 5$, 2, 2
3. $-x^3 + x^2 - 3x + 1$, 3, −1
4. $\frac{1}{3}x^2 + \frac{2}{3}x + \frac{1}{2}$, 2, $\frac{1}{3}$
5. $-3x^4 + 4x^2$, 4, −3
6. $2x^5 - 4x + 3$, 5, 2
7. $2x^2 + 2x - 2$ **8.** $3x^3 - 3x^2 - x - 4$
9. $-x + 3$ **10.** $2x^2 + 6x - 4$
11. $2x^3 - 4x^2 + 3x + 1$ **12.** $-4x^2 - 2x + 4$
13. $7x^3 - 3x^2 - 2x + 1$ **14.** $3x^2 - x$
15. $2x^3 + 6x^2$ **16.** $3x^3 - x^2 + 5x$
17. $x^2 + 3x - 10$ **18.** $x^2 + 4x + 3$
19. $x^2 - 5x + 4$ **20.** $x^3 + 2x^2 - 1$
21. $x^3 - 7x - 6$ **22.** $2x^3 - x^2 - 7x - 3$
23. $x^3 + x^2 - 5x + 3$ **24.** $2x^3 + 5x^2 + x - 2$
25. $2x^3 + 5x^2 - x - 4$ **26.** $x^2 - 1$
27. $x^2 + 6x + 9$ **28.** $x^3 - 6x^2 + 12x - 8$
29. $4x^2 - 4x + 1$ **30.** $4x^2 - 25$
31. $x^3 + 9x^2 + 27x + 27$
32. $x^2 + 42x + 360$
33. $v = -16.2t^3 + 183t^2 + 1352.5t + 11{,}504.1$

Lesson 9.2

1. 3 **2.** 2 **3.** 5
4. Shift graph of f 1 unit to right.
5. Reflect graph of f in x-axis.
6. Shift graph of f 4 units up.
7. Left: rises; Right: falls
8. Left: rises; Right: rises

9. Left: falls; Right: rises
10. Left: rises; Right: rises
11. Left: falls; Right: falls
12. Left: rises; Right: falls
13. b   14. c   15. a

16. 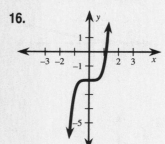   **17.**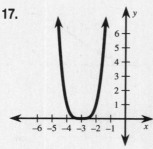

18. 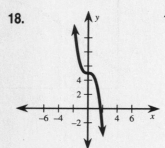   **19.**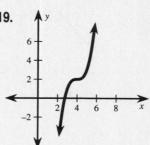

20. 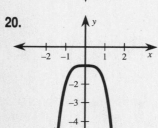   **21.**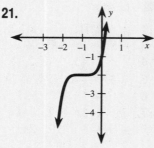

22.

t	S
2	200.8
3	212.2
4	230.8
5	256.0
6	287.2
7	323.8
8	365.2
9	410.8
10	460.0

23.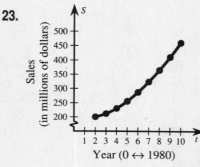

Year (0 ↔ 1980)

24. 1986

■ **Lesson 9.3**

1. $(x + 2)(x - 2)$ **2.** $(2x + 5)(2x - 5)$
3. $(3x + 1)(3x - 1)$ **4.** $(x + 1)(x^2 - x + 1)$
5. $(x - 4)(x^2 + 4x + 16)$
6. $(2x - 1)(4x^2 + 2x + 1)$ **7.** $(x^2 + 4)(x + 2)$
8. $(2x^2 + 3)(x - 3)$ **9.** $(3x^2 - 2)(x + 2)$
10. $(x - 1)^2$ **11.** $(x + 3)(x - 2)$
12. $(2x - 1)(x + 2)$ **13.** $(x + 3)(x + 1)$
14. $(x + 2)^2$ **15.** $(2x + 1)^2$
16. $2x(x + 3)(x - 3)$
17. $(x^2 + 4)(x + 2)(x - 2)$
18. $3x(x - 2)(x + 1)$ **19.** $(x^2 + 3)(x + 1)(x - 1)$
20. $2(3x + 1)(9x^2 - 3x + 1)$
21. $(x + 2)(x - 2)(x^2 + 2x + 4)$
22. $0, -2$ **23.** $0, 2, -2$ **24.** $-5, 3$
25. $0, -4$ **26.** $3, -3, 2, -2$ **27.** -2
28. $0, 3$ **29.** $3, -1$ **30.** $0, 4, -2$
31. $\frac{1}{3}, -2$ **32.** $-1, 5, -5$ **33.** -3
34. 750 ft^3 **35.** $x^3 - 15x^2 + 50x = 750$
36. 15 **37.** $10 \text{ ft} \times 5 \text{ ft} \times 15 \text{ ft}$

■ **Lesson 9.4**

1. $2x + 3$ **2.** $3x - 4$ **3.** $x^2 + x + 1$
4. $x^2 - 3x + 1$ **5.** $2x^2 + x - 3 + \dfrac{5}{2x - 1}$
6. $x + 2 - \dfrac{1}{x^2 + 3x - 1}$
7. $\dfrac{x^3 - 2x^2 - 14x - 5}{x - 5} = x^2 + 3x + 1$
8. $\dfrac{2x^3 + 3x^2 + 3x + 17}{x + 2} = 2x^2 - x + 5 + \dfrac{7}{x + 2}$
9. $\dfrac{x^3 + x - 2}{x - 3} = x^2 + 3x + 10 + \dfrac{28}{x - 3}$
10. $2x^2 + x + 3$ **11.** $x + 5 - \dfrac{2}{x + 1}$
12. $x^2 - 3x + 7 - \dfrac{9}{x + 3}$ **13.** $x^3 + 4 + \dfrac{3}{x - 5}$
14. 29 **15.** -15 **16.** -1 **17.** 0
18. $(x + 8)(x - 2)$ **19.** $(x - 2)^2$
20. $(2x + 1)(x - 1)$ **21.** $(3x + 2)(x - 1)$
22. $x - 2$ **23.** $C = 20x$
24. $R = x(70 - 5x^2)$ **25.** $P = -5x^3 + 50x$

■ **Lesson 9.5**

1. $\pm 1, \pm 2, \pm 4$ **2.** $\pm 1, \pm 2, \pm 3, \pm 6, \pm\frac{1}{2}, \pm\frac{3}{2}$
3. $\pm 1, \pm 2, \pm 4, \pm 8, \pm\frac{1}{3}, \pm\frac{2}{3}, \pm\frac{4}{3}, \pm\frac{8}{3}$
4. $-2, \frac{1}{2}, 3$ **5.** $-\frac{8}{3}, 1, -1$
6. $-\frac{3}{2}, \frac{1}{4}, 2$ **7.** $-2, 5, 1$
8. $-3, -1$ **9.** $\frac{5}{2}, \pm\sqrt{2}$ **10.** $-\frac{3}{2}, \frac{1}{2}, 3$

■ Lesson 9.5 (continued)

11. $3, \pm\sqrt{3}$ **12.** $-2, \frac{1}{2}, \pm\sqrt{2}$

13. $-3, 1, \pm\sqrt{2}$

14. $t^3 - 13t^2 + 65t - 105 = 0$

15. $\pm1, \pm3, \pm5, \pm7, \pm15, \pm21, \pm35, \pm105$

16. $1, 3, 5, 7$ **17.** 1983

■ Lesson 9.6

1. 3   **2.** 6   **3.** 5   **4.** 4   **5.** It is.

6. It is not.   **7.** It is.   **8.** It is.

9. $(x-3), (x-1), (x-2)$

10. $x(x-4), (x+1), (x+2)$

11. $(x+3), (x-i), (x+i)$

12. $(x-4), (x+5), (x-2i), (x+2i)$

13. $f(x) = x^3 - 5x^2 + 2x + 8$

14. $f(x) = x^3 - 5x^2 + 7x - 3$

15. $f(x) = x^3 + 2x^2 + x + 2$

16. $f(x) = x^4 - x^3 + 9x^2 - 9x$

17. $(x-3), (x-1)$

18. $(x+5), (x-1)$ **19.** $(x+90), (x+8)$

20. $x(x+2), (x-5)$ **21.** $f(x) = x^2 - 2x$

22. $f(x) = x^2 + 2x - 3$

23. $f(x) = x^2 + 9x + 14$

24. $f(x) = x^3 - 4x^2 + x + 6$

25. $(x+i)(x-i)(x+1)$

26. $(x+3)(2x+1)(x-2)$

27. $(x+4)(x+3i)(x-3i)$

28. $(x+1)(2x-1)(x+i)(x-i)$

29. $(x+2)(x-2)(x+i)(x-i)$

30. $(x+4)(3x-1)(x+2i)(x-2i)$

31. $(x+1)(x+3)(x-2)$

32. Length: $(x+3)$ **33.** 10
Width: $(x+1)$
Height: $(x-2)$

■ Lesson 9.7

1. 9   **2.** 1.9   **3.** 21

4. $\bar{x} = 2, s \approx 1.054$

5. $\bar{x} = 6.8, s \approx 0.208$

6. $\bar{x} = 105.5, s \approx 0.957$ **7.** b

8. 4   **9.** $\bar{x} = 2.35$ **10.** $s \approx 1.108$

11. 30   **12.** $\bar{x} = 107.4$ **13.** $s \approx 8.052$

14. Machine #1: $\bar{x} = 1.0008$
Machine #2: $\bar{x} = 0.9993$

15. Machine #1: $s = 0.00098$
Machine #2: $s = 0.00095$

16. Machine #2

■ Lesson 10.1

1. All real numbers except 5.

2. All real numbers except -6.

3. All real numbers except 3.

4. All real numbers except -2 and -1.

5. $x = \frac{1}{2}$ **6.** $x = -1, x = 3$

7. $x = 2, x = -2$ **8.** $x = 6, x = -2$

9. $y = 0$ **10.** $y = 2$

11. None   **12.** $y = \frac{1}{2}$

13.

x	$f(x)$
-2	5
-1.5	9
-1.25	17
-0.75	-15
-0.5	-7
0	-3

14.

x	$f(x)$
1	-1
1.5	-3
1.75	-7
2.25	9
2.5	5
3	3

15. b   **16.** c   **17.** a

18.   **19.**

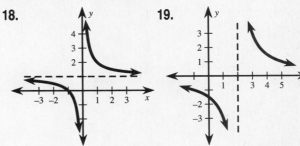

20.   **21.**

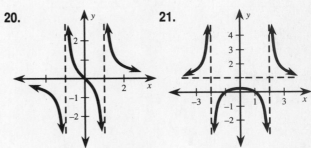

22. $C = 7x + 250$ **24.**

23. $A = \dfrac{7x + 250}{x}$

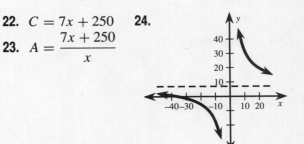

■ Lesson 10.2

1. Directly   **2.** Inversely   **3.** Directly

4. Inversely   **5.** $k = 8, yx = 8$

6. $k = 3, yx = 3$

7. $k = 0.03, yx = 0.03$

8. $k = 3, z = 3xy$ **9.** $k = 3, z = 3xy$

10. $k = \frac{2}{3}, x = \frac{2}{3}xy$ **11.** $k = 12.84$

12. $PV = 12.84$ **13.** 10.7 liters

14. $k = 150,000$ **15.** $px = 150,000$

16. 12,500 units   **17.** $k = 0.055$
18. $I = 0.055tP$ **19.** \$220.00
20. $k = 0.22$ **21.** $H = 0.22mT$
22. 3.9424 kilocalories

■ Lesson 10.3

1. $\dfrac{x-4}{x-3}$ **2.** $\dfrac{x+3}{x+1}$ **3.** $\dfrac{x-6}{x+5}$

4. $\dfrac{x-1}{x+1}$ **5.** $\dfrac{1}{5x^5y^2}$ **6.** $\dfrac{9x^6}{4y^5}$

7. $\dfrac{3x^3y^8}{4}$ **8.** $\dfrac{3x^{11}y}{25}$ **9.** $\dfrac{3}{10}$

10. $\dfrac{4x^2}{3(x-1)}$ **11.** $x - 6$ **12.** $\dfrac{6(x-2)}{x+3}$

13. $\dfrac{x(x-2)}{5}$ **14.** $\dfrac{(x-2)(x+6)}{5x^2}$

15. $x + 3$ **16.** $x + 4$ **17.** $\dfrac{x-11}{x+8}$

18. $\dfrac{7(x-3)}{x(x+5)}$ **19.** $\dfrac{x-1}{x(x-9)(x+3)}$

20. $3(x-2)$ **21.** $\dfrac{6}{5}$ **22.** $\dfrac{5(x+5)}{4x^3}$

23. $\dfrac{(x+10)(x+2)}{(x+8)(x+1)}$ **24.** $\dfrac{x^2(x+4)(x+3)}{x-3}$

25. $\dfrac{4(x+1)}{3(x-2)}$

■ Lesson 10.4

1. $x(x+5)(x-5)$ **2.** $6x^2(x+6)(x-6)$
3. $2x(x+2)(x+2)$ **4.** $x(x+7)(x-7)$
5. It is not.   **6.** It is.   **7.** 0   **8.** 3
9. -4 **10.** $-\dfrac{1}{2}$ **11.** 4, 3   **12.** 6, 5
13. 10   **14.** $\dfrac{9}{7}$ **15.** $\dfrac{7}{4}$ **16.** -2
17. No real solution   **18.** 3   **19.** 20
20. No real solution   **21. c   22. a**
23. b   24. 167, 250, 400   **25.** 750

■ Lesson 10.5

1. $(2x+1)(2x-1)$ **2.** $4(x+4)(x-4)$
3. $x(x+1)(x-1)^2$ **4.** $x(x-2)(x-6)$

5. $\dfrac{x+5}{x+1}$ **6.** $\dfrac{6x+13}{x+3}$ **7.** $\dfrac{2x-1}{(x+2)(x-1)}$

8. $\dfrac{x+5}{(x+1)(x-2)}$ **9.** $\dfrac{6}{(x-6)(x+5)}$

10. $\dfrac{x}{x-1}$ **11.** $\dfrac{2(4x^2+5x-3)}{x^2(x+3)}$

12. $\dfrac{(2x+1)(2x-1)}{2x(x+1)^2}$ **13.** $\dfrac{x^2+3x+9}{x(x+3)(x-3)}$

14. $\dfrac{3x+1}{4x^2}$ **15.** $\dfrac{-11x+2}{3(x^2+x+2)}$ **16.** $\dfrac{x-3}{x}$

17. $\dfrac{x^2+15x+14}{10}$ **18.** $\dfrac{1}{6}$

19. $\dfrac{x(3x+4)}{4x^3+9x-36}$ **20.** $\dfrac{1}{2}$ **21.** $\dfrac{8}{5}$ **22.** 4

23. $R = \dfrac{R_1 R_2}{R_1 + R_2}$ **24.** $\dfrac{4}{3}$ ohm

■ Lesson 10.6

1.

	Bal. before Pay.	Pay.	Intr. Pay.	Prin. Pay.	Bal. after Pay.
1	1500.00	155.55	10.00	145.55	1354.45
2	1354.45	155.55	9.03	146.52	1207.93
3	1207.93	155.55	8.05	147.50	1060.43
4	1060.43	155.55	7.07	148.48	911.95
5	911.95	155.55	6.08	149.47	762.48
6	762.48	155.55	5.08	149.47	612.01
7	612.01	155.55	4.08	151.47	460.54
8	460.54	155.55	3.07	152.48	308.06
9	308.06	155.55	2.05	153.50	154.56
10	154.56	155.59	1.03	154.56	0.00

2.

	Bal. before Pay.	Pay.	Intr. Pay.	Prin. Pay.	Bal. after Pay.
1	2500.00	218.63	18.75	199.88	2300.12
2	2300.12	218.63	17.25	201.38	2098.74
3	2098.74	218.63	15.74	202.89	1895.85
4	1895.85	218.63	14.22	204.41	1691.44
5	1691.44	218.63	12.69	205.94	1485.50
6	1485.50	218.63	11.14	207.49	1278.01
7	1278.01	218.63	9.59	209.04	1068.97
8	1068.97	218.63	8.02	210.61	858.36
9	858.36	218.63	6.44	212.19	646.17
10	646.17	218.63	4.85	213.78	432.39
11	432.39	218.63	3.24	215.39	217.00
12	217.00	218.63	1.63	217.00	0.00

3. \$1000.03   **4.** \$107.47   **5.** \$1653.40
6. \$355.68   **7.** \$771.46   **8.** \$789.92
9. \$277,725.60, \$202,725.60; \$236,976.00, \$161,976.00
10. \$40,749.60
11. d (\$73.49), the other payments are too high.
12. \$69.22   **13.** \$1661.28   **14.** \$57.68
15. \$1384.32
16. First plan doesn't require a down   **17. b**
payment. Second plan has lower
monthly payment.

■ Lesson 11.1

1. $y^2 = 4(4)x$ **2.** $y^2 = 4(1)x$

3. $x^2 = 4(\frac{9}{16})y$ **4.** $x^2 = 4(\frac{1}{32})y$

5. Vertical   **6.** Horizontal

7. Horizontal   **8.** Vertical

9. $(0, \frac{1}{16})$, $y = -\frac{1}{16}$ **10.** $(0, \frac{1}{8})$, $y = -\frac{1}{8}$

11. $(0, -2)$, $y = 2$ **12.** $(-\frac{3}{2}, 0)$, $x = \frac{3}{2}$

13. $(-3, 0)$, $x = 3$ **14.** $(\frac{1}{8}, 0)$, $x = -\frac{1}{8}$

15. $(0, 5)$, $y = -5$ **16.** $(0, -8)$, $y = 8$

17. $y^2 = 32x$ **18.** $x^2 = -8y$

19. $y^2 = -48x$ **20.** $x^2 = 64y$

21. b   **22.** c   **23.** a

24.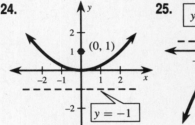

25.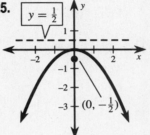

26. **27.**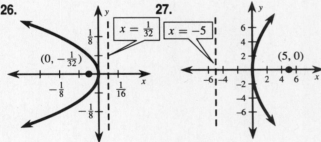

28. $x^2 = 80y$

■ Lesson 11.2

1. $x^2 + y^2 = 4$ **2.** $x^2 + y^2 = 6$

3. $x^2 + y^2 = \frac{1}{9}$ **4.** $x^2 + y^2 = \frac{1}{5}$

5. $x^2 + y^2 = 52$ **6.** $x^2 + y^2 = 5$

7. $x^2 + y^2 = 20$ **8.** $x^2 + y^2 = 29$

9. b   **10.** c   **11.** a

12. **13.**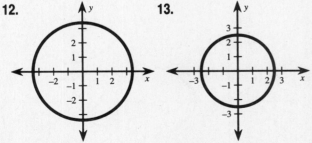

14. **15.**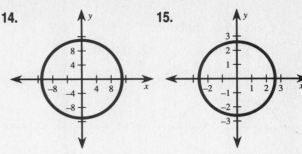

16. $(3, 6)$, $(-3, -6)$ **17.** $(-4, -3)$, $(3, 4)$

18. No points of intersection

19. $(1, \sqrt{2})$, $(1, -\sqrt{2})$ **20.** $x^2 + y^2 = 160{,}000$

■ Lesson 11.3

1. Foci: $(\sqrt{27}, 0)$, $(-\sqrt{27}, 0)$
Vertices: $(6, 0)$, $(-6, 0)$

2. Foci: $(\sqrt{21}, 0)$, $(-\sqrt{21}, 0)$
Vertices: $(11, 0)$, $(-11, 0)$

3. Foci: $(0, \sqrt{48})$, $(0, -\sqrt{48})$
Vertices: $(0, 7)$, $(0, -7)$

4. Foci: $(0, \sqrt{17})$, $(0, -\sqrt{17})$
Vertices: $(0, 9)$, $(0, -9)$

5. $\dfrac{x^2}{16} + \dfrac{y^2}{9} = 1$
Foci: $(\sqrt{7}, 0)$, $(-\sqrt{7}, 0)$
Vertices: $(4, 0)$, $(-4, 0)$

6. $\dfrac{x^2}{4} + \dfrac{y^2}{25} = 1$
Foci: $(0, \sqrt{21})$, $(0, -\sqrt{21})$
Vertices: $(0, 5)$, $(0, -5)$

7. $\dfrac{x^2}{9} + \dfrac{y^2}{(\frac{9}{4})} = 1$
Foci: $(\frac{3\sqrt{3}}{2}, 0)$, $(-\frac{3\sqrt{3}}{2}, 0)$
Vertices: $(3, 0)$, $(-3, 0)$

8. $\dfrac{x^2}{324} + \dfrac{y^2}{225} = 1$
Foci: $(3\sqrt{11}, 0)$, $(-3\sqrt{11}, 0)$
Vertices: $(18, 0)$, $(-18, 0)$

9. $\dfrac{x^2}{9} + \dfrac{y^2}{8} = 1$ **10.** $\dfrac{x^2}{49} + \dfrac{y^2}{25} = 1$

11. $\dfrac{x^2}{32} + \dfrac{y^2}{36} = 1$ **12.** $\dfrac{x^2}{2} + \dfrac{y^2}{5} = 1$

13. b   **14.** c   **15.** a

■ **Lesson 11.3 (continued)**

16. 0.821   **17.** 0.968

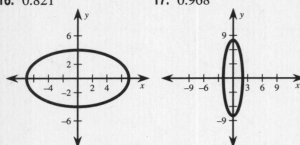

18. 0.866   **19.** 0.997

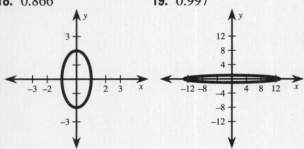

20. 0.500   **21.** 0.700

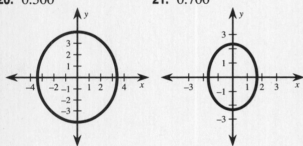

22. $\left(\frac{2}{\sqrt{14}}, \frac{4}{\sqrt{14}}\right)$, $\left(-\frac{2}{\sqrt{14}}, -\frac{4}{\sqrt{14}}\right)$

23. $(2\sqrt{2}, 1)$, $(2\sqrt{2}, -1)$; $(-2\sqrt{2}, 1)$, $(-2\sqrt{2}, -1)$

24. $(3, 0)$, $(-3, 0)$

■ **Lesson 11.4**

1. Vertices: $(5, 0)$, $(-5, 0)$
Foci: $(\sqrt{41}, 0)$, $(-\sqrt{41}, 0)$

2. Vertices: $(0, 7)$, $(0, -7)$
Foci: $(0, \sqrt{58})$, $(0, -\sqrt{58})$

3. Vertices: $(6, 0)$, $(-6, 0)$
Foci: $(\sqrt{61}, 0)$, $(-\sqrt{61}, 0)$

4. Vertices: $(0, 8)$, $(0, -8)$
Foci: $(0, \sqrt{113})$, $(0, -\sqrt{113})$

5. Vertices: $(1, 0)$, $(-1, 0)$
Foci: $(\sqrt{26}, 0)$, $(-\sqrt{26}, 0)$

6. Vertices: $(4, 0)$, $(-4, 0)$
Foci: $(\sqrt{41}, 0)$, $(-\sqrt{41}, 0)$

7. $x^2 - \dfrac{y^2}{36} = 1$
Vertices: $(1, 0)$, $(-1, 0)$
Foci: $(\sqrt{37}, 0)$, $(-\sqrt{37}, 0)$

8. $\dfrac{y^2}{4} - \dfrac{x^2}{9} = 1$
Vertices: $(0, 2)$, $(0, -2)$
Foci: $(0, \sqrt{13})$, $(0, -\sqrt{13})$

9. $\dfrac{x^2}{4} - \dfrac{y^2}{49} = 1$
Vertices: $(2, 0)$, $(-2, 0)$
Foci: $(\sqrt{53}, 0)$, $(-\sqrt{53}, 0)$

10. $\dfrac{y^2}{100} - \dfrac{x^2}{4} = 1$
Vertices: $(0, 10)$, $(0, -10)$
Foci: $(0, 2\sqrt{26})$, $(0, -2\sqrt{26})$

11. $\dfrac{x^2}{16} - \dfrac{y^2}{9} = 1$
Vertices: $(4, 0)$, $(-4, 60)$
Foci: $(5, 0)$, $(-5, 0)$

12. $\dfrac{x^2}{4} - \dfrac{y^2}{9} = 1$
Vertices: $(2, 0)$, $(-2, 0)$
Foci: $(\sqrt{13}, 0)$, $(-\sqrt{13}, 0)$

13. $\dfrac{x^2}{4} - \dfrac{y^2}{5} = 1$ **14.** $\dfrac{x^2}{16} - \dfrac{y^2}{9} = 1$

15. $\dfrac{y^2}{\frac{1}{16}} - \dfrac{x^2}{\frac{15}{16}} = 1$ **16.** $\dfrac{x^2}{9} - \dfrac{y^2}{72} = 1$

17. $y^2 - \dfrac{x^2}{35} = 1$ **18.** $x^2 - \dfrac{y^2}{15} = 1$

19. a   **20. c**   **21. b**

22. $y = \pm\frac{1}{2}x$ **23.** $y = \pm\frac{3}{10}x$

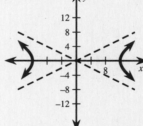
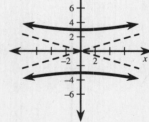

24. $y = \pm\frac{2}{3}x$ **25.** $y = \pm\frac{11}{10}x$

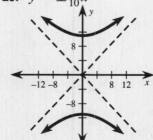

■ Lesson 11.4 (continued)

26. $y = \pm\frac{2}{5}x$ **27.** $y = \pm 4x$

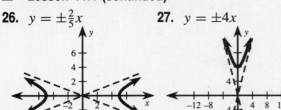

28. Foci: $(2\sqrt{17}, 0)$, $(-2\sqrt{17}, 0)$

29. Foci: $(0, \frac{4\sqrt{10}}{3})$, $(0, -\frac{4\sqrt{10}}{3})$

30. Foci: $(0, \sqrt{5})$, $(0, -\sqrt{5})$

31. $\frac{R^2}{\frac{16}{\pi}} - \frac{r^2}{\frac{8}{\pi}} = 1$; the graph is a hyperbola

■ Lesson 11.5

1. b   **2.** e   **3.** a

4. d   **5.** c   **6.** f

7. $\frac{(y-4)^2}{9} + \frac{(x+1)^2}{4} = 1$

8. $(x-2)^2 = 12(y-2)$

9. $(x+4)^2 + (y+6)^2 = 49$

10. $\frac{x^2}{25} - \frac{(y-5)^2}{24} = 1$

11. $(x-6)^2 + (y+9)^2 = 121$; center: $(6, -9)$, radius $= 11$

12. $(x+3)^2 + (y-2)^2 = 1$; center: $(-3, 2)$, radius $= 1$

13. $(x+5)^2 = 4(1)(y+6)$
Vertex: $(-5, -6)$; Focus: $(-5, -5)$

14. $(y-1)^2 = 4(-4)(x-2)$
Vertex: $(2, 1)$; Focus: $(-2, 1)$

15. $\frac{(x+3)^2}{4} + \frac{(y-1)^2}{1} = 1$
Vertices: $(-5, 1)$, $(-1, 1)$
Foci: $(-3+\sqrt{3}, 1)$, $(-3-\sqrt{3}, 1)$

16. $\frac{(x-1)^2}{4} + \frac{(y+2)^2}{16} = 1$
Vertices: $(1, -6)$, $(1, 2)$
Foci: $(1, -2-2\sqrt{3})$, $(1, -2+2\sqrt{3})$

17. $\frac{y^2}{4} - \frac{(x+1)^2}{3} = 1$
Vertices: $(-1, 2)$, $(-1, -2)$
Foci: $(-1, \sqrt{7})$, $(-1, -\sqrt{7})$

18. $\frac{(y+3)^2}{2} - \frac{(x-1)^2}{18} = 1$
Vertices: $(1, -3+\sqrt{2})$, $(1, -3-\sqrt{2})$
Foci: $(1, -3+2\sqrt{5})$, $(1, -3-2\sqrt{5})$

19. $(x-45)^2 = -\frac{405}{4}(y-20)$

■ Lesson 11.6

1. Ellipse   **2.** Hyperbola   **3.** Parabola

4. Circle   **5.** Hyperbola   **6.** Parabola

7. b   **8.** f   **9.** c   **10.** e

11. a   **12.** d

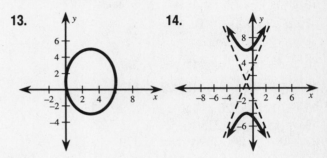

13.   **14.**

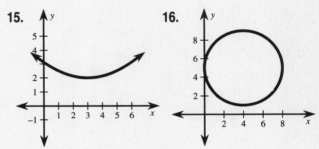

15.   **16.**

17. $(1, 0)$, $(-1, 0)$, $(1, -4)$, $(-1, -4)$

18. $(-3, -3)$, $(-3, 5)$

19. $(0, 0)$, $(0, -4)$ **20.** $(2, 0)$

21. $(-2, 3), (-2, -3)$; $\frac{(x+2)^2}{18} + \frac{y^2}{9} = 1$

■ Lesson 12.1

1. 2, 8, 18, 32, 50   **2.** 5, 3, $\frac{7}{3}$, 2, $\frac{9}{5}$

3. $\frac{1}{2}$, $\frac{4}{3}$, $\frac{9}{4}$, $\frac{16}{5}$, $\frac{25}{6}$ **4.** 5, 7, 9, 11, 13

5. 3, 4, 8, 26, 122   **6.** 6, 24, 120, 720, 5040

7. $\frac{1}{2}$, $\frac{1}{4}$, $\frac{1}{6}$, $\frac{1}{8}$, $\frac{1}{10}$ **8.** 2, $\frac{3}{2}$, $\frac{2}{3}$, $\frac{5}{24}$, $\frac{1}{20}$

9. 1, 2, 5, 26, 677, 458,330   **10.** 1, 1, 3, 7, 17, 41

11. $1 + 4 + 9 + 16 + 25 + 36 = 91$

12. $2 + 6 + 12 + 20 + 30 = 70$

13. $-1 - 4 - 9 - 16 - 25 = -55$

14. $1 + 2 + 24 + 120 + 40320 = 40467$

15. $0 + 4 + 18 + 48 + 100 = 170$

16. $5 + 6 + 9 + 14 + 21 = 55$

Lesson 12.1 (continued)

17. $1 + 2 + 6 + 24 = 33$

18. $9 + 28 + 125 + 726 = 888$

19. $\sum_{i=1}^{6} (2i^2 + 1)$ **20.** $\sum_{i=1}^{6} 2^{i-1}$

21. 325   **22.** 22,140   **23.** 36

24. 1830   **25.** 120

Lesson 12.2

1. It is.   **2.** It is not.   **3.** It is.

4. It is not.   **5.** It is.   **6.** It is.

7. $d = 4$, 23   **8.** $d = \frac{1}{2}$, 7

9. $d = -5$, -24

10. $a_n = 4 - 2n$ **11.** $a_n = 5n - \frac{9}{2}$

12. $a_n = 4n - 7$ **13.** 21   **14.** $-\frac{19}{2}$

15. 8, 12, 16, 20   **16.** c   **17.** a   **18.** b

19. -15 **20.** 2150   **21.** 770   **22.** 1325

23. 4060   **24.** 2800   **25.** 2379

Lesson 12.3

1. It is geometric.   **2.** It is arithmetic.

3. It is neither.   **4.** It is geometric.

5. It is neither.   **6.** It is geometric.

7. $r = 3$, 1458   **8.** $r = -4$, -2048

9. $r = 3$, 1215   **10.** $r = \frac{2}{3}$, $\frac{32}{729}$

11. $r = -\frac{1}{4}$, $\frac{1}{512}$ **12.** $r = \frac{3}{4}$, $\frac{1701}{1024}$

13. 6, 3, $\frac{3}{2}$, $\frac{3}{4}$, $\frac{3}{8}$ **14.** 1, $\frac{3}{5}$, $\frac{9}{25}$, $\frac{27}{125}$, $\frac{81}{625}$

15. $\frac{2}{9}$, $-\frac{4}{3}$, 8, -48, 288

16. 7, 21, 63, 189, 567

17. 15, 10, $\frac{20}{3}$, $\frac{40}{9}$, $\frac{80}{27}$ **18.** 1, $\frac{1}{6}$, $\frac{1}{36}$, $\frac{1}{216}$, $\frac{1}{1296}$

19. $\frac{1}{16}$ **20.** $\frac{2}{125}$ **21.** 354,294

22. $\frac{128}{3125}$ **23.** 6400   **24.** $\frac{1}{1,048,576}$

25. $a_n = 1(\frac{4}{9})^{n-1}$ **26.** $a_n = 100(\frac{1}{20})^{n-1}$

27. $a_n = -5(-2)^{n-1}$ **28.** $a_6 = 1$ **29.** $r = 6$

30. $a_n = 3(4)^{n-1}$ or $a_n = 3(-4)^{n-1}$

31. ≈ 8.00 **32.** 6,046,617.5   **33.** ≈ -12.00

34. \$10.23 for 10 days; \$10,485.75 for 20 days; \$10,737,418.23 for 30 days

Lesson 12.4

1. It does not.   **2.** It does.   **3.** It does not.

4. It does.   **5.** It does.   **6.** It does not.

7. 6   **8.** 16   **9.** 9   **10.** It does not sum.

11. $\frac{20}{3}$ **12.** -5.556 **13.** -2.105 **14.** $-\frac{3}{16}$

15. 0.800   **16.** $\frac{5}{9}$ **17.** $\frac{40}{99}$ **18.** $\frac{18}{99} = \frac{2}{11}$

19. 200 in.^{2} **20.** 8 revolutions

Lesson 12.5

1. 10   **2.** 8   **3.** 35   **4.** 924

5. 1001   **6.** 252   **7.** $x^3 - 12x^2 + 48x - 64$

8. $x^5 + 15x^4 + 90x^3 + 270x^2 + 405x + 243$

9. $16x^4 + 96x^3 + 216x^2 + 216x + 81$

10. $x^6 + 12x^5y + 60x^4y^2 + 160x^3y^3 + 240x^2y^4 + 192xy^5 + 64y^6$

11. $243x^5 - 810x^4 + 1080x^3 - 720x^2 + 240x - 32$

12. $x^4 + 4x^3y + 6x^2y^2 + 4xy^3 + y^4$

13. 576   **14.** 189

15. See page 652 of the text.

16. 21   **17.** 10   **18.** 15   **19.** 4

20. $32x^5 + 80x^4y + 80x^3y^2 + 40x^2y^3 + 10xy^4 + y^5$

21. $x^4 - 12x^3y + 54x^2y^2 - 108xy^3 + 81y^4$

22. $x^6 + 24x^5 + 240x^4 + 1280x^3 + 3840x^2 + 6144x + 4096$

23. $8x^3 - 36x^2z + 54xz^2 - 27z^3$

24. $1024x^5 + 1280x^4 + 640x^3 + 160x^2 + 20x + 1$

25. $x^6 - 18x^5 + 135x^4 - 540x^3 + 1215x^2 - 1458x + 729$

26. $V = 2500(1 - 4r + 6r^2 - 4r^3 + r^4)$

Lesson 12.6

1.

End of Period	Prev. Bal.	Int.	Deposit	New Bal.
1	0.00	0.00	350	350.00
2	350.00	4.67	350	704.67
3	704.67	9.40	350	1064.07
4	1064.07	14.19	350	1428.26
5	1428.26	19.04	350	1797.30
6	1797.30	23.96	350	2171.26

■ **Lesson 12.6 (continued)**

2.

End of Period	Prev. Bal.	Int.	Deposit	New Bal.
1	0.00	0.00	50	50.00
2	50.00	0.38	50	100.38
3	100.38	0.75	50	151.13
4	151.13	1.13	50	202.26
5	202.26	1.52	50	253.78
6	253.78	1.90	50	305.68
7	305.68	2.29	50	357.97
8	357.97	2.68	50	410.65
9	410.65	3.08	50	463.73
10	463.73	3.48	50	517.21
11	517.21	3.88	50	571.09
12	571.09	4.28	50	625.37

3. $1935.93   **4.** $5195.96   **5.** $268.46
6. $12,802.99   **7.** $51,994.37   **8.** $361.03
9. Monthly deposits of $100 at 6%

10. $121,575.73, total balance; $85,575.73 is interest

11. Monthly payments with $8\frac{1}{2}\%$ interest for 10 years

12. $1778.53

■ **Lesson 13.1**

1. $\sin\theta = \frac{6}{\sqrt{85}}$ $\cot\theta = \frac{7}{6}$
$\cos\theta = \frac{7}{\sqrt{85}}$ $\sec\theta = \frac{\sqrt{85}}{7}$
$\tan\theta = \frac{6}{7}$ $\csc\theta = \frac{\sqrt{85}}{6}$

2. $\sin\theta = \frac{3}{\sqrt{13}}$ $\cot\theta = \frac{2}{3}$
$\cos\theta = \frac{2}{\sqrt{13}}$ $\sec\theta = \frac{\sqrt{13}}{2}$
$\tan\theta = \frac{3}{2}$ $\csc\theta = \frac{\sqrt{13}}{3}$

3. $\sin\theta = \frac{3}{5}$ $\cot\theta = \frac{4}{3}$
$\cos\theta = \frac{4}{5}$ $\sec\theta = \frac{5}{4}$
$\tan\theta = \frac{3}{4}$ $\csc\theta = \frac{5}{3}$

4. $\sin\theta = \frac{1}{\sqrt{26}}$ $\cot\theta = 5$
$\cos\theta = \frac{5}{\sqrt{26}}$ $\sec\theta = \frac{\sqrt{26}}{5}$
$\tan\theta = \frac{1}{5}$ $\csc\theta = \sqrt{26}$

5. $\sin\theta = \frac{1}{6}$ $\cot\theta = \sqrt{35}$
$\cos\theta = \frac{\sqrt{35}}{6}$ $\sec\theta = \frac{6}{\sqrt{35}}$
$\tan\theta = \frac{1}{\sqrt{35}}$ $\csc\theta = 6$

6. $\sin\theta = \frac{5}{\sqrt{34}}$ $\cot\theta = \frac{3}{5}$
$\cos\theta = \frac{3}{\sqrt{34}}$ $\sec\theta = \frac{\sqrt{34}}{3}$
$\tan\theta = \frac{5}{3}$ $\csc\theta = \frac{\sqrt{34}}{5}$

7.

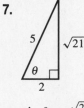

$\sin\theta = \frac{\sqrt{21}}{5}$ $\cot\theta = \frac{2}{\sqrt{21}}$
$\cos\theta = \frac{2}{5}$ $\sec\theta = \frac{5}{2}$
$\tan\theta = \frac{\sqrt{21}}{2}$ $\csc\theta = \frac{5}{\sqrt{21}}$

8.

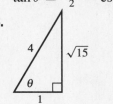

$\sin\theta = \frac{\sqrt{15}}{4}$ $\cot\theta = \frac{1}{\sqrt{15}}$
$\cos\theta = \frac{1}{4}$ $\sec\theta = 4$
$\tan\theta = \sqrt{15}$ $\csc\theta = \frac{4}{\sqrt{15}}$

9.

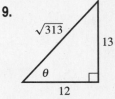

$\sin\theta = \frac{13}{\sqrt{313}}$ $\cot\theta = \frac{12}{13}$
$\cos\theta = \frac{12}{\sqrt{313}}$ $\sec\theta = \frac{\sqrt{313}}{12}$
$\tan\theta = \frac{13}{12}$ $\csc\theta = \frac{\sqrt{313}}{13}$

10.

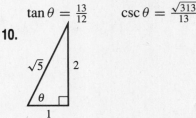

$\sin\theta = \frac{2}{\sqrt{5}}$ $\cot\theta = \frac{1}{2}$
$\cos\theta = \frac{1}{\sqrt{5}}$ $\sec\theta = \sqrt{5}$
$\tan\theta = 2$ $\csc\theta = \frac{\sqrt{5}}{2}$

■ Lesson 13.1 (continued)

11.

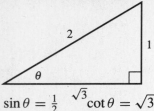

$\sin\theta = \frac{1}{2}$ $\cot\theta = \sqrt{3}$

$\cos\theta = \frac{\sqrt{3}}{2}$ $\sec\theta = \frac{2}{\sqrt{3}}$

$\tan\theta = \frac{1}{\sqrt{3}}$ $\csc\theta = 2$

12.

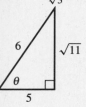

$\sin\theta = \frac{\sqrt{11}}{6}$ $\cot\theta = \frac{5}{\sqrt{11}}$

$\cos\theta = \frac{5}{6}$ $\sec\theta = \frac{6}{5}$

$\tan\theta = \frac{\sqrt{11}}{5}$ $\csc\theta = \frac{6}{\sqrt{11}}$

13.

$\sin\theta = \frac{3}{4}$ $\cot\theta = \frac{\sqrt{7}}{3}$

$\cos\theta = \frac{\sqrt{7}}{4}$ $\sec\theta = \frac{4}{\sqrt{7}}$

$\tan\theta = \frac{3}{\sqrt{7}}$ $\csc\theta = \frac{4}{3}$

14.

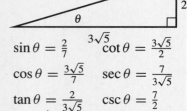

$\sin\theta = \frac{2}{7}$ $\cot\theta = \frac{3\sqrt{5}}{2}$

$\cos\theta = \frac{3\sqrt{5}}{7}$ $\sec\theta = \frac{7}{3\sqrt{5}}$

$\tan\theta = \frac{2}{3\sqrt{5}}$ $\csc\theta = \frac{7}{2}$

15.

$\sin\theta = \frac{5}{\sqrt{26}}$ $\cot\theta = \frac{1}{5}$

$\cos\theta = \frac{1}{\sqrt{26}}$ $\sec\theta = \sqrt{26}$

$\tan\theta = 5$ $\csc\theta = \frac{\sqrt{26}}{5}$

16. $\frac{\sqrt{5}}{3}$ **17.** $\sqrt{3}$ **18.** $\frac{\sqrt{10}}{3}$

19. $\frac{2\sqrt{6}}{5}$ **20.** $\frac{4}{\sqrt{41}}$ **21.** $\sqrt{15}$

22. $\frac{2}{\sqrt{3}}$ **23.** $\frac{1}{\sqrt{3}}$ **24.** 0.259   **25.** 0.682

26. 2.145   **27.** 3.236   **28.** 1.103

29. 0.532   **30.** ≈66.78 ft or 66 ft 9 in.

■ Lesson 13.2

1. They are coterminal.

2. They are coterminal.

3. They are not coterminal.

4. They are coterminal.

5. They are coterminal.

6. They are not coterminal.

7. They are coterminal.

8. They are coterminal.

9. 30°   **10.** 75°   **11.** 18°   **12.** $\frac{3\pi}{8}$

13. $\frac{\pi}{14}$ **14.** $\frac{\pi}{4}$ **15.** $\frac{7\pi}{20}$ **16.** $\frac{9\pi}{26}$

17. 75°   **18.** 5°   **19.** 120°   **20.** 145°

21. $\frac{\pi}{6}$ **22.** $\frac{\pi}{4}$ **23.** $\frac{3\pi}{5}$ **24.** $\frac{11\pi}{15}$

25. 585°, −135°   **26.** 700°, −20°

27. 180°, −180°   **28.** 420°, −300°

29. $\frac{2\pi}{5}$, $-\frac{8\pi}{5}$ **30.** $\frac{3\pi}{2}$, $-\frac{\pi}{2}$

31. $\frac{2\pi}{3}$, $-\frac{4\pi}{3}$ **32.** $\frac{6\pi}{5}$, $-\frac{4\pi}{5}$

33. $\frac{3\pi}{4}$ **34.** $\frac{2\pi}{9}$ **35.** $\frac{13\pi}{9}$

36. $\frac{43\pi}{36}$ **37.** $-\frac{17\pi}{9}$ **38.** $\frac{7\pi}{6}$

39. 105°   **40.** −150°   **41.** 120°

42. 585°   **43.** 480°   **44.** 30°

45. b   **46. a**   **47. c**   **48.** 4.655°

■ Lesson 13.3

1. $\sin\theta = -\frac{3}{5}$
$\cos\theta = -\frac{4}{5}$
$\tan\theta = \frac{3}{4}$

2. $\sin\theta = -\frac{1}{\sqrt{5}}$
$\cos\theta = \frac{2}{\sqrt{5}}$
$\tan\theta = -\frac{1}{2}$

3. $\sin\theta = \frac{5}{\sqrt{106}}$
$\cos\theta = \frac{-9}{\sqrt{106}}$
$\tan\theta = -\frac{5}{9}$

4. $\sin\theta = \frac{8}{\sqrt{89}}$
$\cos\theta = \frac{5}{\sqrt{89}}$
$\tan\theta = \frac{8}{5}$

5. $\sin\theta = \frac{1}{\sqrt{2}}$
$\cos\theta = \frac{-1}{\sqrt{2}}$
$\tan\theta = -1$

6. $\sin\theta = \frac{7}{\sqrt{58}}$
$\cos\theta = \frac{3}{\sqrt{58}}$
$\tan\theta = \frac{7}{3}$

7. $\sin\theta = \frac{-1}{\sqrt{26}}$
$\cos\theta = \frac{-5}{\sqrt{26}}$
$\tan\theta = \frac{1}{5}$

8. $\sin\theta = \frac{-9}{\sqrt{97}}$
$\cos\theta = \frac{4}{\sqrt{97}}$
$\tan\theta = -\frac{9}{4}$

9. $\sin\theta = \frac{5}{\sqrt{41}}$
$\cos\theta = \frac{-4}{\sqrt{41}}$
$\tan\theta = -\frac{5}{4}$

◼ Lesson 13.3 (continued)

10. $\theta' = 45°$
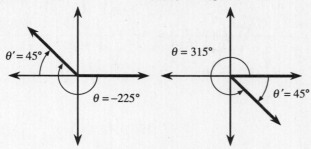

11. $\theta' = 45°$

12. $\theta' = 30°$
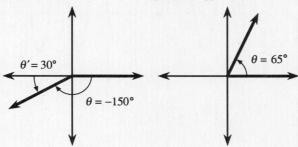

13. $\theta' = 65°$

14. $\theta' = \frac{\pi}{4}$
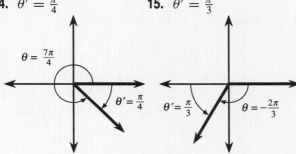

15. $\theta' = \frac{\pi}{3}$

16. $\theta' = \frac{\pi}{4}$
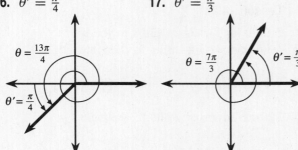

17. $\theta' = \frac{\pi}{3}$

18. $\theta' \approx 1.083$
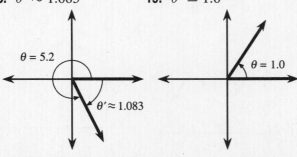

19. $\theta' = 1.0$

20. $\theta' \approx 0.0584$ **21.** $\theta' \approx 0.442$
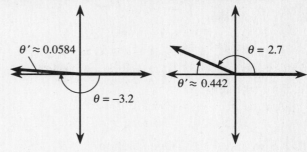

22. True **23.** True **24.** True
25. False **26.** False **27.** True
28. $\frac{\sqrt{3}}{2}$ **29.** $-\sqrt{2}$ **30.** $-\sqrt{3}$
31. $-\sqrt{2}$ **32.** $\frac{\sqrt{3}}{2}$ **33.** $-\sqrt{3}$
34. $\sqrt{2}$ **35.** $-\frac{\sqrt{3}}{2}$ **36.** 0.9659
37. 0.7071 **38.** -1.0009 **39.** 0.5774
40. -0.5248 **41.** 1.4945
42. ≈ 152 ft/sec, ≈ 722 ft

◼ Lesson 13.4

1. 33.690°, 0.588 **2.** 36.870°, 0.644
3. 44.427°, 0.775 **4.** 39.806°, 0.695
5. 18.435°, 0.322 **6.** 36.870°, 0.644
7. $-30°$, $-\frac{\pi}{6}$ **8.** $-30°$, $-\frac{\pi}{6}$ **9.** 0°, 0
10. 60°, $\frac{\pi}{3}$ **11.** $-45°$, $-\frac{\pi}{4}$ **12.** 45°, $\frac{\pi}{4}$
13. 30°, $\frac{\pi}{6}$ **14.** 120°, $\frac{2\pi}{3}$
15. 36.870°, 0.644 **16.** 138.590°, 2.419
17. 77.471°, 1.352 **18.** 104.478°, 1.823
19. 84.261°, 1.471 **20.** $-68.199°$, -1.190
21. 64.158°, 1.120 **22.** $-23.578°$, -0.412
23. 35.797°, 0.625

◼ Lesson 13.5

1. $C = 105°$, $b \approx 14.1$, $c \approx 19.3$
2. $C = 110°$, $b \approx 22.4$, $c \approx 24.4$
3. $B \approx 21.4°$, $C \approx 116.6°$, $c \approx 29.4$
4. $B \approx 21.6°$, $C \approx 122.4°$, $c \approx 11.5$
5. $B = 10°$, $b \approx 69.5$, $c \approx 136.8$
6. $A \approx 10.2°$, $C \approx 154.3°$, $c \approx 11.0$
7. $A \approx 25.6°$, $B \approx 9.4°$, $a = 10.5$
8. No solution

■ Lesson 13.5 (continued)

9. Two solutions:
$B \approx 70.4°$, $C \approx 51.6°$, $c \approx 4.2$
$B \approx 109.6°$, $C \approx 12.4°$, $c \approx 1.1$

10. $C = 66°$, $b \approx 38.1$, $c \approx 46.1$

11. Two solutions:
$A = 61.50°$, $C = 70.37°$, $c = 5.62$
$A = 118.50°$, $C = 13.37°$, $c = 1.38$

12. No solution   13. One solution
14. Two solutions   15. One solution
16. No solution   17. Two solutions
18. 2288.87 sq units   19. 10.39 sq units
20. 1675.19 sq units   21. 9.58 ft

■ Lesson 13.6

1. $B \approx 74.9°$, $A \approx 47.7°$, $C \approx 57.4°$
2. $A \approx 95.1°$, $B \approx 24.9°$, $c \approx 27$
3. $A \approx 26.7°$, $C \approx 33.3°$, $b \approx 140.5$
4. $A \approx 52.4°$, $B \approx 82.6°$, $c \approx 16.4$
5. $A \approx 54.2°$, $B \approx 79.8°$, $c \approx 100$
6. $A \approx 57.5°$, $B \approx 71.5°$, $c \approx 282.9$
7. $B \approx 42.5°$, $C \approx 20°$, $a \approx 9.9$
8. $A \approx 27°$, $B \approx 34°$, $C \approx 119°$
9. $A \approx 40.9°$, $B \approx 82.2°$, $C \approx 56.9°$
10. $A \approx 102.2°$, $B \approx 38.4°$, $c \approx 81.8$
11. $A \approx 153.5°$, $B \approx 15.5°$, $C \approx 11.0°$
12. 16.25 sq units   13. 41.23 sq units
14. 96.82 sq units   15. 10.44 sq units
16. 1350.22 sq units   17. 1.62 sq units
18. 6.0 sq units   19. 54.0 sq units
20. 0.47 sq units   21. $B : \approx 52.6°$ E of S
$C : \approx 25.3°$ W of S

■ Lesson 14.1

1. 4, 4π 2. $\frac{1}{2}$, $\frac{\pi}{2}$ 3. 1, $\frac{\pi}{4}$ 4. $\frac{1}{3}$, π
5. 10, 4π 6. 6, $\frac{2}{3}$ 7. $\frac{1}{2}$, 4 8. 4, $\frac{1}{2}$
9. c   10. b   11. a

12. 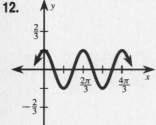   13.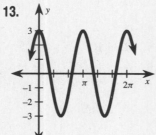

14. 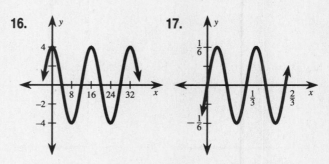   15.

16.   17.

18. $y = 2 \sin \frac{\pi}{2} x$ 19. $y = \frac{1}{8} \sin \frac{1}{4} x$
20. $y = 4 \cos 4x$ 21. Minimum at
$\frac{3\pi}{4}$, $\frac{7\pi}{4}$
Maximum at
$\frac{\pi}{4}$, $\frac{5\pi}{4}$

22. Minimum at 2, 6; Maximum at 0, 4

23. **a.** 4 sec **b.** 15 **c.**

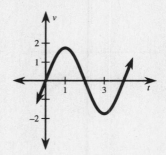

■ Lesson 14.2

1. 5 units up   2. π units to the left
3. 4 units down, $\frac{\pi}{4}$ units to the right

4. 2 units up, $\frac{\pi}{2}$ units to the left

5. 2 units down, π units to the right

6. $\frac{\pi}{4}$ units to the left
7. b   8. a   9. c   10. $y = -\frac{1}{2} + 3 \sin \frac{1}{2} x$
11. $y = 2 + 3 \cos(x + \pi)$

12. 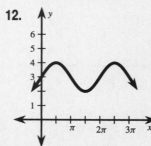   13.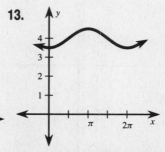

■ **Lesson 14.2 (continued)**

14.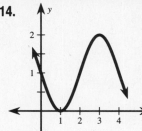

15.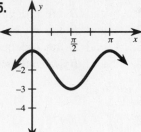

16.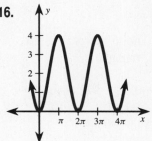

17. Minimum at $x = 0, \; \pi$
Maximum at $x = \frac{\pi}{2}, \; \frac{3\pi}{2}$

18. $y = -3 + \sin(\frac{1}{3}x - \pi)$

19.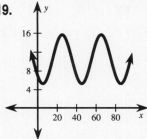

Brightest: 25th, 65th
Dimmest: 5th, 45th

■ **Lesson 14.3**

1. $\cos x$ **2.** $\csc x$ **3.** $\tan^2 x$ **4.** $\sec x$
5. $\sin x$ **6.** $\sec^2 x$ **7.** $\cot x$ **8.** $-\tan x$
9. $\sin x$ **10.** Answers vary.
11. Answers vary.   **12.** Answers vary.
13. Answers vary.   **14.** Answers vary.
15. Answers vary.   **16.** Answers vary.
17. Answers vary.   **18.** Answers vary.
19. Answers vary.   **20.** Ellipse

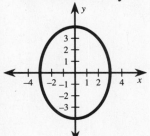

21. Answers vary.

■ **Lesson 14.4**

1. $\tan 2x = -\frac{1}{\sqrt{3}}, \; 2x = \frac{5\pi}{6}$
2. $\sin x = 1, \; x = \frac{\pi}{2}$
3. $\sec x = 2, \; x = \frac{5\pi}{3}$
4. $\sin x = 0, \; x = 0$
5. $\cos x = -\frac{1}{\sqrt{2}}, \; x = \frac{5\pi}{4}$
6. $\tan x = -1, \; x = \frac{7\pi}{4}$ **7.** $\frac{\pi}{3}, \; \frac{2\pi}{3}$
8. $\frac{\pi}{4}, \; \frac{3\pi}{4}, \; \frac{5\pi}{4}, \; \frac{7\pi}{4}$ **9.** $\frac{\pi}{6}, \; \frac{5\pi}{6}, \; \frac{7\pi}{6}, \; \frac{11\pi}{6}$
10. $0, \; \pi, \; \frac{3\pi}{2}$ **11.** $\frac{\pi}{2}, \; \frac{3\pi}{2}, \; \frac{2\pi}{3}, \; \frac{4\pi}{3}$
12. $\frac{\pi}{2}, \; \frac{3\pi}{2}, \; \frac{2\pi}{3}, \; \frac{4\pi}{3}$ **13.** $\frac{\pi}{6}, \; \frac{5\pi}{6}, \; \frac{7\pi}{6}, \; \frac{11\pi}{6}$
14. $\frac{2\pi}{3}, \; \frac{4\pi}{3}$ **15.** $\frac{\pi}{4}, \; \frac{3\pi}{4}, \; \frac{5\pi}{4}, \; \frac{7\pi}{4}$
16. $\frac{\pi}{3}, \; \frac{2\pi}{3}, \; \frac{4\pi}{3}, \; \frac{5\pi}{3}$ **17.** $\frac{7\pi}{6}, \; \frac{11\pi}{6}, \; \frac{\pi}{2}$
18. $\frac{\pi}{2}, \; \frac{3\pi}{2}, \; \frac{\pi}{3}, \; \frac{5\pi}{3}$ **19.** $\frac{3\pi}{2}$
20. $0, \; \pi, \; \frac{\pi}{6}, \; \frac{5\pi}{6}$ **21.** $\frac{\pi}{2}, \; \frac{3\pi}{2}, \; \frac{7\pi}{6}, \; \frac{11\pi}{6}$

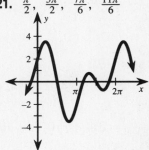

■ **Lesson 14.5**

1. $\frac{\sqrt{6}-\sqrt{2}}{4}$ **2.** $\frac{\sqrt{2}-\sqrt{6}}{4}$ **3.** $\frac{\sqrt{3}+1}{\sqrt{3}-1}$
4. $\frac{-\sqrt{6}-\sqrt{2}}{\sqrt{6}-\sqrt{2}}$ **5.** $-\frac{4}{\sqrt{6}+\sqrt{2}}$ **6.** $\frac{4}{\sqrt{2}-\sqrt{6}}$
7. $\sin 72°$ **8.** $\cos(-\frac{5\pi}{42})$ **9.** $\tan 175°$
10. $\sin(1.8)$ **11.** 0 **12.** $\frac{\sqrt{6}-\sqrt{2}}{4}$
13. Undefined   **14.** $\frac{\sqrt{2}-\sqrt{6}}{4}$
15. Answers vary.
16. Answers vary.   **17.** $\frac{3}{5}$
18. $\frac{-44}{125}$ **19.** $\frac{5\pi}{4}, \; \frac{7\pi}{4}$
20. $\frac{\pi}{3}, \; \frac{5\pi}{3}$ **21.** $0, \; \pi$ **22.** $\frac{3\pi}{2}$
23. Answers vary.   **24.** $\frac{\sqrt{2}+\sqrt{6}}{4}$

■ **Lesson 14.6**

1. $4\sin x \cos^3 x - 4\sin^3 x \cos x$
2. $2\cos x - \sec x$ **3.** $\cos x$ **4.** $\csc x \sec x$
5. $1+\sin x-2\sin^2 x$ **6.** $2\cos^2 x+\cos x-1$
7. $\frac{7\pi}{6}, \; \frac{11\pi}{6}, \; \frac{\pi}{2}$ **8.** $\frac{\pi}{3}, \; \frac{5\pi}{3}, \; \pi$
9. $\frac{\pi}{6}, \; \frac{5\pi}{6}, \; \frac{7\pi}{6}, \; \frac{11\pi}{6}$ **10.** $0, \; \frac{2\pi}{3}, \; \frac{4\pi}{3}$
11. $\frac{\pi}{2}, \; \frac{3\pi}{2}, \; \frac{\pi}{4}, \; \frac{3\pi}{4}, \; \frac{5\pi}{4}, \; \frac{7\pi}{4}$
12. $0, \; \pi, \; \frac{3\pi}{4}, \; \frac{5\pi}{4}$ **13.** $\frac{\sqrt{2-\sqrt{2}}}{2}$
14. $-\frac{\sqrt{2-\sqrt{3}}}{2}$ **15.** $-2+\sqrt{3}$

■ **Lesson 14.6 (continued)**

16. $\frac{\sqrt{2-\sqrt{2}}}{2}$ **17.** $\frac{\sqrt{2}}{2-\sqrt{2}}$ **18.** $\frac{\sqrt{2+\sqrt{2}}}{2}$

19. $\sin\frac{u}{2} = \frac{1}{\sqrt{10}}$, $\cos\frac{u}{2} = \frac{-3}{\sqrt{10}}$, $\tan\frac{u}{2} = -\frac{1}{3}$

20. $\sin\frac{u}{2} = \frac{7}{5\sqrt{2}}$, $\cos\frac{u}{2} = \frac{1}{5\sqrt{2}}$, $\tan\frac{u}{2} = 7$

21. $\sin\frac{u}{2} = \frac{3}{\sqrt{10}}$, $\cos\frac{u}{2} = -\frac{1}{\sqrt{10}}$, $\tan\frac{u}{2} = -3$

22. $\sin\frac{u}{2} = \frac{1}{\sqrt{26}}$, $\cos\frac{u}{2} = \frac{-5}{\sqrt{26}}$, $\tan\frac{u}{2} = -\frac{1}{5}$

23. $r = 300$ ft, $\theta \approx 36.87°$

■ **Lesson 15.1**

1. $\frac{1}{2}$ **2.** $\frac{5}{12}$ **3.** $\frac{1}{3}$ **4.** $\frac{1}{4}$
5. 0.125 **6.** 0.0425 **7.** 0.01 **8.** 0.28
9. 0.63 **10.** 0.13 **11.** $\frac{2}{9} \approx 0.222$
12. $\frac{6}{9} \approx 0.667$ **13.** $\frac{4}{9} \approx 0.444$

■ **Lesson 15.2**

1. 6 **2.** 24 **3.** 120 **4.** 720
5. 120 **6.** 720 **7.** 1920 **8.** 12
9. $\frac{1}{40,320} \approx 2.48 \times 10^{-5}$ **10.** $\frac{1}{720} \approx 0.014$
11. 471,074,400

■ **Lesson 15.3**

1. 3 **2.** 6 **3.** 10 **4.** 15 **5.** 1
6. 4 **7.** 10 **8.** 20 **9.** 6
10. 126 **11.** 220 **12.** 90 **13.** 126
14. a 0.1176, **b** 0.0002, **c** 0.0005

■ **Lesson 15.4**

1. 0.00; A and B are mutually exclusive.
2. 0.10; A and B are not mutually exclusive.
3. 0.8; A and B are not mutually exclusive.
4. 0.80; A and B are not mutually exclusive.
5. 0.70; A and B are not mutually exclusive.
6. 0.35; A and B are not mutually exclusive.
7. 0.68 **8.** 0.19 **9.** $\frac{17}{70}$ **10.** $\frac{32}{65}$
11. 0.240 **12.** 0.6
13. 0.27 single, 0.73 married
14. 0.38 single, 0.62 married

■ **Lesson 15.5**

1. A and B are independent.
2. A and B are dependent.
3. A and B are independent
4. A and B are independent
5. $\frac{1}{3}$ **6.** 0.08 **7.** 0.8 **8.** 0.8
9. 0.5 **10.** 1.0 **11.** $\frac{1}{4} = 0.25$
12. $\frac{399}{400} = 0.9975$ **13.** 0.985
14. ≈ 0.216 **15.** ≈ 0.019 **16.** ≈ 0.784

■ **Lesson 15.6**

1. $0, fair game **2.** $1, no **3.** $0.75, no
4. $0, fair game **5.** $0, fair game
6. $-$0.57, no
7. A: $64,000; B: $36,000; C: $72,000;
D: $45,000; E: $108,000;
F: $105,000; Total = $430,000

8. $646,000
9. Player A, 0 **10.** Player A, $\frac{1}{2}$
Player B, 0 Player B, $-\frac{1}{2}$